T0149038

FORBIDDEN LIVES

For my wife Julie Carpenter with love and thanks

FORBIDDEN LIVES

LESBIAN, GAY, BISEXUAL AND TRANSGENDER
STORIES FROM WALES

NORENA SHOPLAND

FOREWORD BY JEFFREY WEEKS

Seren is the book imprint of
Poetry Wales Press Ltd
Nolton Street, Bridgend, Wales

www.serenbooks.com
facebook.com/SerenBooks
Twitter: @SerenBooks

© Norena Shopland, 2017
Foreword © Jeffrey Weeks, 2017

The right of Norena Shopland to be identified
as the Author of this Work has been asserted
in accordance with the Copyright, Designs
and Patents Act, 1988.

ISBN 978-1-78172-410-1
Ebook: 978-1-78172-414-9
Kindle: 978-1-78172-418-7

A CIP record for this title is available from
the British Library

All rights reserved. No part of this publication
may be reproduced, stored in a retrieval system,
or transmitted at any time or by any means
electronic, mechanical, photocopying, recording
or otherwise without the prior permission
of the copyright holders.

The publisher works with the financial assistance
of the Welsh Books Council

Printed by 4edge Ltd

Contents

Foreword

Human beings are story tellers and imbibers of stories. Stories tell us where we came from, who we are, how we live and should live, where we want to go. They are the links between past, present and possible futures. They weld our identities, connecting us to those we think we are like, and differentiating us from people we believe are different from us. Stories give us comfort and support, warnings and memories, hope and aspiration. Without them we are lost from history. With them we can make links across the chasm of time and difference.

This is a book of stories about LGBT lives from Wales. When I was growing up in the Rhondda in the 1950s and 1960s the only stories I heard were of guilt and self-loathing, embarrassment and shame. My move to London in the mid 1960s as a student was in part in order for me to discover stories I could recognize myself in. It took me some time to find them, and when I eventually did they formed the basis of the histories of LGBT lives, identities and politics that I began to write. But I always felt there was a void where the history of LGBT life in Wales should be. Gradually stories have emerged – through myths, memoirs and biographies, oral history, accounts of trials and scandals and so on that have provided hints about what a Welsh LGBT history could look like, in all its richness and complexity. Now Norena Shopland has brought together for the first time a collection of these stories. They are gripping in their own right, but they also provide the necessary outline of what a full history of LGBT life in Wales will be.

Historians have now begun to show Wales has a rich sexual history that is in many ways quite distinct from that of the rest of Britain. Yet even within the boundaries of quite a small country there is considerable diversity, as these stories illustrate: between rural Wales and the valleys, the upper and middle classes and the working class, with considerable change over time. What we have learnt from LGBT historians is that there is not a single LGBT history but many histories. Through these stories we can begin to see that clearly for the first time in Wales.

Jeffrey Weeks

Introduction

It was in 1991 that the term heteronormativity was first used in a major work. This word encapsulates the belief that gender is binary, as in man/woman, and that sexual orientation is also binary, the attraction of opposite sexes. However this term with all its attendant connotations causes concern. After all, anything which includes 'normal' implies that everything else is 'not normal' and that can often lead to stigmatism, marginalisation or oppression.

Due to the way that laws have been constructed over the centuries there have been many legal requirements to remain within the heteronormative narrative of the state supported by or enforced by religious and societal beliefs. This can make it very difficult for researchers looking for examples from the past to illustrate that 'normal' doesn't exist. Particularly as many established histories have been constructed from a heterosexual viewpoint. It may never occur to them, or they deliberately ignore, the subtle clues that may indicate hidden or forbidden lives. Only by looking at material from a sexual or gender fluid openness can some lives begin to make sense. But for many examples we are often left reading between the lines and raising questions rather than making bold statements.

This is particularly true of Wales where the history of LGBT people and events has rarely been told. Just as sexual orientation and gender identity have been subsumed into a heteronormativity history so Welsh people and events have been subsumed into an English or British history.

In 2010 I applied to the HLF for a grant to collect material to do the first exhibition of Welsh lesbian, gay, bisexual and transgender people. Once outside the famous names such as Ivor Novello, the Ladies of Llangollen and more modern people such as Sarah Waters and Gareth Thomas things became harder. Trying to find the everyday lives of people became an exercise in 'bit picking' from other works. For much of what had existed has been shattered. For example, Frances Power Cobbe destroyed both her and her partner Mary Lloyd's letters and diaries. Nothing they did was illegal, women were not affected by a ban in law the way that men were, but society did not approve and so the material was destroyed. Consequently we are left to pick around in the letters and diaries of others to piece together stories about LGBT people in history.

Over the years I have done much picking at bits and pieces and this book represents that. This is the first work highlighting real lives of lesbian, gay, bisexual and transgender people and events in and from Wales.

I am grateful to my parents Pam and Bob Shopland who have helped and supported this book enormously; Susan Edwards, Glamorgan Archives; Matthew Williams, Cardiff Castle; Massimo Moretti, Studiocanal; Llinos Wynne; Ross Burgess, Campaign for Homosexual Equality; Peter Scott-Presland; Bjorn Weiler; Jeffrey Weeks.

1. Here Lived Peggy Evans

A story which illustrates the need to question 'heteronormativity' is that of Margaret uch Evans, also known by the names of Marged ferch (or Verch) Ifan or Peggy Evans. The main reason we know of her is through Thomas Pennant.

In 1776 Pennant, a prolific writer, traveller and antiquarian who specialised in the study of Wales, its nature and people set off from his home at Downing Hall, Flintshire. He was gathering information for his new book *A Tour in Wales*. This three volume work chronicled three trips he made on horseback between 1773 and 1776, and is still regarded as one of the best travel books of the period.

In the second volume, *Journey to Snowdon* published in 1781, Pennant relates how he had made his way to a small stone cottage near Capel Cerig on the edge of Llanberis Lake in North Wales, to meet a particular woman. He had obviously been given directions to find her and he certainly had preconceptions about her as he was "disappointed in not finding [her] at home". He never did meet her and instead had to rely on information provided to him, by whom we don't know, to relate her story.

"Near this end of the lake," he began, "lives a celebrated personage... This is Margaret uch Evans of Penllyn, the last specimen of the strength and spirit of the ancient British fair. She is at this time

LLANBERIS LAKE

about ninety years of age." Pennant says 'about' as this was a period
when births, deaths and marriages were not widely recorded,
particularly in rural areas, so confusion about people's age was
common. In the printed versions of her life Marged's age is given either
as 70, 92, 100 or 105. In the *Oxford Dictionary of National Biography*,
Ceridwen Lloyd-Morgan states that she was probably born in
Beddgelert, Caernarvonshire and baptized in the parish church on 10
May 1696. She was one of at least eleven children born to Ifan Powell
and his wife, Elizabeth Hughes.

Pennant claims this "extraordinary female was the greatest hunter,
shooter, and fisher, of her time. She kept a dozen at lest [sic] of dogs,
terriers, grehounds [sic], and spaniels, all excellent in their kinds. She
killed more foxes in one year, than all the confederate hunts do in ten;
rowed stoutly and was queen of the lake; fiddled excellently, and knew all
the old British music; did not neglect the mechanic arts, for she was a
good joiner; and at the age of 70 was the best wrestler in the country, and
few young men dared to try a fall with her. She had a maid of congenial
qualities; but death, that mighty hunter, at last earthed this faithful
companion. Margaret was also blacksmith, shoe-maker, boat-builder,
and maker of harps. She shod horses, made her own shoes, built her own
boats whilst she was under contract to convey the copper ore down the
lakes. All the neighbouring bards paid their address to Margaret, and
celebrated her exploits in pure British verse. At length she gave her hand
to the most effeminate of her admirers, as if predetermined to maintain
the superiority which nature had bestowed upon her."[1]

This description was cited for many years afterwards as an example
of the extraordinariness of certain women. Many writers simply
re-printed Pennant's description, but the first to provide further
commentary was *The Gentleman's Magazine*, which in 1820 included a
contribution by William Hutton, a poet and historian who made sixteen
Welsh tours described in his book *Remarks Upon North Wales* (1803).
In it he included his poem on 'The Welch Wedding' (written on 13
September 1799) in which he describes the "simple manners of the
natives of this retired spot of the principality":

> We see life sustained with the most simple fare;
> Their health and their harmony are not disjointed,
> For, as they expect not, they're not disappointed.

Robust are the females, hard labour attends them,
With the fist they could knock down the man who offends
them.

It is not known if Hutton met Marged, but continuing in his 'robust females' theme he describes her:

Here lived Peggy Evans, who saw ninety-two,
Could wrestle, row, fiddle, and hunt a fox too;
Could ring a sweet peal, as the neighbourhood tells,
That would charm your two ears – had there been any bells;
Enjoy'd rosy health in a lodging of straw,
Commanded the saw-pit, and wielded the saw:-
And though she's deposited where you can't find her,
I know she has left a few sisters behind her.[2]

Hutton in his poem claims that many women of the area were robust and even after Marged's death "left a few sisters behind her". This is borne out by evidence of other women. In the *Harleian Miscellany*, a collection of stories co-edited by Samuel Johnson and published between 1744 and 1753, there is a piece in the eighth volume entitled 'Wonderful news from Wales'. The story concerns Jane Morgan whom it is claimed was 130 years old, and her biographical notes included a portrait of her masculine mother: "Jane Lloyd was married at twenty years of age to one Evan Morgan, an able fanner's Son, who was the activest [sic] and strongest in his country at wrestling." Evan had just beaten all the neighbours and strangers when Jane put on "man's apparel, entered the round, and gave him three falls; upon which she bore away the little silver bell that was the conqueror's due." When her identity was revealed Evan was so smitten that he "fell so deeply in love with her" that he married her and they lived together for forty-five years. She didn't give birth until the age of sixty-six when she had her daughter, Jane Morgan. "Many masculine and heroick acts did this virago mother do," said the *Harleian Miscellany*. When she was close to 100 she went to Oswaldstrey (modern Oswestry) market, three miles away but "because of its ruggedness and length, she had better have gone from London to Barnet". Filling her apron with "cumbersome necessaries" she was about to begin the long walk back when a

sceptical bystander made the mistake of trying to help her. He
remarked it would be impossible for her to walk all the way home so
laden. But Jane, looking at his horse with two heavy pieces of coarse
Welsh cotton on its back, scornfully replied "If you put those two
pieces, which your horse seems almost to shrink under, upon my
shoulders, I will for a wager, undertake to carry them as far as my
house, before you and your horse can come thither."

The man, a neighbour of hers, indignantly pointed out that he had
been trying to ease her troubles not increase them. However another
man in the watching crowd took up the bet and he, with three or four
curious neighbours, got horses and followed them. After 2½ miles they
overtook the man "belabouring his weary horse" and asked where Jane
was. Swearing loudly and complaining bitterly that he had suffered two
or three falls he said he had no idea. The men rode on and found Jane
"sitting in her chimney corner, smoaking [sic] tobacco in a comfortable
short pipe at which they were astonished."

Another example is Catherine Thomas, also from Llanberis, who
went by the nicknames of Caddy or Catrin of Cwm-glâs. David
Hughson, in *Cambria Depicta: A Tour through North Wales*, recalls
meeting her early in the 1800s. "Her appearance was very singular, and
not until I gained better information, could I be persuaded that she was
not a man in female habit. Her voice was strong and deep-toned, and
her shape masculine to a degree; the shoulders being broad like those
of the male, while the *glutei muscles* contracted so, as scarcely to enable
her to keep on her petticoats. She seemed to cultivate a beard with
some care, which had already grown bushy through age."

The *North Wales Chronicle* in 1837 stated that she "...had been
celebrated by most of the modern Welsh tourists as the far famed
Catrin of Cwmglas, who in her younger days was gifted with greater
bodily strength than any man in the country, of which many anecdotes
are recorded." One of these anecdotes concerned Mr Jones of the
copper mine (the same Llanberis mine for which Marged Uwch Evans
had worked). He often teased Catrin about her supposed strength,
refusing to believe the stories. One day as he was standing on the bank
of the pier she crept up behind him and lifted him up and out over the
water. "Now, Sir (said she) I suppose you will believe that I am
tolerably strong; you must confess it, or I shall throw you in." Mr Jones
immediately confessed it.

An article published in *Y Drych* in 1917 recalled that she could "gludo sachaid o wenith ar ei gwar o Gaernarfon i uchaf Llanberis" (transport a sack of wheat on her neck from Caernarfon to Llanberis top). "In appearance," said the *North Wales Chronicle*, "she exactly resembled a strong man dressed in female attire, with extraordinary deep gruff voice, and strong black beard which she shaved regularly." She rarely came into town for the boys would run after her and call her 'the woman with a beard.' Catrin had a fairly extensive mountain farm under local landowner Mr. Assheton Smith, and was much esteemed as a kind and hospitable neighbour. "Charitable to the poor, and exemplary in the whole of her conduct," Catrin had but one singularity which was that she never allowed "any individual whatever to sleep a night in her house."

Another woman who defies heteronormativity was Grâs y Garth or Grace Parry, who worked the Anglesey ferry, first with her family and then by herself. There is a description of her by the Rev. Richard Warner in his book *A Second Walk through Wales in August and September 1798*. She was says, Warner, a short, thick, squat female of about 60 who was "as strong as a horse, and as active as one of her own country goats." She told him that she looked down on men, whom she considered as inferior animals and regarded only as a necessary evil. Her excellence in rowing and managing the ferry was unrivalled through the coast. And although married she rarely allowed her husband to help her as he could not do it half as well as herself. One day on discovering someone had stolen her boat she, and a 'stout fellow', walked 60 miles to Liverpool, where it had been taken. Regaining her property she rowed it back to Garth Point through heavy seas, "as perilous a voyage as ever was performed". The Rev. Warner having heard of her violent hatred of the English decided to pay her double the ferry fare for one trip, and so grateful was she and so strongly did she shake their hands that she almost dislocated their fingers.

These extreme forms of masculine women fascinated people. Yet little or no attempt was made to understand how it was that women's physical appearance could be so closely similar to that of a man. Given that many 'normal' women by necessity of the harsh conditions they lived in had to be robust, these 'masculine' women must have been extraordinarily robust to have generated such copious interest and discussion. Similarly women today such as the athlete Caster Semenya have been tested as to their 'true' gender because their appearance and strength have been questioned.

To return to Marged uch Evans, in his 1854 book *The Heroines of Welsh History,* Thomas Jeffery Llewelyn Prichard noted that "If female worth deserves to be recorded, surely the accomplishments of Margaret should not be passed over unnoticed. Few ladies in North Wales have attained so much renown as Margaret of Penllyn, whose abilities were by no means circumscribed by etiquette, or confined within the sphere of the general occupations of a woman." Prichard didn't expand on Marged's 'renown' and provided no new details about her, but speculated on how different her life might have been had she not been from such a lowly background. "Although occupying but a homely position in life, as the human race are all creatures of circumstances, it is not uninteresting to surmise what she might have been had fortune cast her lot in another sphere and era, and given a fair field to her genius. It is undeniable that this rustic heroine of a comparatively lowly lot possessed more of what is called the master mind than many who have been born to empire, swaying the fate of nations, and conducting them to eminence and glory."

Prichard goes on to speculate which great leaders would take a woman of such masculine appearance. "What a congenial partner would she have been for such a man, who, of all others, would have valued those original but masculine qualifications, so repulsive to the generality of mankind."[3] The idea of masculinity in a woman is still considered 'repulsive' by certain members of society even today.

Other information about Marged is to be found in a work by Isaac Foulkes, a Welsh author and printer who was dedicated to preserving the Welsh language and its literature. Between 1862 and 1864 he compiled a three-part work, *Cymru Fu,*[4] a collection of Welsh fables, romances and traditions. Included in this work is a piece entitled 'Margred uch Ifan' by Wmffre Dafydd (Humphrey David).

The *Oxford Dictionary of National Biography* identifies Marged's husband as the harpist Richard Morris, who died in 1786. The couple kept an inn called Telyrni between Nantlle and Drws-y-coed in the parish of Llandwrog, frequented by copper miners for whom Marged and Richard probably played. Pennant also notes, "All the neighbouring bards paid their address to Margaret, and celebrated her exploits in pure British verse." It is more likely she was written about than composed many songs herself. A number of ancient airs about her share the same theme – that Margaret owned two items one small and one large such as:

> Mae gan Marged fwyn ach Ifan
> Grafanc fawr a chrafanc fechan,
> Un i dynnu'r cŵn o'r gongol,
> A'r llall i dorri esgyrn pobol.

> Fair Margaret daughter of Evan has
> A large claw and a small claw,
> One to drag the dogs from the corner,
> And the other to break people's bones.[5]

The most enduring story about Marged is in Wmffre Dafydd's account of her small dog, Ianto, which made its way into a miner's house and ate his food. Infuriated, the miner killed the dog. Marged offered to pay for the food if the miner paid for the dog but when he sarcastically refused Marged set him "flush to the floor". It is this story about Marged which has survived and has been reprinted several times, often accompanied by images of a pretty feminine woman. But the original sources are not stated and the story does not appear in print until 84 years after Pennant, who never mentions the dog – surely he would not have missed such a good yarn?

When local copper mining declined Richard and Marged moved to Pen-llyn at the north-western end of Padarn lake in the parish of Llanddeiniolen, sometime before 1764. It was here her reputation was established.

The recurring theme in all accounts of her life is that after refusing many marriage offers Marged finally agreed to give her hand "to the most effeminate of her admirers". 'Effeminate' is a Latin word made from 'ex' meaning a change of state and '*femina*' or woman. The most common definition today is that of a man or boy having the characteristics generally regarded as typical of a woman. The term is generally a derogatory one highlighting lack of masculinity. It can also imply weakness, or 'something-not-quite-right', such as an 'effeminate government'. Given Marged's renowned strength the description of her husband may refer to his weaker physical strength, particularly if he was a professional harpist, but it may also be that he was a man who appeared feminine.

Wmffre Dafydd says Marged chose a most cowardly-hearted life partner so she could maintain control. "O'r diwedd dewisodd yn gymar bywyd y mwyaf llwfr-galon y gwyddai am dano, fel y byddai yr arglwyddiaeth yn ei llaw yn yn gyfangwbl." And the article in *Y Drych* in 1917 mentioned "Medrai Marged uch Ifan gario ei gwr dan ei chesail i'r siamber gefn, ond yr oedd haiarn yn ei hesgyrn hi am ei bod wedi byw ar laeth enwyn a maip". (Margaret uch Ifan could carry her husband under her armpit to the back chamber, there was iron in her bones because she had lived on buttermilk and turnips.)

Richard may also have been the victim of domestic violence. She gave him "two severe beatings: after the first, he married her, on 8 May 1717 in Beddgelert, and after the second he joined the Methodists."[6] (She also apparently dropped into the lake the local magnate Thomas Assheton Smith of Vaenol when he made sexual advances towards her. When he begged to be pulled out she refused until he had paid her half a guinea.) Despite his supposed effeminacy, Richard and Marged had at least three children, a son and two daughters.

The two accounts by Thomas Pennant and Wmffre Dafydd both mention Marged's maid. Servants were rarely written about and there would be no reason to mention the maid unless there was an extraordinary closeness between them. Pennant noted that Marged "had a maid of congenial qualities" and Wmffre Dafydd in his final lines about Marged noted how she had died shortly after her long-serving maid: "Bu ei hoff forwyn farw ychydig o'i blaen, wedi ei gwasanaethu am ddeugain a dwy o flynyddau" (Her favourite maid who died just before her had served for forty-two years). Marged died in January 1793 at Penllyn and was buried in Llanddeiniolen churchyard, though the grave no longer survives.

Although we cannot draw any definitive conclusions about Marged's sexual orientation or gender identity, it is apparent from accounts of her that Marged was so extraordinary in her masculinity that it placed her beyond the boundaries of 'heteronormativity' – and if someone can be placed outside those boundaries it meant they never really existed in the first place.

2. The Welsh Sappho

Katherine Philips was an Englishwoman who spent most of her life in Wales. From her home in Cardigan she was to write poetry that marked her out as the first significant female British poet. She was also the first woman to have a commercial play staged. Well known in her own time, she fell into obscurity and it was not until the late twentieth century that her true worth was recognised. When feminist writers began to focus on her poetry she was finally acknowledged as one of the most influential women poets in the English language.

Much discussion around Katherine's life and poetry concentrates on whether she was a lesbian, for the emotional focus of her poetry was on women and the passionate relationships she had with them. Regardless of Katherine's own sexual orientation they are the first British poems which express same-sex love between women.

Early biographical material about Katherine is scant. Most of the information is supplied by the antiquarian and author John Aubrey. In his most famous book, *Brief Lives*[1], he brought together short biographical sketches of notable individuals and, where possible, interviewed those who had known his subjects. For his piece on Katherine one source was his own cousin Mary, who played such a pivotal role in Katherine's life.

Katherine Phillips was born in Bucklersbury, in the City of London on 1 January 1632, the daughter of John Fowler and Katherine Oxenbridge. John was a wealthy cloth merchant while his wife came from a distinguished family. The young Katherine was extremely precocious, she could read the Bible before she was four years old and had an excellent memory. She was extremely religious, praying for hours, and at ten could repeat verbatim entire sermons she had heard only once. She wrote poetry avidly and kept her work in a 'table book'. She was, said her cousin, very good-natured, not high-minded, pretty fat, not tall, with a reddish face.

Katherine's preciousness had a lot to do with her parents, who hosted literary gatherings in the years before the outbreak of the Civil War. John Aubrey would have attended, as did Henry Vaughan, the Welsh poet, and many others. They also chose to send Katherine to school – a rare occurrence for a girl at this time. But female education was not the same as that of young boys – the emphasis was on social graces and the skills for becoming a good wife. Katherine did however continue her love of poetry and Aubrey comments that she "loved poetrey at schoole, and made verses there", so was certainly not restricted by the idea that women did not write.

Katherine's closest friends at school were Mary Aubrey and Mary Harvey. The latter would become influential in British arts as the first published British woman composer. Katherine and her friends set up a literary salon, the Society of Friendship, on the model made fashionable by Henrietta Maria, the French wife of Charles I. The Queen had made popular the idea of 'Platonic love', which became the rage at court in all art forms. Part of this fashion was to set up societies of friendship whose members adopted pastoral names from classical works. In Katherine's school version she became Orinda, a name she seems to have made up for herself, and Mary Aubrey became Rosania.

However Katherine's childhood was interrupted at the age of ten when her father died, leaving his wife, daughter and son Joshua some £3,300 (about half a million pounds today). Three years later in 1646 the widow re-married, to Sir Richard Philipps the 2nd Baronet of Picton Castle in Pembrokeshire. This was a step up for the three of them as they married into one of the most ancient and powerful families in Wales.

In time Katherine also married – probably through her mother's influence. She was seventeen and her husband was a widower of fifty-four[2]. James Philipps was a distant cousin and son-in-law of her step-father, whose first marriage had been to Sir Richard's daughter.

Following her marriage Katherine moved into James' home, Cardigan Priory in Cardiganshire (now the Cardigan Memorial Hospital). Her new husband was generally regarded as a kind man who was a colonel of the Parliamentary army, a member of the High Court of Justice and MP for Cardigan.

The civil war in Britain had been raging since 1642 as the royalists, or cavaliers, fought to uphold the king whilst the parliamentarians, also known as roundheads, under Oliver Cromwell sought to change the way Britain was governed. In 1646 the first civil war ended with a victory for the parliamentarians. The Philipps family had been one of the few Welsh families for Cromwell, and James and his brother Hector gained notoriety by confiscating property from royalists. James, in particular, was known for the suppression of royalists through his position at court, and had even ordered executions.

This was a problem for Katherine, who w as a devout royalist. Most of her influential friends in London and Wales were of the same belief, like John Aubrey's extended family at Llantrithyd, John Jeffreys of Abercynrig and the poet Henry Vaughan. James did not seem to mind his young wife's support of the monarchy and initially it caused little tension between them.

Despite the close connection between Wales and London it must have been hard for the young Katherine to begin a new life away from all she had known. The Wales she had moved to was predominantly rural – towns were small and far apart. Letter writing was the main way of keeping in touch and people wrote copious amounts, sharing a vast and continuous exchange of news. A bright and lively girl, she made the best of it and wrote of how much more peaceful and less political the country was. She quickly made friends in the area and extended her Society of Friendship, with its logo of two interlinked burning hearts, to include new members.

Katherine was a charming and interesting character who captivated people, and few refused her invitations. How effective this early 'society' was is open to interpretation. Some see it as an productive group whilst critics view it as the desperate imaginings of a lonely girl imposing her poetry on the group's members.

The group included a number of women and it is Katherine's relationships with these women that has attracted so much attention. She lived in a society where the two sexes were shaped by radically different expectations and experiences. Close relationships were bound to be formed when spending so much time with members of the same sex. Most did not have a sexual element but there were those which, measured against the non-sexual close friendships, stand out for their exceptional emotional and romantic content.

The first person to whom Katherine devoted all her passion was Mary Aubrey or 'Rosania'. There is no record of Mary's response and so it is only Katherine's feelings we can take into account. In her poem on friendship she writes of their becoming 'one' in 'L' Amitie:[3] To Mrs. Mary Awbrey'

But we by Love sublim'd so high shall rise,
To pity Kings, and Conquerours despise;
Since we that Sacred Union have engrost
Which they and all the sullen World have lost.

Friendship with Katherine came at a high price. One member of the
group was Regina Collier for whom Katherine had written a poem on
the loss of her daughter. Regina's husband died in January 1650 and
Katherine tried to make a match for her with the Breconshire royalist
John Jeffreys. Regina had not been interested and returned to her home
in Antwerp. A furious Katherine penned a highly critical poem to her
former friend entitled 'To the Queen of Inconstancy, Regina Collier'.
Worse was to come when in 1652 Mary Aubrey married but neither
informed or invited Katherine to the wedding. It is not known why.
Perhaps Katherine's intensity of feeling for her was too much for Mary,
perhaps she wanted to spare her the pain. Whatever the reason,
Katherine was furious. Acting like a lover scorned she demeaned Mary
for denying the higher calling of 'friendship' which now "Ly's gasping
in the crowd of common things".
    Katherine poured out her grief in a series of self-obsessed verses:

Lovely apostate! what was my offence?
Or am I punish'd for obedience? ...
... And you kill me, because I worshipp'd you.
But my worst vows shall be your happiness,
And nere to be disturb'd by my distress.
And though it would my sacred flames pollute,
To make my Heart a scorned prostitute;
Yet I'le adore the Authour of my death,
And kiss the hand that robbs me of my breath.[4]

Yet like many a wounded lover Katherine quickly transferred her
affections to another, a local woman she had known about a year. Anne
Owen lived at Landshipping near Katherine's mother's old home at
Picton Castle. She came originally from Prysaeddfed in Anglesey but
had moved south to marry John Owen of Orielton, Pembrokeshire. She
joined Katherine's Society of Friendship and was given the name
Lucasia. Katherine lost no time parading her emotions for her new

friend before her old flame in 'On Rosania's Apostacy, and Lucasia's Friendship':

> Hail, Great Lucasia, thou shalt doubly shine:
> What was Rosania's own is now twice thine;
> Thou saw'st Rosania's Chariot and her flight,
> And so the double portion is thy right:
> Though 'twas Rosania's Spirit, be content,
> Since 'twas at first from thy Orinda sent.

For ten years Katherine and Anne remained the closest of friends, visiting each other and staying in each other's houses. Katherine was devoted to her and wrote probably her greatest and most quoted poem, 'To My Lucasia, in Defence of Declared Friendship':

> O My Lucasia, let us speak our Love,
> And think not that impertinent can be,
> Which to us both doth such assurance prove,
> And whence we fine how justly we agree.
> If I distruct, 'tis my own worth for thee,
> 'Tis my own fitness for a love like thine;
> And therefore still new evidence would see
> T'assure my wonder that thou canst be mine.

Katherine's passion first for Mary Aubrey and then Anne is undeniable. If written today her poems would be defined as lesbian or homoerotic, and her relationships with both women far exceed the criteria for 'romantic friendship'. How far their relationships went we will never know. Same-sex eroticism between women was known at this time and commentators varied in their opinions as to whether it was deviant or non-threatening to heterosexual relationships. Katherine herself mentioned Sappho[5] in her poetry (she was the first English language poet to evoke Sappho in verse). After she had died her friend Sir Charles compared her to Sappho, but aware of the poet's reputation he sought to distance Katherine from that association and 'shame':

> They talk of Sappho, but alas! the shame
> Ill Manners soil the lustre of her fame.

We know that Katherine had a sexual relationship with her husband. He may have waited until his young bride was a little older because six years after they were married Katherine gave birth to their first child Hector, who died shortly afterwards. A heartbroken Katherine poured out her grief in poetry. They were to have one other child, a daughter, also called Katherine, born two years later, who eventually married Lewis Wogan of Boulston, Pembrokeshire. Katherine and Lewis had sixteen children though only one daughter survived. Her mother never mentions her daughter in her writings.

Meanwhile in 1650 Parliament had appointed a Commission to change the way religion was practised in Wales. The Puritan religion was to replace the Anglican Church and so obliterate any traces of Catholic influence. The Commission for the Propagation of the Gospel in Wales was established and as part of this James was charged with increasing the number of Puritan preachers in his locale. This led him into contact with a principal advisor to the Commission, Vavasor Powell, a fiery, controversial Welsh Puritan preacher. For three years Powell removed any priest that he deemed unfit and replaced them with preachers of his choosing. He became a regular visitor to Cardigan Priory, dining often with James and Katherine. She loathed him – still a devoted royalist she was appalled by his views.

Powell had recently published a rhyme celebrating the regicide of Charles, the reaction of the public and the disrespect done to the king's body. Disgusted, Katherine published her own response: 'Upon the Double Murder of King Charles in Answer to a Libellous Rhyme made by V.P.' It was her first foray into political writing and she is one of the first women to do so in British literature. She was, herself, aware of the novelty and she excused her writing as "the breach of nature's laws".

Sending her poems to those in her Society of Friends always posed a problem in that they could fall into unfriendly hands. And an opponent did obtain a copy and threatened to publish, thereby humiliating James, unless Katherine wrote an open apology to Vavasor Powell. James himself weighed into the argument and also insisted on an apology. Katherine reluctantly did so in a poem which expressed her regret that James should be criticised for something she had written. But her feisty response, whilst distancing her views from James, afforded her an ideal opportunity to subtly reinforce her beliefs. And it was only through the influence of James did she manage to escape any further trouble.

By 1658 Cromwell had died and the political crisis that followed cleared the way for Charles II to accede to the throne. Katherine was ecstatic. James was in trouble. Having condemned a local royalist to death he was now under attack by his opponents. It was left to his twenty-eight year old wife to rescue him. Calling on her royalist friends in court, such as Sir Charles Cotterell, and using her attack against Vavasor Powell to illustrate her unswerving loyalty, she pleaded for her husband.

Katherine was obviously very fond of James. Marriage was necessary for women at this time and there are many instances of couples living separate lives or openly hating each other. Had Katherine been unhappy with James his fall from political grace would have been an excellent opportunity for her not just to leave him but to stand aside and see him executed. But she saved him.

Yet despite her fondness for James it was to the women in her life that she expressed most affection. Sir Charles Cotterell was Katherine's great friend and it was to him that she poured out her heart about her love for both Mary and Anne. Her letters to him include constant references to Anne at times almost in 'couple speak' referring to 'we' and 'us'. She also kept up a regular correspondence with Mary ('Rosania') and had to remind Sir Charles on several occasions not to tell Mary things she had said in her letters to him.

In 1663 Katherine's beloved Anne decided to marry. Anne's first husband had died whilst staying with Katherine and James at the Priory – during the same year that Katherine lost her son – and the two had comforted each other. Over time Katherine had hatched a plot for Anne to marry Sir Charles, who was now 45 years old, but Anne preferred the advances of Marcus Trevor, Viscount Dungannon from County Down, Ireland. Katherine, unsurprisingly, couldn't stand him and went to stay with Anne at Landshipping in an attempt to persuade her not to marry. But her friend would not be convinced and she duly married Dungannon.

On this occasion Katherine was invited the wedding and although she went with them to Ireland she was bitter and heartbroken. Writing to Sir Charles:

> on Sunday last the ceremony was performed to the great
> satisfaction of them all: for I alone of all the company was
> out of humour; nay, I was vexed to that degree, that I could

> not disguise my concern, which many of them were
> surprised to see, and spoke to me of it; but my grief was too
> deep rooted to be cured with words. Believe me dear
> Poliarchus, I have wept so much, that my eyes almost refuse
> me this present service.

She added: "she pretends to be the most satisfied creature in the world, and is very much concerned when she sees me melancholy." Katherine's behaviour strained her relationship with Anne to the limit and accepting her friendship was now over. Katherine wrote, "… we may generally conclude the marriage of a friend to be the funeral of a friendship."

The trip to Ireland was not simply to see Anne married. Katherine had gone there in an attempt to claim lands belonging to her father to aid her husband's ailing finances. A great lover of plays she decided to translate *La Mort de Pompée* by the French writer Corneille, but added material by herself and others from the Society. She probably chose the play deliberately as it concerns the aftermath of civil war, its understanding and forgiveness – possibly to aid her husband. It was performed in February 1663 at the Smock Alley Playhouse paid for by Roger Boyle and Sir Edward Deering. The whole of Dublin society turned out and it was an enormous success. It is the first commercial play by a woman to be performed on a British stage.

After a year in Ireland Katherine returned to Cardigan. She was depressed and lonely without Anne, and James' financial difficulties and local reputation were making life hard. He had tried to retain his Parliamentary seat for Cardigan, but was rejected. Instead they turned their attention to support Sir Charles as MP for Cardigan – an obvious pay-back for the help he had given James and his support for Katherine's play.

Katherine's last female passion was Berenice, to whom she wrote begging her to visit Cardigan to console her over Anne's loss. Higher in society than Katherine, the four letters which exist are ingratiating and fawning. But little is known about Berenice outside these letters and it is not known if she ever visited Katherine.

In 1664 Katherine went to London for three months but whilst there she contracted smallpox. In the few days she suffered she was nursed by none other than her first great love, Rosania, Mary Aubrey – and she died in Mary's arms.

ORINDA.
From the Engraving by Faithorne prefixed to the first authorised edition of the Poems (1669).

Three years after her death Katherine's poems were published to great acclaim, and became an inspiration for other women poets. The book had been compiled as a personal gift for Rosania, and in the front was a letter by 'Polexander' whose identity is unknown. He writes consoling Rosania:

> Orinda, though withdrawn, is not from you;
> In lines so full of Spirit, sure she lives;
> And to be with you, is that only spell,
> Can share her with the bright abodes;
> Your Eyes, her heaven on Earth;
> Your Noble Heart her Centre.

3. The man with the upside-down arms

In the splendid banqueting hall of Cardiff Castle is a series of stained glass windows depicting the castle's owners throughout history. In one corner is the fourteenth century proprietor Hugh Despenser the Younger. But there is one aspect of this image which differs from all the others. His heraldic coat of arms has been placed upside-down – to show his fall from grace, through treason.

Hugh Despenser window (by kind permission of Cardiff Castle).

Hugh's image in the window is all golden haired and glorious holding a hawk in one hand and gazing off into the distance, but this is a Victorian invention, for hardly any images of the real Hugh survive. And far from being glorious, he was a cruel vindictive man who wielded complete power over, and caused the ultimate destruction of, the English king Edward II.

There is one fact that almost everyone knows about 'gay' King Edward. That he was killed by a red hot poker up the rectum. But it's not true – this was a much later invention, possibly as a commentary on his alleged 'sodomy'. The other 'fact' that everyone seems to know is that Edward's father, having promised the Welsh a prince who could not speak English, held up his baby son on the balcony of Caernarvon castle. Again not true.

These inventions are not particularly surprising in the light of the complicated and controversial life of an extraordinary individual. Opinion varies on whether Edward was a good or bad king, a good or bad man, gay, straight or bisexual. One thing is certain – due to the mass of discussion around his sexual orientation Edward is placed firmly in that history, irrespective of whether he did or did not have sex with men.

Edward's reputation as a 'gay' king deals predominantly with his relationship he had with his favourite at court Piers Gaveston. From the sixteenth century onwards numerous depictions portray them in a manner which we would recognise today as homosexual. This started as early as 1593 in Christopher Marlowe's play, *Edward II*. Marlowe, subject to much speculation about his own sexual orientation, wrote a sympathetic and complex portrayal of Edward. But modern workings have tended to make Edward's sexuality more explicit and more central to his character, the most notably in 1991 by Derek Jarman – himself an out gay man. Other works have been extremely negative, such as the 1995 film *Braveheart*, in which the king is portrayed as camp and stereotypical. Perhaps this is hardly surprising given the other historical inaccuracies in the film.

Edward's sexuality has been picked over for centuries. And as soon as modern LGBT historians tried to examine Edward's life the traditional outcry of 'no proof of sex' and 'brotherhood-in-arms' was the response. Nevertheless the proof, albeit mostly circumstantial, is enough to justify Edward's inclusion in sexual orientation history. The unknown author of the *Vita Edwardi Secundi* (Life of Edward Second) written around 1326 and so contemporary to Edward, writes "I do not remember to have heard that one man so loved another. Jonathan cherished David, Achilles loved Patroclus. But we do not read that they were immoderate. Our king, however, was incapable of moderate favour."

The *Flores Historiarum* (Flowers of History) two Latin chronicles of the fourteenth century by Robert of Reading says that Edward had "illicit and sinful unions".[1] That his friendship with Gaveston went beyond the bounds of moderation and that Edward desired "wicked and forbidden sex". The *Monastic Chronicles of Meaux*, although written much later, stated that Edward took too much delight in sodomy. These and other statements sum up how far Edward exceeded the concept of 'brother-in-arms' and 'romantic friendship'. The desire to constantly be with the other person, the excessive gift giving, the devotion, etc are not seen in heteronormal friendships. Trying to prove, or not prove, a physical relationship then becomes pointless.

After Gaveston was murdered by powerful barons who wanted him out of the king's life Edward had a number of 'favourites' – for he seemed incapable of functioning without close male support. But he then began the relationship which would destroy his life.

Hugh Despenser has received less coverage than Gaveston in LGBT history despite his having a much bigger impact on Edward's life. Both he and his father, also named Hugh, were closely associated with the royal court. They were wealthy and powerful, and Edward I, in debt to Hugh the Elder, arranged a marriage in 1306 between his granddaughter Eleanor de Clare and the younger Hugh. They had ten children in seventeen years, and it was reported to be a good marriage. One of Eleanor's sisters was also the widow of Piers Gaveston.

When Eleanor's brother died at Edward's disastrous Battle of Bannockburn in 1314 he left no children. So Eleanor became co-heiress, inheriting lands in Glamorgan, with her two sisters. However Hugh was not satisfied with his wife's inheritance and began to systematically cheat her sisters and others, particularly women, out of their lands until he owned almost the entire southern coast of Wales.

These lands had suffered a troubled past both before and during Hugh's ownership. Sir Payn Turberville during the Great Famine which hit Europe in 1315-17, extorted money from his unfortunate tenants and treated them appallingly. Llywelyn Bren, Lord of Senghenydd and Meisgyn, appealed to Edward to curb the excesses of Sir Payn. However Edward refused to meet Llywelyn and instead accused him of trouble making. Llywelyn began a rebellion by attacking Caerphilly Castle, and the revolt quickly spread through Glamorgan. Edward, anxious to prevent the whole of Wales rising against him, quickly sent men to crush the rebellion. Llywelyn was overcome and fled to the Brecon Beacons where he offered to give himself up if the rest of his followers were allowed to go free. Senior barons spoke to Edward on his behalf asking for leniency so Edward sent Llywelyn and his family to the Tower of London for safety. To keep the peace he replaced Sir Payn with someone less avaricious. However Hugh removed Llywelyn from the Tower sometime in 1318 and executed him in Cardiff. Technically this was murder as Hugh had no permission from the king to carry out such an act. However he received no punishment because he had replaced Gaveston in the king's affections, and could act with impunity.

According to Thomas Nicholas in *The History and Antiquities of Glamorganshire*, "The wholesale spoliation and cruelty practised by the latter family towards the inhabitants burnt deep into the native mind. Whenever a man's lands were cleared of cattle, or his house of goods, it was known that Despencer had been at work. Hence arose the popular saying (which to this day plays on the lips of the peasantry), when anything was hopelessly lost, 'It's gone to Caerphilly'."[2] Caerphilly was owned by Hugh and Nicholas goes on to relate that around 1380 the Welsh poet Dafydd ap Gwilym also recognised the reputation of Hugh's lands:

> A gên y gwr gan ei gi, a'i gorff el i Gaerffili!
> Let his soul pass into his dog, and his body go to Caerphilly!

In the same year that Hugh had Llywelyn executed he was promoted to Chamberlain to Edward, replacing all his previous favourites. He seized yet more lands and wielded almost absolute power – if anyone wanted an audience with Edward it had to be authorised by him. By nature Hugh was a cruel, avaricious man and like Gaveston before him his power and unpopularity placed him in a dangerous situation.

The chronicle the *Scalacronica*, a history of Britain written in the mid-fourteenth century, says that "the great men had ill will against him [Edward] for his cruelty and the debauched life which he led, and on account of the said Hugh, whom at that time he loved and entirely trusted". What the writer meant by 'debauched' is not known.

The powerful barons that surrounded the king despised both Despensers and in 1321 they struck. The Earl of Hereford and the Earl of Lancaster, along with Roger Mortimer, attacked the lands of the Despensers at Newport, Cardiff and Caerphilly in what became known as the Despenser Wars. With the country in chaos it was left to the Queen to bring about peace.

Edward had married Isabella of France in 1308 when she was twelve.

Like most royal marriages it was an arranged one but it is unlikely they had sex until she was old enough to conceive. It is known that Edward had been with other women as he acknowledged a son, Adam, who was born about 1307 and died fighting the Scottish in 1322.

Edward and Isabella's first child was born in 1312, when Isabella was sixteen. They went on to have three more children, John in 1316, Eleanor in 1318 and Joan in 1321. Examination of the couple's itineraries show that they were together nine months before the conception of each child so there is no reason to suppose that Edward was not the father. Kathryn Warner, in her biography of Edward, states, "Isabella was his loyal and supportive companion and ally, and their relationship was far more successful than commonly supposed."[3] There does seem to be a genuine affection between the two, as can be seen from their few surviving letters.

Yet at Edward's coronation it had been Gaveston who took a central role, generating outrage from both the English and French who felt that Isabella had been snubbed. But then not many twenty-four year-old men would want to spend time with a twelve year-old child. However, their relationship seemed, for an arranged one, adequate. Isabella appears to have tolerated Gaveston, and she and Edward got on fairly well. As Katheryn Warner has pointed out, they conceived their first child during Lent. This was a time of abstinence from many things, including sex. If Edward was completely homosexual this would have been an ideal opportunity for him not to have to undertake his royal 'duties'. It was not until Edward was being controlled by Hugh that his relationship with Isabella came to an end.

In history Isabella has been described as a 'she-wolf', and as wicked for usurping Edward. However her reputation has been viewed in a more balanced way through works such as Alison Weir's *Isabella: She-Wolf of France, Queen of England* and others. The queen was an intelligent woman and often acted as a mediator between Edward and his barons. But it was the younger Despenser who broke her loyalty to Edward. She never expressed any anger towards Edward, although he too could be a cruel and avaricious man – all her hatred was for his favourite.

Isabella's intervention in the Despenser Wars was crucial. It was she who publically knelt and begged Edward to send Hugh and his father into exile. Reluctantly Edward agreed. However before long the barons fell out amongst themselves and Edward plotted his revenge. In a convoluted plan Isabella went on a pilgrimage during which she visited Leeds Castle, owned by one of Edward's opponents. When the Queen was refused admittance Edward was given an excuse to begin hostilities again. This time he defeated his enemies, and having regained his power, Edward immediately sent for Hugh and his father to return from exile.

However Roger Mortimer continued to resist the king and fighting once again broke out in Wales. Again Edward was victorious and Hugh, back at Edward's side, tried to persuade the king to execute Roger. He had a long-standing hatred of the Mortimer family as his grandfather had been killed by Roger's grandfather and he had sworn vengeance. Edward however refused Hugh's demands and Mortimer escaped his imprisonment in the Tower, and fled to France.

Hugh's power was now absolute. It was he who was in control and even Isabella had to ask his permission to see her husband. She loathed him – he was by all accounts a misogynist and was particularly known for his cruelty to women.

Edward also had a new problem. As the owner of lands in France, he was expected to pay fealty to the French king, Isabella's brother. Edward was extremely reluctant to go; he disliked the idea of one king kneeling to another. In addition to the political ramifications he knew only too well that if he took Hugh with him to France there were many only too willing to assassinate him. Yet if he left Hugh behind without the king's protection, he was equally vulnerable.

So Isabella went. There she met and began a relationship with the one man who hated Hugh more than any other – Roger Mortimer. Louis X, the French king, refused to accept fealty from Isabella so she suggested that Edward send their young son Prince Edward. Agreeing to this was a crucial mistake by Edward. Isabella now held the heir to the throne and France was full of influential people who had reason to hate both Hugh and Edward. Despite several attempts to negotiate Isabella's return she wrote to powerful people, including the Pope, saying she could not until Hugh was removed, as she feared he would kill her. And she took to wearing widow's weeds to mourn, she said, the death of her marriage. But Edward would not remove Hugh and instead rejected his wife, his son and his country in order to keep his favourite. The result was a plot to invade England and overthrow Edward and the Despensers, with the Prince to be placed on the throne with Isabella as regent.

In October 1326 Isabella and Mortimer invaded. Their small force of 1,500 quickly gathered support. Shortly afterwards the Bishop of Hereford, Adam Orleton, publicly denounced Edward as a sodomite, in a sermon. Edward, with Hugh and his father, fled London and headed west. Kathryn Warner notes that in the annals of Newenham Abbey, written shortly after the event, is the line *rex et maritus eius* (the king and his husband) fled to Wales, indicating that some contemporaries thought there was a deeper, more sexual relationship.

From Gloucester the pair headed for Chester and took a boat, possibly for Ireland. But bad weather forced them to put in to Cardiff after five days spent sailing nowhere. Having left land technically the king had forsaken the country and Isabella quickly used that fact to appoint the Prince Keeper of the Realm, for whom Isabella could act.

From Cardiff Edward and Hugh made their way to Caerphilly Castle, a strong fortification which could hold out for many months. Whilst there they heard that Hugh's father who had been holding Bristol castle had been defeated and hanged. Edward tried to raise an army amongst the Welsh – they had always been fond of their king and shown him much loyalty. But they hated Hugh. They had not forgiven Hugh's excesses against them and in particular the execution of the rebel leader Llywelyn Bren.

For reasons which are unknown, Edward and Hugh then left the security of Caerphilly Castle and made for Neath Abbey where they remained for two weeks. Very little is known about their activities during that fortnight. In the late nineteenth century David Thomas, a well-known mining and civil engineer of Neath, claimed that an ancestor from the James family of Gelly Lenor, a farm near Maesteg, employed Edward as a farm servant when on the journey from Neath back to Caerphilly. Although this is probably an apocryphal story it may illustrate Edward's reported great love for 'ordinary life', for which he was greatly criticised by his contemporaries. Someone who had been ordained by God shouldn't be rubbing shoulders with the hoi polloi. However some modern interpretations see Edward as a man with the common touch.

It was a dark and stormy night on the 16 November 1326 when Edward and Hugh were captured. They were pursued by a group of men which included two sons of Llywelyn Bren. As they made their way on the ancient highway they were guided by Rhys Hywel, a

Cistercian monk and supporter of Roger Mortimer, who is supposed to have betrayed their whereabouts to Isabella. As the small group travelled down a track beyond a bend Isabella's forces were waiting. Pouncing on the king they were attempting to arrest him when Hugh managed to escape – but he was quickly recaptured. 583 years later Morien, a journalist for the *Cardiff Times*, had a plaque erected in an area which had been re-named to commemorate the capture, Pant-y-Brad (Hollow of Treachery), near Tonyrefail.[4]

"Pant-Y-Brad, Opposite on Nov. 16th 1326 was captured King Edward 2nd, (Edward of Caernarvon), The guide of captors was Rev. Rhys Hywel (Rhys o'r Mynydd)" Nov 16th 1909.

This dramatic capture, on the road from Neath to Caerphilly is as questionable as other parts of Edward's story – it is possible that they never left Neath Abbey at all. Edward was taken to one of Hugh's castles at Llantrisant for the night before being moved to Berkeley Castle in Gloucestershire.

Realising that Mortimer would kill him, Hugh, tried to starve himself to death. Unsure if he could survive a move to London Isabella and Roger put Hugh on trial in Hereford on 24 November 1326. He was brought before the jury, which included Isabella and Roger, and accused of theft of lands, murder, returning from exile without authority, usurping royal authority and high treason. Among these numerous charges was the accusation that he had come between the king and the queen and hindered their relationship. Having been found guilty he was stripped of his clothes and made to wear a crown of thorns, with his coat of arms reversed as a sign of treachery. Biblical passages were written over his body. He was dragged to his place of execution and hanged from a 50 foot gallows so the crowd could see him, cut down alive, tied to a ladder and drawn and quartered. Roger and Isabella witnessed it. The execution was depicted in the chronicles of Jean Froissart, who also stated that Hugh's genitals were cut off and burnt before his eyes. This was not generally included in the tortures of others who suffered this type of execution and was seen to be a commentary on Hugh's homosexuality.[5]

Edward meanwhile languished for ten months in Berkeley Castle. Two rescue attempts were made but in September 1327 it was announced he was dead. Controversy surrounds what happened to Edward. Some say he was murdered at the castle others say he was helped to escape and spent the remainder of his life travelling around Europe. A review of the evidence, which is quite compelling, can be seen on Dr. Ian Mortimer's blog *A Note on the Deaths of Edward II*, and Kathryn Warner's *Longlive the King: The Mysterious fate of Edward II*.[6] Irrespective of whether he did or did not die at Berkeley his lavish tomb can still be seen at Gloucester Cathedral.

Isabella and Roger went on to reign on behalf of Edward III but they had learnt no lessons from Edward and Hugh. Their own avaricious behaviour was brought to a halt when Edward III had Roger executed and Isabella sent to a convent.

So much discussion about Edward, Piers and Hugh's sexuality has been to do with homosexuality. Yet all three were married and all fathered children. We cannot make any definitive statements about the nature of their relationships with the women particularly as they were all arranged marriages. But to assign one sexuality to these men is short sighted – regardless of whether that one is hetero or homosexuality. Modern historians tend to recognise that their situation is much more complex and that people like Edward, Piers, Hugh and other should be seen as more sexually fluid.

4. Extraordinary Female Affection

In 1829 the *Cambrian Quarterly Magazine* carried a short piece on the death of Lady Eleanor Butler. "There are few of our readers," it stated, "who have not heard of the Ladies of Llangollen". This was followed by a quotation of the Comtesse de Genlis saying she would travel a long way to see two persons so united by friendship. "Then," she was told, "you should go to Llangollen, where you will see a model of perfect friendship."

There are few readers of LGBT history who do not know the Ladies of Llangollen, either. Probably the most famous 'lesbian' couple in history, they are included in almost every timeline or book on gay history and feature frequently in women's or societal studies. They do so for a number of reasons. Their story has a rattling good plot – an elopement, social exclusion and derision which gives way to acceptance and affection. Pilgrimages were, and are, made to their front door. And it has what every good story should have – undying love.

It began in 1739 when Lady Eleanor Butler was born in Dublin to an ancient Irish family. As part of her ancestry Eleanor could claim descent from the sixteenth century Margaret FitzGerald, Countess of Ormond. Described as one of the most remarkable women of her age and country she was a very active woman, "manlike and tall of stature, liberal and bountiful, a sure friend and a bitter enemy."[1]

Eleanor's family were Catholics and like many, in order to avoid the troubles in Ireland, they quite often lived abroad. Consequently Eleanor was born in a convent in France. She appears to have had quite a lonely childhood and taking up residence in her Irish home did not fit in well. She was described as too 'satirical' and masculine to attract men. Her family feared she would end up an old maid in an era when a women's main goal in life was to marry. But then something happened which would change everything.

When Eleanor was twenty-nine a neighbouring family wrote to the Butlers asking if they could watch over their niece. Thirteen year-old Sarah Ponsonby was to attend Miss Parke's school for girls and Eleanor was given the task. It was a good match for they were both avid readers and shared many interests and over the next five years they formed a friendship which steadily grew into much more.

Sarah had been born in 1755, also to a prominent Irish family. However her mother had died when she was three and her father when she was seven. With the birth of her half-brother and her step-mother's re-marriage she became an unwanted family member and was shipped off to a cousin at Woodstock who enrolled her in Miss Parke's school.

Both women were living miserable lives. The orphaned Sarah was receiving unwanted advances from her uncle and Eleanor's family were urging her to enter a convent as she was quite clearly unmarriageable. Their only sanity was the secret letters they constantly wrote to each other. When Eleanor was 34 and Sarah 18 they planned an escape.

On 3 April 1778 Sarah's aunt sent a letter to her friend in great panic "I cant Paint our distress. My Dr Sally[2] lept out of a Window last Night and is gon off. We learn Miss Butler of the Castle is wt her. I can say no more. Help me if you can. We are in the utmost distress and I am sure you pitty us. God Bless you. ever Yours E.F." With a postscript, "Mr Butler of ye Castle has sent here in search of his daughter."[3]

Sarah, it seemed, had dressed in men's clothing, armed herself with a pistol and taking her small dog Frisk had climbed out of a downstairs window. A labourer in on the plan took her to the barn where Eleanor was waiting. Eleanor had left her house around 10pm, also in men's clothes, and had ridden to join Sarah with the intention to ride to Waterford and get a boat to England.

In the morning everyone was searching for the fugitives. But it seems for some reason the two women either did not reach the boat or it did not sail, and they were forced to shelter for two days in a barn. Then they were caught. Sarah's family arrived first and was planning to take both women back to Woodstock when Eleanor's family arrived insisting she go back with them. Despite much begging and pleading that she might be allowed to go with Sarah her father's orders were to remove her. Crying hysterically Eleanor begged further until she was dragged onto the coach and they left.

As they made their way back home Sarah's aunt demanded to know the reason for the strange escape. They wanted to go to England, said Sarah, take a house and live together. Later her aunt wrote of the relief that there had been no man involved – that it had all been just a Romantic Friendship. But the local area was abuzz with rumours causing the family to worry for what was seen as a ruined future for both women.

Sarah, who had caught a cold from hiding in the barn, became extremely ill and Eleanor was kept a virtual prisoner at her sister's house. She was writing daily to Sarah but the distress her letters caused made her aunt ask Eleanor to stop.

Eleanor's family was even more determined to send her to a convent but Sarah vowed that she would do anything to save her friend from this fate. Sending members of her family they pleaded for Eleanor but the Butlers would not be moved. Finally it was decided – Eleanor was to be sent to France. They did make a last minute offer that she would only have to go for two years if she agreed never to see Sarah again. Eleanor refused and in a last show of kindness the two families allowed the friends to meet for the final time. But in the half hour they were given they hatched a new plot to run away again.

Once again Eleanor escaped, and hid in Sarah's bedroom, aided by a housemaid Mary Carryl. They were discovered 24 hours later and kept in the house for ten days as they were lectured and berated to come to their senses. But they were adamant about their decision to go away together.

Suddenly help came from an unexpected quarter. The Butlers had given up. They sent a solicitor to say that they would no longer stand in their way and faced with this news Sarah's family also capitulated. However a family friend could not resist one last try and warned Sarah that Eleanor had a 'debauched mind' and was only acting in her own interests and not those of the one she professed to love. Sarah's uncle fell to his knees, apologising for his conduct and offered her twice her allowance if only she would only stay. Sarah's reply was that she wanted to "live and die with Miss Butler."

Two days later, laughing happily, they got into a coach with Mary Carryl and left Ireland on 9 May 1778 never to return. Arriving in Milford Haven Sarah began writing a journal '*An Account of a Journey in Wales … By Two Fugitive Ladies*' and dedicated it to her 'most tenderly Beloved Companion'. With money running short and finally finding themselves in Llangollen they determined to remain in the place with which they would forever be associated.

Despite the family's relief that their relationship was nothing more than a 'romantic friendship' there was an underlying understanding that this could be so much more. The word 'romantic' had originally meant anything that was fanciful or idealised and did not have such a link to love as it does today. Romantic friendships had developed in the eighteenth century to describe passionate relationships between women. With both sexes spending most of their time apart the growing number of middle and upper-class bored ladies was also growing. Having become quite a phenomenon, 'romantic friendships' were promoted as a shared interest in the finer things in life and there are a wide range of texts illustrating the fashion. One familiar theme was the idea of retirement to some idyllic location to devote oneself to scholarly pursuits and pastoral life. Eleanor and Sarah were seen as the zenith of this ideal and so their fame grew.

The 'ideal' was, however dogged by rumour and speculation about the exact nature of two women excluding themselves from society and living together. And that rumour and speculation was being applied to Eleanor and Sarah's 'friendship.' They were particularly annoyed by an article in London's *General Evening Post* which in 1790 ran a story headlined 'Extraordinary Female Affection'. The piece described their flight from Ireland and of their finances and life together with, as Elizabeth Mavor says in her book, an "unmistakable innuendo of perversity". The paragraph which caused most annoyance described the pair almost in 'butch-femme' language. Eleanor was "tall and masculine, wears always a riding habit, hangs her hat with the air of a sportsman in the hall, and appears in all respects as a young man, if we except the petticoats which she still retains. Miss Ponsonby, on the contrary, is polite and effeminate, fair and beautiful." The article was worrying for a number of reasons. The two women depended on their families back in Ireland for financial support as well as the government for a pension. Any hint of perversity and they could be cut off from both sources. No wonder Eleanor was so anxious to stop articles of this kind appearing. They enquired about suing for libel but were advised against it. However the air or perversity remained and so over the following years the Ladies set about crafting their lives very carefully.

Through family contacts they were introduced to high society in the area and were slowly accepted. People travelling to Ireland would often stop en-route in Llangollen as it was a popular place on the tourist map. As knowledge about the Ladies grew, more and more visitors wanted to view this extraordinary pair but they admitted only those they could trust, and themselves called only on people they knew would not cause trouble. The extensive landscaping they had done at Plas Newydd turned it into a kind of historic house visit and was on any proposed itinerary for travel in the area. Eleanor and Sarah would hide away as visitors tramped around the garden. The press bought into the carefully constructed image and wrote lavishly of the house its gardens and its occupants. By 1801 the Ladies of Llangollen were international celebrities.

As their fame grew so did the people of distinction visiting them – Robert Southey, William Wordsworth (who wrote a rather doggerel verse about them), Sir Walter Scott, Gladstone, the Duke of Wellington and Josiah Wedgewood. Caroline Lamb, the lover of Byron, was related to Sarah and also visited. International visitors from minor royalty to writers and artists came. But the problem of so many visitors was that the Ladies could not guarantee what would be written about them. The celebrated comic actor Charles Mathews described their appearance: "there is not one point to distinguish them from men; the dresses and powdering of the hair, their well-starched neckcloths, the upper part of their habits (which they always wear, even at a dinner party) made precisely like men's coats, with regular black beaver hats, everything contributing to this semblance. To crown all, they had crop heads, which were rough, bushy, and white as snow."[5]

The Scottish writer John Gibson Lockhart visited in 1825 and writing to his wife gave a slightly flawed history and mixed Eleanor and Sarah up. He wrote:

> "It was many a day, however, before they could get implicit credit for being the innocent friends they really were, among the people of the neighbourhood; for their elopement from Ireland had been performed under suspicious circumstances; and as Lady Eleanor arrived here in her natural aspect of a pretty girl, while Miss Ponsonby had condescended to accompany her in the garb of a smart footman in buckskin breeches, years and years elapsed ere full justice was done to the character of their romance ...
>
> Imagine two women, one apparently seventy, the other sixty-five, dressed in heavy blue riding habits, enormous shoes, and men's hats, with their petticoats so tucked up, that at the first glance of them, fussing and tottering about their porch in the agony of expectation, we took them for a couple of hazy or crazy old sailors."[6]

Nowadays with the benefit of their published journals and the letters and texts of others we can see that the rumours were not ill founded.

They shared the same bed for fifty years, a large four-poster of richly carved oak. In their diaries and even in letters to friends they constantly referred to each other as 'beloved' or the matrimonial implication 'my better half'. In her will Eleanor left everything 'to the beloved of my heart' and when she was ill was tended by 'My Sweet Love.' Everything they owned was embossed with their intertwined initials and their letters were jointly signed. They spoke of 'we' and 'our'.

In addition the friends to whom they were closest to tended to be other women involved in questionable romantic friendships. They included Anna Seward, the leading female poet of day whose work is now a staple of lesbian literature, and who referred to them as the 'Rosalind and Celia of real life' (after the Shakespearean transvestite characters). In 1796 Anna wrote the poem 'Llangollen Vale' which was widely read and added to the cult of celebrity around Eleanor and Sarah. Not everyone was comfortable with their questionable reputation. Other women in partnerships wanted to keep a low profile and disliked the speculation surrounding Eleanor and Sarah. Edith Somerville, who had a partner Violet Martin, referred to them as a 'grotesque romance'. Hester Thrale, the diarist and author who provides an important source of information on eighteenth century life, referred to them as 'dammed sapphists' and writes that women would not stay overnight with them unless accompanied by a man.[7]

Eleanor and Sarah lived together for fifty years with the ever faithful Mary Carryl, who had been instrumental in their escape. In Ireland she had been known as Molly the Bruiser, was masculine, and could certainly hold her own having been dismissed for throwing a candlestick at a fellow servant. She took no wages but lived with them for the rest of her life. When she died in 1809 Eleanor and Sarah were heartbroken and built a triangular monument in St Collen's church with a loving epitaph engraved on one side.

As the years passed Eleanor became almost blind and was led around the house by Sarah, famously depicted in a painting by Lady Delamere. Eleanor died in 1829 and Sarah two years later. They were interred under the triangular monument next to their faithful Mary.

Ever since LGBT people were first able to claim their history the Ladies have been the subject of intense discussion as to whether they were a lesbian couple in the sense we understand today. One of the criteria of those who argue for friendship over relationship is that there is no proof that they had sex. This assumes that only sex makes you gay – an argument which devalues non-sexual relationships between any couple. No relationship can be measured on such narrow criteria. Equally, given that a huge number of marriages throughout history have been arranged or forced, and even when we knew sex took place it does not confirm a relationship, particularly in those days when men and women lived such separate lives. When married couples without children feature in history there is not the same amount of intense speculation as to whether they did or did not have sex. However the mere fact of trying to prove sexual activity puts the Ladies firmly into the history of sexual orientation. So in many ways it's irrelevant. Equally the descriptions of them as 'masculine' or wearing masculine attire puts them firmly into gender identity history.

With many forbidden lives from the past we are left to excavate fragments in order to provide a narrative of people's lives. With the Ladies the same is true of their image. They were adamant about not having their portraits made but in 1828 Mary Parker (later Lady Leighton) visited. Whilst her mother distracted the Ladies Mary made two sketches of their faces from under the cover of a table. Sarah was in profile but as Eleanor was now very blind it was possible to sketch her full face without being seen. The picture was not completed until three years later, after both Sarah and Eleanor had died. Mary visited Plas Newydd before it was dismantled and sketched the library with all the items on the table exactly as it had been and then transposed her sketches of their faces onto imagined bodies. The completed picture

was then engraved by Richard James Lane and sold by Mary to raise money for charity.

However the most famous image of the ladies is by James Henry Lynch. Taking Mary Parker's image he made a pirated copy sometime between 1833 and 1845 of the ladies standing outside in riding habits.

This was widely circulated in the latter part of the nineteenth century[8] and became the defining image of Eleanor and Sarah. It appears on myriad Victorian/Edwardian souvenirs from postcards to tea-cups. There was even a dinner service depicting an idealised image of the women on horseback amid a not very Welsh background. A copy of this was produced by Swansea (Cambrian) pottery later owned by the cross-dressing Amy Dillwyn, who had her own same-sex relationship.

After their death Plas Newydd was bought by Charlotte Andrews and Amelia Lolly who had been 'impersonating' the Ladies, but they could not emulate them effectively. By 1861 they too were both dead, and buried beneath their own Gothick obelisk in Llantysilio churchyard. But the legend of the Ladies was now unstoppable. Mary Louisa Gordon, one of the first women doctors to be trained in Britain, visited following a dream. Inside the house she had a vision of the

Ladies and went away to study them. Eight months later she was back
seeing another vision of them outside. Arranging with the apparitions
to meet them back at the house she broke into Plas Newydd and spent
the night chatting to them. The result of this spiritual tête-à-tête was
Mary's 1936 book *Chase of the Wild Goose*[9], published by Hogarth
Press. Mary also donated a marble relief of the Ladies which can still
be seen in Saint Cullen's church.

Since their deaths Eleanor and Sarah have been invoked by many
people for many reasons. The marketed image of the 'Ladies of
Llangollen' have been held up as an ideal – the romantic escape from
harsh environments, fighting against all odds to be together,
acceptance from neighbours and the wider world, influencing others,
and becoming internationally famous. It encompasses all the elements
of LGBT history, and LGBT fiction, in a way many other stories
cannot.

A final note. In 2012 this author, aware that no National or Poet
Laureate anywhere in the world had written a poem dedicated to the
LGBT people of their country, invited the National Poet of Wales
Gillian Clarke to contribute to LGBT History Month Cymru. Gillian
kindly wrote and appeared in person at the Senedd to read 'Sarah at
Plas Newydd, July 5th, 1788'. As the first poem of its kind in the world
it is fitting it commemorates the most famous historic 'lesbian' couple
in the world:

> And our good neighbours, who warmed us when,
> the hounds of disapproval at our heels,
> the valley took us in, out of the storm,
> Come. See our vines, our roses. Be our witness
> that honest love can shape the wilderness.

5. Frances and Mary

"Miss Frances Power Cobbe lived in Wales, but she belonged to the world, and women everywhere owe her more than they will realize."[1]

So began the *Cambrian News* obituary for one of the most unsung heroes of women's suffrage. Virtually unknown outside the papers of academia, Frances was in her time a powerful women who wrote extensively on a vast number of topics – around 320 books and pamphlets. She founded a number of animal charities and helped form the nascent RSPCA. All her life she fought for the abolition of vivisection. She was a founding member of the first group in Britain to campaign for women's rights, the National Society for Women's Suffrage in 1867 decades before the more well-known Emmeline Pankhurst's ultimately successful campaign in 1903. Her pamphlet *Wife Torture* directly influenced the Matrimonial Causes Act 1878 which gave women the right to separation with maintenance and with custody of a child under ten if the husband was violent.

Born into the prominent landed Cobbe family in Dublin, Frances was well educated and independent. She had enough family income to travel extensively and met numerous influential people whom she often called upon to help in her work. Through friends she was introduced to Mary Carpenter, a social reformer, one of the foremost public speakers of her time on anti-slavery, women's suffrage and education. Mary had established various poor, or 'ragged', schools, including one in Bristol. Mary, looking for someone to share her work, invited Frances to move in and it is believed they had a relationship, which did not work out.

Frances' wide circle of friends included the American actor Charlotte Cushman. Charlotte had gained great fame in America before deciding to make her name in Britain. She was renowned for her 'breeches' roles, or cross-dressing to play male leads, her most famous being Romeo. Victorian audiences saw nothing odd in a woman dressed as a man playing a romantic role with another woman. They believed it represented a purer, more spiritual way of expressing love without the taint of sexuality getting in the way. Throughout her life Charlotte was openly lesbian. She took a number of wives including in the UK the immensely popular poet Eliza Cook, followed by the writer Matilda Hays.

Charlotte, like many with wealthy and artistic talent, was attracted to Rome where numerous artists, sculptors and writers went to live or visit. Such company took a more liberal attitude which women in particular found attractive. And this was particularly true of women sculptors. At least nine worked in Rome at this time, four of whom had been encouraged and supported by Charlotte and her large entourage of lesbian and non-lesbian women. They included Edmonia Lewis, an African-Native American and the only black woman sculptor of the time; Harriet 'Hatti' Hosmer, the most famous American female sculptor of the nineteenth century, and Emma Stebbins, Charlotte's last 'wife'. Her most famous work, and New York's first commissioned statue by a woman, is the *Angel of the Waters* (1873) fountain in Central Park. The statue with its large soaring wings has always captured imagination and it has been extensively copied in many media. It even comes to life in *Angels in America* a TV miniseries centred on a gay man living with AIDS.

Charlotte constantly used her influence to promote members of her group and she had arranged for Hatti Hosmer to meet John Gibson. He had been born in north Wales from very humble origins but his talent had seen him rise to become one of the most famous sculptors of the time. He is now all but forgotten. In 1856 he had caused enormous controversy with his 'Tinted Venus'. Gibson believed rightly that classical statuary had been coloured and so he painted his version of Venus – an act which shocked Victorian society. A naked woman in pristine white marble was art; a naked woman coloured in flesh tones was simply rude.

In Rome Gibson was extremely close to another Welsh artist, Penry Williams. As with many people with forbidden lives there is little direct evidence to support claims that the two men had a relationship. However a close reading of accounts left by contemporaries provides enough circumstantial evidence to strongly support the relationship. Unlike other artists, Gibson rarely took pupils but he had a close friendship with Mary Charlotte Lloyd.

Mary was born on 23 January 1819, one of seventeen children, to Edward Lloyd and Frances Maddocks. She came from an ancient family and members had married into the Wynns one of the most earliest and important families in Wales. The Lloyds lived in the fourteenth century Rhagett Hall, near Corwen, which Edward had acquired in 1804. In her extensive biography of Frances Power Cobbe[2], Sally Mitchell could find no record of Mary's early life, and speculates that she may have lived with her spinster aunt Margaret. Margaret and the Lloyd family were friends of that most famous of historical lesbian couples, the Ladies of Llangollen. The Ladies' diaries record visits by the Lloyd family, and Margaret had a number of books inscribed to her by the Ladies which she left to Mary. It is unknown if Mary ever met the Ladies if she did so she must have been a child, as they died in 1829 and 1831.

Mary inherited money from both her father and her aunt which gave her independence. She studied art and sculpture with Rosa Bonheur, who is now considered to be the most famous female painter of the nineteenth century. By 1853, aged 34, Mary was in Rome working in John Gibson's studio. Also working there was Hatti Hosmer. Charlotte's influence had worked and Gibson had been so impressed with the young American that he broke his rule never to take on pupils for her. It was in his studio that Mary and Hatti began a life-long friendship.

The presence of so many artists in Rome brought streams of visitors to see them working in their studios. Their legacy is a large number of diaries, letters and other writings which provides us with detailed accounts of Charlotte's group of women artists. Their masculinity, independence and habit of wearing male dress made them curious to behold and fodder for many commentaries. The women were un-married, riding around town unchaperoned, drinking coffee in cafes and working with their hands, which shocked more 'respectable' visitors. Nathaniel Hawthorne described them in his novel *The Marble Faun*, and Henry James derisively dismissed the female sculptors as 'the White Marmorean Flock'.

A visitor to the 'flock' was Frances Power Cobbe. She visited Italy six times between 1857 and 1879 and in her autobiography wrote: "In Florence my friends had been principally literary men and women. In Rome they were chiefly artists. Harriet Hosmer, to whom I had letters, was the first I knew. She was in those days the most bewitched sprite the world ever saw." She described John Gibson as "a most interesting person; an old Greek soul, born by hap-hazard in a Welsh village." And she found "brightness, freedom and joyousness" in the company of the American women, comparing them to "we quiet English ladies ...

taught from our cradles to repress such signs, and to cultivate a calm demeanour under all emergencies."[3]

Sometime in the winter of 1861-2 Frances and Mary met – she was 39 and Mary 43. "One day when I had been lunching at her house," Frances recalled in her autobiography, "Miss Cushman asked whether I would drive with her in her brougham to call on a friend of Mrs Somerville, who had particularly desired that she and I should meet, – a Welsh lady, Miss Lloyd, of Hengwrt. I was, of course, very willing indeed to meet a friend of Mrs. Somerville.[4] We happily found Miss Lloyd, busy in her sculptor's studio over a model of her Arab horse, and, on hearing that I was anxious to ride, she kindly offered to mount me if I would join her in her rides on the Campagna. Then began an acquaintance, which was further improved two years later when Miss Lloyd came to meet and help me when I was a cripple, at Aix-les-Bains."

During the next two years Frances and Mary's friendship grew, with Frances returning to Rome several times to visit Mary. In 1857 she was determined to go despite having fallen and injured her foot which never fully recovered and plagued her for the rest of her life. "My last journey but one to Italy was taken when I was lame ... Miss Lloyd rejoined me at Genoa in the spring to help me to return to England, as I was still (after four years!) miserably helpless. We returned over Mount Cenis which had no tunnel through it in those days; and, on the very summit, our carriage broke down. We were in a sad dilemma, for I was quite unable to walk a hundred yards; but a train of carts happily coming up and lending us ropes enough to hold our trap together for my use alone, Miss Lloyd ran down the mountain, and at last we found ourselves safe at the bottom."

By 1864 they had set up house together in Kensington, London: "Miss Lloyd – one morning before breakfast – found, and, in an incredible short time, bought the dear little house in South Kensington which became our home with few interruptions for a quarter of a century, No 26, Hereford Square." Mary, thanks to her inheritance, paid for it, and they split the household bills. They shared many interests, in animals, women's rights and social welfare, but they were very different. Whereas Frances was outgoing, fun and lively, Mary was introverted and often unsociable. Constance Battersea, the daughter of Baron de Rothschild, and friend of Frances noted how Mary was

devoted to Frances but "so unlike her. Pessimist, unsociable, gloomy …
rather alarming at first; a stern moralist; a hater of cant, with no belief
in humanity or I fear in God."

Once they had moved in together they began a relationship of which
Frances wrote, "and from that time, now more than thirty years ago,
she and I have lived together. Of a friendship like this, which has been
to my later life what my mother's affection was to my youth, I shall not
be expected to say more."

In London the two threw themselves into activism, particularly with
regard to animals. Mary was an executive for the Home for Lost Dogs
which later moved to Battersea. She and Frances mortgaged their
home, raising money to help Battersea Dogs Home out of a financial
crisis.

They still travelled alone in various directions. Mary often went back
to Wales to visit her family, and in 1866 she left for Rome to visit
Gibson who had been taken ill. Frances, writing to her friend Mary
Somerville, says "… as if I were going to let my wife run about the
world in that manner like an unprotected female & leave me behind."
But Frances, unable to accompany Mary, wrote about her sadness not
to have her partner with her that winter. Later, when Mary went to
Wales without her, Frances again wrote to Somerville that Mary was
coming "home to me like a truant husband."[5]

Gibson had suffered a stroke and Hatti wrote to his friend Lady
Eastlake, "Very early on the morning of Mr Gibson's death Miss Lloyd
and I were summoned hastily to his room – she remained with him till
the last, but I left a kiss on his forehead and came away. Oh! How cold
and drear the stars looked that morning as I walked slowly home! I saw
the beloved master a moment after death. Grand and calm and
beautiful his face was! Then I left Rome for a time. One of my best
friends was taken from me when the master died."[6]

In his will Gibson left Mary £200 (about £17,000 today). Apart
from a fund to look after his Tinted Venus he left the rest of his estate
to Penry Williams.

Back in London Mary and Frances designed the new house so that
she could have studio in the garden, "Behind us we had a large piece
of ground, which we rented temporarily and called the 'Boundless
Prairie', where we gave afternoon tea to our friends under the limes,
when they were in bloom. On a part of our garden Miss Lloyd erected

a sculptor's studio. The house itself, though small, was very pretty and airy; every room in it lightsome and pleasant, and somehow capable of containing a good many people. We often had in it as many as fifty or sixty guests. In short, I had once more a home, and a most happy one; and my lonely wanderings were over."

However Mary, ever the country girl, was never completely happy in town and it probably added to her grumpy old woman persona. She was very anxious about their relationship, insisting that Frances keep her name out of all their work and on her death left orders for all of her correspondence to be destroyed. So we have no writings by Mary – or pictures. Everything known about her has either been written by others or by Frances.

Despite her unhappiness with town life Mary stayed to support Frances' work. They tried to ease her need for the countryside by moving to the outskirts of London. In *The Duties of Women* Frances put marriage and friendship as equal. With no other term available to her it was necessary to use the word 'friendship' as the only way to describe her marriage. "I think," she wrote "that every one, at least some time or other in life, must have the chance offered to them of forming a true marriage with one of the opposite sex or else a true friendship with one of their own, and that we should look to such marriages and friendships as the supreme joy and glory of mortal life, – unions wherein we may steep our whole hearts."[7]

They had become a couple and were recognised as such by all their friends. Letters would be address to "you and Miss Lloyd" and Frances peppered her own writings with 'our house', 'our garden', 'we' and other shared terminology. In 1869, when Mary was once more away, Frances wrote to Somerville whom Mary was stopping to see: "I thought ere this you would have had my better half with you... Poor old darling, I am comforted by knowing she is happy and enjoying her little fling. Her life can never have too much of that to make up for the past – but I am very lonely and sad without her."[8]

Frances' work in anti-vivisection was not going well and was meeting with resistance at every turn. Infighting had made the work difficult and as several successive secretaries left the work fell heavily on her and Mary. She recalled, "... the heart-wearing work combined with my own increasing years (made) my life in London less and less a source of enjoyment and more of strain than I could bear. In 1884 Miss Lloyd, with my entire concurrence, let our dear little house in Hereford Square to our friend Mrs. Kemble, and we left London altogether and came to live in Wales."

Initially they rented a cottage, as the house in which Mary had inherited a one third share in, with her sisters, was being rented out to provide an income. One of their neighbours was Charles Darwin. They received a stream of visitors and Frances described themselves as "The Ladies of Hengwrt – not to be confused with the Ladies of Llangollen". The Imp, Hatti, arrived in 1867, "I have made a jump and landed on the Welsh hills," and she wrote to a friend. "We have been on a most delightful excursion nearly all day, under the guidance of Miss Lloyd. She has reason to be proud of her country as far as its atmosphere and beauty are concerned ...Miss Lloyd is hospitality itself, Miss Cobbe jollity itself, and we three are as snug as possible ... The air is perfectly delicious, like champagne, only much better, for that I never drink, but the air! I walk with my mouth wide open to get as much of it as I can ..."

Later Hatti and Mary went on pilgrimage to find the humble cottage near Conwy in which John Gibson had been born.

In 1892 Frances received an inheritance which allowed them to quit their rented cottage and move into Mary's house, Hengwrt. Mary's home ownership must have rankled with Frances though. The 1869 Municipal Franchise Act meant Mary was able to vote, while Frances, who had done so much to fight for the rights of women, was not. The house was a delight to them both. "No spot in the kingdom," wrote Frances, "I think, not even in the lovely Lake country, unites so many elements of beauty as this part of Wales." And there Mary flourished.

Despite their happiness they were both getting old and Mary in particular suffered badly with arthritis. She was no longer able to work in the garden and look after the house, and as movement became more difficult so did her mood. By 1895 her health was bad. A year later she suffered a heart attack. When Frances wrote describing Mary's death she said she had died "bravely resting on my arm and telling me we should not long be separated."

Mary was buried in Llanelltyd churchyard in the village that Frances could see from the windows of Hengwrt, in a double plot with a single headstone with views down to the sea and surrounded by woods. To Frances Mary's death was a 'mortal blow' – "I have yet to learn how I am to live without the one who has shared all my thoughts and feelings for so long." She described their relationship as "thirty-four years of a friendship as nearly perfect as any earthly love may be – a friendship in which there never was a doubt or break – or even a rough word – and which grew more tender as the evening closed."

Frances carried on writing, working and living at Hengwrt but wrote to friends describing herself as a 'poor lonely woman' or 'lonely beyond words'. Her friend the writer Blanche Atkinson, who had moved nearby to Dolgelly, later wrote, "The sorrow of Miss Lloyd's death changed the whole aspect of existence for Miss Cobbe. The joy of life had gone. It had been such a friendship as is rarely seen – perfect in love, sympathy, and mutual understand. No other friend – though Miss Cobbe was rich in friends – could fill the vacant place, and henceforward her loneliness was great even when surrounded by those she loved and valued. To the very last she could never mention the name of 'my dear Mary', or of her own mother, without a break in her voice. I remember once being alone with her in her study when she had been showing me boxes filled with Miss Lloyd's letters. Suddenly she turned from me towards her bookshelves as though to look for something, and throwing up her arms cried, with a little sob, 'My God! how lonely I am!'

Every morning Frances rose early to visit Mary's grave. She planted roses from Mary's garden on the grave and whenever she was troubled or sad she would sit there to "find a closer communion ... with one who had been her counsellor in all difficulties, her helper in all troubles."

Frances would spend hours re-reading the letters and records of their life together. In the spring of 1891-92 Blanche Atkinson was walking with Frances through the grounds at Hengwrt and asked if she would write an autobiography. But Frances thought she had done nothing of worth, but also "she did not think her friend, Miss Lloyd, would like it." However she relented and wrote the first volume in 1894.

Her life continued – she discussed donating her library to Barmouth but when falsely accused of ill-treating her horse she was so angry she wanted to withdraw the offer. That she who had fought so hard all her life for animal rights should be so accused. Furious at the judiciaries, the press, the police, she needed to get away for a while and travelled to Bristol to visit her old flame Mary Carpenter. But she was glad to return home.

A year later Frances re-wrote her autobiography with Blanche's help. She had relaxed slightly in her adherence to Mary's orders not speak of her and wrote, "It would be some poor comfort to me in my loneliness to write here some little account of Mary Charlotte Lloyd, and to describe her keen, highly-cultivated intellect, her quick sense of humour, her gifts as sculptor and painter (the pupil and friend of John Gibson and of Rosa Bonheur)." And there creeps in a note of sadness that she cannot speak so freely of the woman she loved, "the reticence which belonged to the greatness of her nature made her always refuse to allow me to lead her into the more public life whereto my work necessarily brought me, and in her last sacred directions she forbids me to commemorate her by any written record. Only, then, in the hearts of the few who really knew her must her noble memory live." And she included a poem she had written to Mary twenty-five years earlier adding, "They have a double meaning for time has come for me to need her most ..."

> In joy and grief, in good and ill,
> Friend of my heart: I need you still,
> My Guide, Companion, Playmate, Love,
> To dwell with here, to clasp above,
> I want you,– Mary.

"God has given me two priceless benedictions in life," Frances wrote. "In my youth a perfect Mother; in my later years, a perfect Friend ...To live in companionship, almost unbroken by separation and never marred by a doubt or a rough word, with a mind in whose workings my own found inexhaustible interest, and my heart its rest; a friend who knew me better than any one beside could ever know me, and yet – strange to think! – could love me better than any other, – this was happiness for which, even now that it is over, I thank God from the depths of my soul."

Frances died on the 5 April 1904 and was buried alongside her beloved Mary in the grave with a single headstone.

6. Cranogwen

When Sarah Jane Rees died in 1916 the *Carmarthen Journal's* obituary said "It can safely be claimed that no other Welsh woman enjoyed popularity in so many public spheres as Cranogwen did."

Cranogwen was the bardic name for which Sarah was to become famous – a fusing of Saint Cranog, after whom Llangrannog was named, and Hawen the local river. And she certainly covered a lot of ground in her life. She was a sailor, teacher, award-winning poet, writer and editor, and lay preacher. She did an enormous amount for the advancement of Welsh women writers, but today is little known.

Sarah Jane Rees was born on January 9, 1839 in the small coastal village of Llangrannog, Cardiganshire. She was the youngest child of John Rees and his wife Frances who lived in a small thatched cottage two miles inland. Having two older brothers her birth was welcomed by the family and she was named after her father's mother, who lived with them. Her early life was dominated by women, unsurprising in a town where many of the men were at sea for long periods. Sarah says in her autobiographical writings that she was a tomboy (rhoces) and copied her brothers in all they did.[1]

From her earliest days it was obvious Sarah was extremely precocious. Her parents took the unusual step of allowing her to be educated, not just in the usual female arts of housekeeping but at the village school alongside the boys. The schoolmaster, Hugh Davies, accepted her and in later life taught her Latin and astronomy.

Finishing her education around the age of fifteen Sarah was sent to start a job in Cardigan as an apprentice dressmaker. However this was not to her liking and it quickly transpired that this choice of career was unsatisfactory. Returning home she stated she wanted to go to sea with her father.

John Rees was the master of his own vessel, in which he traded up and down the coastline to Liverpool or Swansea, and occasionally to France and Holland. He was also a part-time school master. When he took his daughter with him it was not uncommon for a girl or woman to go to sea. For many years sailors had taken their wives and children with them. These women were not out to break social taboos – they were simply there to accompany their men. In 1869 the Admiralty ruled that no more women were to be allowed on Royal Navy ships. As the *Flintshire Observer* noted, "the Admiral to be commanded by the Admiral's wife, who thus commands the fleet – is certainly inconvenient".

Many more women went to sea in merchant than naval vessels, particularly those ships which sailed short routes up and down the coast as John Rees did. In 1845, around the time that Sarah first went to sea with her father, there are some thirty mentions in the Welsh press of the wives, some with children, who drowned at sea. Whilst daughters at sea are mentioned, rarely are names or ages given. When Sarah sailed with her father there was no mention in the local or national press, indicating that this was not sufficiently unusual to be worthy of comment.

A great deal has been written about women who go to sea for long periods of time in ocean-going ships but little attention has been paid to those on thousands of local vessels. One reason we know about some of the women is through seafaring tragedies. In 1878 the *South Wales Daily News* quoted a Board of Trade inquiry into the loss of the steamer *Democrat,* which had sunk off the Isle of Man. The captain was found guilty of careless navigation and the judge said, "this was another instance of a vessel lost when the master had his wife on board. If he were a shipowner he would not allow a master to have his wife on board."[2] A similar note was sounded by the columnist Cosmos in his *South Wales Notes.* In a piece entitled 'Wives on board ship' he says, "The managing shipowner does not view with any degree of favour the presence of a captain's wife on board. It is true that there are many objections to a captain of a tramp steamer taking his spouse with him. She often commands the ship, and the consequence is that it is difficult to secure officers who will put up with the dictation of a woman."[3]

Many of these women who went to sea with their husbands did so as part of the family business. They had to be willing and able to protect their property and Sarah, it seems, was no exception. On one occasion when a storm rose her father wanted to turn inland but she argued that it would be safer to go further out to sea. After a furious row between them, she won.[4] There is an indication that her father may have been an alcoholic, which would have played a part in his decision making.

After three years working on the family boat and being taught by her father, Sarah returned to education, this time to learn navigation. She went first twelve miles up the coast to New Quay, which had a number of small navigation schools. It was a predominantly male populated town in the 1840s attracting men from all over Wales and beyond, most of whom worked on building ships or other maritime occupations. It must have been a daunting time for a young woman – Sarah was undoubtedly regarded as something of a curiosity. Whilst most men would have been accustomed to women at sea, a woman studying alongside them was unusual. Leaving New Quay, presumably with a qualification, Sarah moved down the coast to Cardigan to another school, probably to gain more specialist knowledge. She then went to London to finish her education and emerged with a master's certificate which allowed her to captain a vessel anywhere in the world – a rare achievement.

Most female captains had become so through experience not official examination. The record of female captains in the nineteenth century is predominantly American but there are British examples. The *Pembrokeshire Herald* in 1852 told of Betsy Miller who for the last twenty years had been a 'sailing master' trading between Ardrossan and Irish ports. Her father was a ship owner and "Miss Betsy, before she went to sea acted as ship's husband to her father; and, seeing how the captains in many cases behaved, her romantic and adventurous spirit impelled her to go to sea herself. Her father gratified her caprice, and gave her command of the *Clietus* ... and she has weathered the storms of the deep when many commanders of the other sex have been driven to pieces on the rocks." Betsy died in 1864 at Glasgow, and was so successful she became very prosperous.

Few known transvestite women or transmen achieved sea-going high rank – possibly because they wished to avoid detection. Captain John Weed was a transman who had commanded transatlantic vessels for years, and was mentioned in the *Evening Express*. In 1904 he had cut his own throat at a sailors' home in New York and only on medical examination was Weed found to be a biological woman. It begs the question how many more undetected transmen there were at sea.

Once qualified Sarah did not return to sea but instead set up a navigation school in her home village of Llangrannog, in 1859. Navigation schools for young men and women were growing in popularity and flourished during the second half of the nineteenth century. The old method of sending children on board a ship to gain their education afloat was being replaced by the idea of training them on land first.

Sarah was not the only woman to run a navigation school in Wales. Ellen Edwards was the daughter of Captain William Francis, who set up a school on Anglesey which became one of the best in north Wales. Indeed it was so popular that he decided on another in Carnarvon, in 1830. The twenty year-old Ellen, the same age as Sarah when she set up her school, was put in charge. Unfortunately the idea of a school being run by woman had its critics, particularly from the local church and school. Many years later Ellen was cited as a biased example of how uncivilised the Welsh were in the *Report of the Commission of Inquiry into the State of Education in Wales*, commonly referred to as the 'Treachery of the Blue Books' due to its inaccurate portrayal of Welsh society. However, a number of influential men defended Ellen – many of them ship's captains who had been taught by her. She died in 1889 at the age of 79 and her daughter, who started as a teacher, eventually took over the school. When Sarah opened her school in 1859 there was no mention of it in the Welsh press indicating it was perhaps not that unusual for a woman to run a navigation school.

There is no record that Sarah ever suffered criticism, as Ellen Edwards had. In fact, so successful was she that she opened her classes to adults. She was tall and commanding, with a strong husky voice like a man's. Russell Davies in his book *Hope and Heartbreak* stated that she was a "dried spinster of ferocious irritability, [who] often clouted her navigation pupils so hard that they saw stars."[5]

At home Sarah's family life appeared to be quite normal – an unmarried woman who lived with her parents. However next door lived Jane Thomas who was, as Cranogwen's biographer put it, her 'constant companion and support'. It was not Sarah's first relationship with a woman. Jane Aaron, in her writing on Cranogwen, quotes from a two-part autobiographical essay Cranogwen wrote in 1886 in which she recalled her grief over the death of Fanny Rees.

Fanny, a milliner's daughter from Troedyraur near to Llangrannog, shared a similar career path to Cranogwen. She had published works under her bardic name of Phania and like Cranogwen had managed to persuade her parents to let her leave mill-work to move to London to study. Unfortunately she contracted tuberculosis and around 1874 returned to Wales to die. But she moved not into her family's home but that of the Reeses, and died in Sarah's arms. As Aaron says, that Fanny chose to spend her last days with Cranogwen and not her own family implies "a requited affection stronger than friendship".[6] Sarah, in her essay, admitted she had "an unusual attachment to her and admiration of her", and it was only after some twelve years had passed that she had been able to plant a flower on her grave.

Some years after Fanny's death Jane Thomas lived in the house next door. When her parents died Cranogwen sold her house and moved in with Jane, and they remained partners for the next twenty-five years until Cranogwen's death in 1916.

In one of her most well-known poems she speaks of her love for 'Fy Ffrynd' (My Friend).

> Ah! Annwyl chwaer, 'r wyt ti i mi,
> Fel lloer I'r lli, yn gyson;
> Dy ddilyn heb orphwyso wna
> Serchiadau pura'm calon,
>
> I seren dêg dy wyneb di
> Ni welaf *fi* un gymhar ...
> Mae miloeed eraill, sêr o fri,
> Yn gloewi y ffurfafen;
> Edmygaf hwy, ond *caraf* di,
> Fy Ngwener gu, fy 'Ogwen'.

> Oh! My dear sister, you to me
> As the moon to the sea, constantly,
> Following you restlessly are
> My heart's pure affections
>
> To the fair star of your face
> *I* see no equal ...
> A thousand other stars of distinction
> Brighten the firmament;
> I admire them, but I *love* you,
> My beloved Venus, my 'Ogwen.'

Jane Aaron points out that Ogwen was the female love object of a popular romantic ballad of the period and so Cranogwen is placing herself in the role of the lover. Aaron also illustrates how through her writings Cranogwen was dependent on her emotional relationships with women. Her involvements with women do not seem to cause her any difficulties, which is true of many of the other women in same sex relationships. There was a whole coterie of lesbian women flourishing at the same time as Cranogwen. Frances Power Cobbe and Mary Lloyd had moved to west Wales in 1884 although there is no evidence they met for Cranogwen was by then was touring south Wales.

Cranogwen wrote about women who did not fit into the heteronormative narrative of society. One example was her essay on 'Esther Judith' which appeared in the magazine *Y Frythones* between 1880 and 1881. Esther was a neighbour in Llangrannog where she worked her whole life as a farm labourer but who was also a gifted orator. Whilst lamenting her loss to the world as a preacher Cranogwen said "Whoever else was called upon to 'keep house' and look after a family, Esther was *not*." Esther seems to fit in perfectly with the women such as Margaret uch Evans and others mentioned earlier in this book.

It was through her writing that Cranogwen became a celebrity almost overnight. In 1865 she entered that quintessentially Welsh cultural event, the Eisteddfod. At the National in Aberystwyth she entered a poem 'Y Fodrwy Briodasal' (The Wedding Ring). Entry is anonymous so when it was revealed a woman had won there was genuine shock. She had been competing against established and renowned male writers who were, the *Cambrian News* reported, 'disgusted'[7]. And *Seren Cymru* added a note of caution about a young girl of twenty-six winning against 'men of talent', hinting that fraud was well-known at the Eisteddfod with people passing off other's work as their own.[8] Not that they were pointing fingers.

'Y Fodrwy Briodasal' considers four different women reflecting on their marriage and whilst it considers many aspects of marriage it, as Aaron points out, "at no point features a bridegroom".

Cranogwen went on to have enormous success at eisteddfodau. The following year she won a substantial prize at the Chester National Eisteddfod with the poem 'Longing' and took the chair at the local Aberayron in 1873 for a poem 'The Wreck of the North-fleet'. *Y Quiet a'r Dydd* noted: "pa hysbysiad a dderbyniwyd gyda tharanau o

gymeradwyaeth, gan mai dyma y ddynes gyntaf a gyrhaeddodd Gadair Eisteddfod'" (which was received with thunderous approval, because this was the first woman to win a 'Chair Eisteddfod').[9] Sarah presented the chair to Capel Bancyfelin in Llangrannog but when it closed it was removed to Capel Penmorfa near Penbryn.

Sarah's eisteddfodau successes brought her great acclaim and now known by her eisteddfodic name of Cranogwen she was invited to speak across Wales. She published a book of poems, *Caniadau Cranogwen* (Songs of Cranogwen), in 1870 dedicated to her mother Frances. And she was making enough money to stop teaching. Devoutly religious and dedicated to temperance she became a travelling lay preacher. She did not give up writing and in 1878 she became editor of a Welsh language women's journal *Y Frythones* (the Woman's Journal) devoted to women's issues. It was thirty pages of jam-packed articles in small print in double columns, which appeared each month.

There had been a Welsh magazine for women before. *Y Gymraes* had been set up in 1850 by Ieuan Gwynedd but most of the writers were male and it promoted the male-centric 'ideal woman' scenario. Working women were generally ignored. It was predominantly read by men and as it closed Ieuan Gwynedd bitterly commented "*Y Gymraes* was never supported by the women of Wales."[10] Not surprising really.

In England there had been women's magazines and journals since the eighteenth century, some run by known lesbians. In 1847 Matilda Hays, the English 'wife' of the American actor Charlotte Cushman, had attempted to set up a journal but it had come to nothing. Eliza Cook, another English 'wife' of Charlotte's, set up her eponymous journal shortly afterwards with contributions by Matilda. They wrote extensively on women's education, temperance and the plight of working women. Matilda went on to found the *English Woman's Journal* in 1858. Both Eliza and Matilda were members of the 'the White Marmorean Flock' – that collection of predominantly British and American gay women living in Rome. Whilst there is no evidence that Cranogwen knew or interacted with any of them she would undoubtedly been aware of their publications and writings.

Twenty years after *Y Gymraes* closed Cranogwen became the first woman editor of a Welsh woman's magazine. But in many ways *Y Frythones* took over from where *Y Gymraes* left off – the articles predominantly promoting the 'ideal woman' image. Some things had changed though, Cranogwen was a great believer in women's and girl's education which she promoted through the pages of *Y Frythones*. However, working women still received little attention. For example, a recent law banned women and girls from working in mines, which put a lot of working-class women out of work. Despite a well-publicised struggle to keep their jobs, *Y Frythones* made no comment and the only mention in the magazine came in the letters column from a correspondent advocating the ban.

One of the astounding contributions Cranogwen has made to Welsh culture was her determination to promote women's writing. And she proved to be one of, if not the biggest, influence on women writers in Wales. Through the many competitions in the journal and through her constant chiding more women and girls to get involved she opened the way for women to write. The deeply flawed and unfair reporting in the 'Treachery of the Blue Books' still rankled with the Welsh. It had been particularly critical of Welsh women and over the following decades many Welsh writers wrote extensively on the morality of their countrywomen. *Y Frythones* was deliberately published in Welsh to show that Wales had a strong culture, to give those who could not speak English a platform and to promote a sense of Welsh belonging. Certainly Cranogwen felt patriotically towards Wales and the Welsh language. In the poem 'My Country' she wrote, "My country, I shall spend my life in service unto you."

In other pages of the journal marriage, despite being a part of 'ideal woman' scenario, received short shrift. In an 1880 letter writer, 'R.A.' from Cwmceri, asks "Are there not many more girls in the world than boys?" To which Cranogwen answers "No, the number is pretty equal. Not 'all' of them choose marriage presumably ... Be comforted, sisters, and try to find something to do." This echoes Frances Power Cobbe some twenty years earlier in her pamphlet 'What Shall We Do With Our Old Maids?', written shortly after meeting Mary, in which she proposed that single women could be as happy as married ones. She cheerfully referred to herself and other independent women with reputations as poets, novelists, artists and sculptors as 'old maids'. Frances and others in same-sex relationships saw themselves in a completely different light to those of their heterosexual married sisters.

Knowledge of same-sex relationships between women was more widely known than has been acknowledged. Certainly during Katherine Philips' time, the Ladies of Llangollen, and Frances and Mary and their extended circle of lesbian women, all couples were recognised and discussed in letters and diaries. Whilst descriptions lacked the vocabulary used today it can be clearly seen that many of these comments concerned the disturbing aspect of their 'friendships'. Whilst lesbianism as we know it today – which includes a greater openness in society and a holistic understanding of life relationships – was not known during these times; it was recognised that women living non-heteronormative lives could be in 'perverted' relationships.

Between 1869 and 1870 Cranogwen toured the United States lecturing on women's issues and temperance. In 1889 she resigned as editor of *Y Frythones* (which thereafter it lost its way rather and shut down in 1891). Eleven years later, at the age of sixty, Cranogwen co-founded Undeb Dirwestol Merched y De (UDMD), the South Wales Women's Temperance Union. Jane Aaron quotes the poet Nantlais, who portrays Cranogwen in what would traditionally be a masculine role:

> She was born to lead an army,
> the front line was her place;
> God gave her an army,
> the army of the brave Women of the South.

By the end of the first year it had ten branches just in Glamorgan, and by the time of her death in 1916 there were 140 branches throughout the whole of Wales. But Cranogwen's preaching was not always welcomed and she often suffered from depression and self-doubt. In her poem 'Evening Meditation' she wrote of "how heavy is my load, my weight of sin, of tedious guilt" and "so weak, so feeble, lonely on my road."[11]

This is perhaps not surprising when, as Rev. D.J. Jones of Pontardawe in his biography of Cranogwen recalled "that women and wives were things to be kept shut up in houses and wait upon the menfolk ... When they saw Cranogwen in the pulpit addressing a crowd of men they thought that the end of the world had come. They thought it excellent to suggest that she was a man in female form, or woman in masculine form, and we heard some suggest that she belonged to neither one sex nor the other.'[12]

Often she was denied access to the pulpit in chapels and had to preach from the deacon's pew but the Rev. Jones reports "She was looked upon as a great wonder ... The village poets were gratified to have the honour of seeing her walk down the street; truly, they thought of her as a supernatural being.'[13]

Cranogwen led the temperance movement for sixteen years before retiring though ill health. She died aged eighty-one in Cilfynydd, at the house of her niece, and was buried back home under a large obelisk in the churchyard at St. Crannog in Llangrannog.

7. Too absurd to be seriously entertained

The small town of Abercanaid, named as the place where the River Canaid sparkled and frothed into the River Taff, was a small farming community until it was transformed into an industrial village in the 1860s. It lay in the coalfield just two and a half miles south of Merthyr Tydfil, clustered around its two mines the Glyndyrys Pit and the Plymouth Colliery. The mines were important, their output high enough to warrant running the Glamorganshire Canal through Abercanaid in 1849 on its way from Merthyr to Cardiff, and it was the only point on the canal to have a double dock.

The two mines stood one north and one south of the town and it was in the north's Glyndyrys engine house that the Phillips family lived. They had moved to Abercanaid from Llantrisant as James Philips improved himself from a pitman and handy man to a foreman at the Glyndyrys mine. His wife Margaret, originally from Pontypool, and their five children lived squeezed into the four rooms of the engine house. Their two eldest sons, Evan and Joseph, had moved away, while their four daughters and a baby boy were still at home. On Monday 1 October 1901, their fifteen-year-old daughter Edith Gertrude went missing.

Margaret described the last time she had seen her daughter: "I left home … to go to Merthyr to deliver some vegetables from the garden … at half past two o'clock, and the girl was then taken in the house, so that she did not go away before dinner. When I came back she was missing."[1] Despite an extensive search by the family and their neighbours the girl's whereabouts had not been discovered and on Tuesday James called the police.

By Wednesday afternoon concern was such that PC Dove, the local constable, decided to drain part of the Neath canal, but nothing was found. On Thursday another length was drained from Upper Abercanaid to the double lock, and to general alarm Edith's bodice was discovered near Quay Row and her skirt in the old basin. Fearing foul play the whole length of the canal from the double dock to the Merthyr laundry was let out but there was no sign of a body. As people began to despair that they would ever find the girl alive PC Dove received news on the Friday evening that Edith was alive and well. She was living in lodgings nearby – her story so strange that the press rushed there clamouring for interviews.

She had been in school, Edith told the *Carmarthen Weekly Reporter*, until she was twelve and having left had been acting as a domestic servant for her mother. She had turned fifteen in January and had been growing increasing unhappy with the severity with which she was treated by her mother so she decided to run away. "Towards dinner time on Monday," Edith said, "when the coast was clear, I undressed in the back garden and put on a shirt and an old suit of clothes belonging to my brother Joseph, which were hanging on some bushes, and cut my hair short with a pair of scissors and went off. I threw my own clothes into the canal, and went for a walk round the Cwm pit."

Her father, who worked nights, was asleep upstairs and the only other person present was her invalid sister. The house was in an isolated position near the canal and it would have been easy for her to undress outside without being seen. In the evening she walked to Dowlais, about four and a half miles from Abercanaid, and "tried to get work there, calling at Mr Thomas Jones's, a manager in the Dowlais Works. He told me to come at six o'clock on the next day." Edith walked about Dowlais for the whole night, and "on Tuesday morning I went to the coke ovens at a quarter to 6 o'clock, and one of the labourers told me there was no work there for me."

Disappointed, Edith returned to Abercanaid but rather than go home she "went across to the South pit, Plymouth, where I stayed until the men came up. I saw a collier named Matthew Thomas, who promised to give me work with him and the next day, and on the following morning I saw him at the lamp room and went down to work with him in the No 1 pit as his boy, the arrangement being that he should pay me 15s per week. I worked all that day, having got lodgings at Mrs White's, in Nightingale-street, Abercanaid. I worked also on the Thursday and on the Friday, and still lodged at Mrs White's, where, after I had washed on Friday night, Police Constable Dove found me. Each night at my lodgings I slept with a male lodger, but he had no suspicion of my sex, which, of course, I carefully concealed."

Mrs White, it seemed had no idea her new lodger was actually a girl and whilst speaking to the journalists continued to refer to Edith as a boy. "He came to my house about five o'clock on Tuesday evening, and asked, "Please can you give me some lodgings?" I asked

him where came from and he said 'From Cwmbach.' I asked him
further if he had a father, and he said 'Yes,' but he told me that his
mother had been dead about two years... I suspected nothing until
Thursday night, when another lodger who saw the boy washing in
the tub, made a communication to me." Mrs White said she spoke to
the boy about the lodger's suspicions, but could get no satisfactory
answers from him so "On Friday night...I told him he had better look
for another place and he said, 'All right.' Between 7 and 8 o'clock that
night my daughter, Mrs Griffith Jones, called in, and upon carefully
looking at the boy, identified him as Edith Phillips. She did not
pretend that she had recognised him, but she went and told Mr
Phillips, the father."

Once Mrs Jones had gone to fetch Edith's father, Mrs White turned
on the girl saying, "What is this game you are carrying on?" Edith gave
no reply but started to cry. "Meanwhile," Mrs White told the journalist,
"Police Constable Dove was sent for, and he came, and, the youngster
having had his clothes taken off, some neighbours provided him with
proper female attire, and he was taken away." When PC Dove had
arrived he "saw the girl, happily, safe and sound" and dressed in a shirt
and trousers. Initially his intentions had been to return Edith to her
family but "she resolutely declined to allow herself to be taken home"
and became quite hysterical at the idea. So much so that concerned
about her mental health PC Dove "conveyed her by the nine o'clock
Rhymney train to Merthyr, and took her to the workhouse, where she
still remains in the Infirmary."

Edith had told PC Dove that her mother had beaten her on the
Saturday and things were so bad she feared to return to the house. But
when interviewed by the press Margaret Phillips denied it saying, "I
don't remember beating her on Saturday at all, but I recollect that I had
occasion to scold her. Her brother, who is married, lived up at Mardy,
came up to see us on Sunday, and she seemed very much annoyed
because we wouldn't allow her to go to the station to see him off. It is
not true that I am in the habit of ill-treating her. She is of a rather sulky
disposition, and whenever I asked her to do anything she did not seem
willing to do it." This seems a strange answer, 'not remember' if she had
beaten the girl, but James who was present when his wife was being
interviewed stated that as far as he knew there had been no cruelty on
his wife's part.

Edith's brother Joseph was also interviewed and he told the journalist that on Wednesday evening he had seen a person dressed as a boy in Glebeland Street, in Merthyr, and felt certain it was his sister though he did not speak to her fearing he may have been mistaken. He followed her for a considerable distance through various streets until eventually he lost sight of her by the throttle valve[2] at the bottom of High Street. When he got home he related the affair to his parents, but they treated the idea of the girl being dressed as a boy as too absurd to be seriously entertained. It seems, though, that Joseph was right because Edith later admitted to being in town that evening having gone to purchase a shirt.

Edith's story was further verified when the press spoke to Matthew Thomas of Gethin Street, Abercanaid. The miner told journalists, "The boy, as he appeared to me, came to me after I got to the top of the pit on Tuesday evening, and asked me if I could give him work. I asked him if he had been working underground before, and he said he had not, but that he had been working on the top of the pit at Pontypridd ... He then went to the colliery office to sign the book, and he signed on as John Williams ... He seemed to be a bit weak, but he did his work as a helper well, and gave such perfect satisfaction that I had intended keeping him on permanently."

Matthew Thomas never doubted that Edith was a boy and in everyone's description she is described as very convincing. The journalist from the *Carmarthen Weekly Reporter* said that Edith had a somewhat boyish face, a strong voice, in walking took a good stride and was able to pass herself off as male very well. Although, he added, "she was not capable of doing it sufficiently well to escape occasional suspicion", deliberately ignoring the fact that Edith was only caught because she was accidentally seen whilst washing.

There is not a great deal of information about Edith's family life and how she was treated, but certain things she says and does are telling. Whilst giving versions of her story to both Matthew Thomas and Mrs White she said that her father was alive but that her mother was dead, indicating an antipathy against her. The very idea of her returning home affected Edith so badly that PC Dove was concerned enough not to force her but instead took her to the Infirmary. One may argue that she was simply throwing a temper tantrum but consistent evidence indicates that she was deeply uncomfortable about returning home.

She also had money which she offered to Mrs White for the lodgings. It is unlikely that she would have been paid after only one day's work as most were paid weekly. Yet she certainly had money as she stated that she had visited Merthyr to buy a shirt. Nobody in the family accused her of stealing so she must have gained it by other means. If she had saved it she must had done so for some time, indicating that her plan to leave was not a sudden one.

Edith was described by one journalist as having great strength of character as she moved about in her own village among people who knew her. She was aided by the idea that, as her parents told Joseph, a girl dressing as a boy was "too absurd to be seriously entertained". However that 'absurdity' was not borne out in the world at large. Numerous cases concerning sexual orientation and gender identity had appeared in the press in the 1890s, more frequently than in previous years. One of the reasons was the change in taxation on newspapers. They were now much cheaper and there was a proliferation of new titles all chasing good stories. Part of the increase in articles on gender fluidity was the huge rise of women who were dressing, acting or living as men.

At the beginning of the century only a handful of cases were being reported in the Welsh press. However by the 1890s the number had shot up to around 352 cases averaging about 29 stories a month. This rise in coverage also reflects the controversy around ordinary women wearing trousers as part of women's suffrage. They are included here as these women were regarded as 'unnatural'.

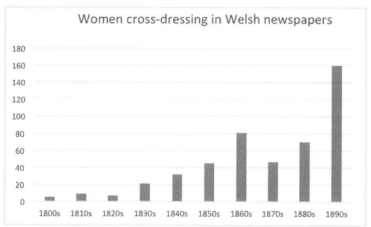

The articles covered women all over the world, which reflected the improved transmission of knowledge internationally. Many of the stories were similar to Edith's – girls who wanted to escape from the harsh realities of their life. But in an age when women had few rights a significant number turned themselves into men. Passing undetected sometimes for their entire lives these women's secrets often only revealed themselves upon death. Some did it for economic reasons to support a family with no man around, and some did it for personal freedom. A number did it because they were transgender or lesbian, and often set up home with a woman – several even getting married in church.

The media appeared singularly sanguine about the whole thing. There was no in-depth analysis of why women wanted to live as men and no explanation as to how they had achieved the transformation. If men and women were so different, as they believed them to be, how could a woman look, walk, talk and act like a man so convincingly that nobody noticed? On the whole it was all treated with a slightly bemused indulgent attitude. But as the number of cases grew the interest of the press started to wane. The *Pembrokeshire Herald* in its piece on Edith sighed about "the latest instance of a girl donning masculine attire" as did the English newspaper the *Tamworth Herald* – "the latest member of her sex to disown the petticoat in favour of masculine attire."

When the press asked why women wanted to appear as men the answer was often 'for a lark', a phrase so frequently used it became almost a stock answer. Edith told the *Pembrokeshire Herald* that she thought it "would prove the best and shortest way to emancipation." What is significantly different about Edith's story compared to most of the others on record is that she remained in her home town. Dressing as a man was invariable a means of escape and most women left their local areas.

What gave Edith her confidence to remain among people who knew her is unknown. If her family's attitude that a girl dressing as a boy was absurd, where did Edith get both the idea and the confidence to carry it out? Everybody who spoke of the young girl described her as quite bright, and she was educated enough to read – it's quite possible she was familiar with instances of girls donning masculine attire through reading newspapers. Certainly her resolve never wavered. She must have known that the canal had been drained on the Wednesday and the

Thursday; Abercanaid was not a big town and rumours would have been rife. Having just come up from the pit on the Friday she may not have known about the attempt to drain the pond but it seems that Edith deliberately allowed the town to assume she was dead, perhaps in the hope that she could start a new life or earn enough money to escape.

However having been caught and removed to Merthyr her story didn't stop there. Arguments raged whether she should be allowed into the workhouse, because she wasn't destitute, or whether she should be forced to return home. Some thought she should be found a job, with one workhouse board member commenting "Work might do her good" – ignoring the fact that Edith had been working extremely hard down the mine. Inquiries confirmed that life at home was not happy for Edith, and she was permitted to go into the workhouse. Initially housed in the infirmary, whenever she was moved into the general populace she suffered some kind of mental attack and was returned to the infirmary. Edith, it seemed, knew how to get her own way.

Her unusual story had tugged at the hearts of the local miners, who set about raising funds for her so she could be trained in order to find a more suitable job. The fund raised £27. Using the money Edith was moved to the Salvation Army Rescue Home, Charles Street, Cardiff, with the Chairman of the fund Mathew Blackwell seeing her off from Rhymney Railway Station. The *Carmarthen Weekly Reporter* who followed her there described Edith as having a "masculine appearance, is very bright and happy in her new surroundings, and evidently appreciates fully the efforts made on her behalf by her collier friends in the Merthyr district. Arrangements are being made to give her a good training, but it is not yet decided whether she will be kept at Cardiff or sent to some other of the many admirable institutions connected with the social work of the Salvation Army."

Little more is heard of Edith until three years later in 1904 when it was reported she was very ill. The fund for her finally reached £30 but had become exhausted in August 1903. Edith was now in bad health and as she was unable to work it was necessary for her to be discharged from the Salvation Army accommodation. She could not be induced to return to her parents and as the doctors felt she would not live long John Morgan of the Merthyr Board of Guardians asked that she be brought back to the Merthyr workhouse, which was agreed.[3]

Although Edith survived her ill health in 1904, very little is known about her subsequent life. She appears on the 1911 census as a domestic servant when she is 25, single, and working for Laurence Pearson a maker of artificial teeth in Thorncroft, Penydarren, Merthyr. She died in 1963 aged 77 – there is no record of her ever marrying or of her ever donning masculine attire again.

Society has in the past, and to a certain extent continues to be so today, wedded to the idea of a binary gender – male, female. Many struggle to understand how an individual can change gender so effectively that family, friends and society no longer recognises that individual. Edith, and others in this book, clearly show that boundaries between genders are much more blurred than is realised.

8. The Girl Who Would a Sailor Be

In October 1898 a sixteen year-old American girl, Alice Amelia McKinley, arrived at the Sailor's Institute in London, sent there by well-wishers after undertaking a voyage as a sailor. Journalists rushed to interview her, an appeal raised money for her, and everyone wanted to know about her adventures. How could a woman disguise herself so completely that everyone believed she was a man?

Her story was no means unusual. From the earliest of times, according to the evidence of prehistoric graves, there have been hundreds and hundreds of stories of women who dressed as men, lived as men, married women, and as far as society was concerned were men. But how was it possible for these women, who lived before gender reassignment surgery or medicine, to blur the lines of gender so effectively?

Nowadays society in many areas of the world sees nothing wrong with women wearing trousers. Yet in some countries it is still either illegal or socially unacceptable. In 2015, nine Sudanese women faced forty lashes for being dressed 'inappropriately'. On the other hand, men wearing women's clothes do not enjoy the acceptance that many women expect when wearing men's clothes.

Cross-dressing is an age-old tradition around the world. It has often been used to illustrate the disruption of the natural world in much the same way as role reversal traditions. However as society became more religious it was religious texts, not the law, which underlay the enforcement of dress codes. Women who wore men's clothes were often arrested on suspicion of disguising themselves for nefarious purposes – it was beyond the comprehension of the police and the judicial system that women would want to wear trousers. But with no law to fall back on the accuser's only option was to quote Deuteronomy 22:5 "the woman shall not wear that which pertaineth unto a man, neither shall a man put on a woman's garment: for all that do so are abomination unto the Lord thy God."[1] Trouser-wearing Christian women can often be seen condemning homosexuality on the grounds of Leviticus 18:22 – but conveniently ignore their own status of abomination.

If gender definitions are caught up in what clothes men and women put on, where does that leave us when writing about people from history who cross-dressed? There can be little or no comment about their sexual orientation unless there is direct evidence of it, but what can we say about those who blur the lines of gender?

The late nineteenth century saw an enormous amount of press attention on women who cross-dressed as men. The reasons given are various. Many did it simply to escape, reluctant to put themselves at risk whilst travelling. Others did it for nefarious purposes such as house burglaries or fraud. At a time when women's wages were a fraction of the pay of men (even when doing exactly the same job) some did it to earn better wages. When a man left home sometimes the woman did it to support her family. Women had little or no recourse to help as victims of domestic violence and so a number simply ran away and disguised themselves. There were practical considerations as well. Women in the mines found skirts too cumbersome and adopted a sort of half-way solution. They kept the skirt as a pseudo-apron over trousers – much to the horror of many.

There were numerous reasons why women decided to dress and live as men. But the two areas which fascinated society then and now were those women who lived as male soldiers or sailors. And it was the latter which was to dominate during the nineteenth century. So much so that in 1843 *The Welshman* wrote: "Every newspaper had its paragraph announcing the discovery of a female sailor. The result was a thorough conviction in the public mind that all sailors were female sailors – that there were no other sailors than female sailors in disguise; and now the curiosity would be the discovery of a male sailor, if such a phenomenon could be well authenticated."[2]

The number of articles in Welsh newspapers runs to several hundred and in the whole British media into thousands. From these articles 156 individual women have been identified from the period 1800 to 1899. Most appear after the 1840s when newspapers became more prolific, with the greatest number (41) during the 1840s. The stories came from around the world and the Welsh press reported on 103 of them. The majority of the women are from England (60), Wales has 12, Scotland 7, Ireland 6, and the USA and France and 5 each, with single examples from Canada, Sweden, Denmark, Russia, Holland, Australia, Spain and India.

The Welsh examples illustrate some of the reasons why women cross-dressed. The story of female sailors had been a popular theme in seventeenth century ballads which were printed and sold in the streets and shops in thousands. These stories of female sailors conformed to a strict stereotype. Usually pulled from her lover's arms by various hardships the woman dons male attire to seek her love. However she is always depicted as rather feminine, which bore no relevance to real-life female sailors, and always reverted back to her womanly ways once she had found her true love.

Some of the real-life stories conformed to this ballad stereotype. In 1806 *The Cambrian* had a story about a young Welsh woman who signed as a volunteer on board a tender[3] in Swansea. This was during the Napoleonic Wars, which meant that as a volunteer she avoided a medical examination. When the tender arrived in Plymouth she met up with her young man. At this time when men could be 'pressed into service' or forcibly made to serve in the armed forces particularly when the country was at war. The young man in question had obviously been pressed and the young woman was anxious to marry him because as soon as she got there they were duly wed.

In many of the stories, particularly during the early part of the century, the press was quite reluctant to name the women involved. By doing so they brought shame and disgrace not only on the woman but on their families. Only after the 1840s are more women named. An example appears in a story of 1842.

In September that year a sailor by the name of Edward Williams signed on the *Lady Charlotte,* a packet carrying mail and passengers. However just as they were about to sail from Cardiff the attention of PC Perkins was drawn to the sailor. He had been flashing money about carelessly and seemed very anxious as to when the packet was to sail. Perkins approached him and asked where he had acquired the money but he refused to answer. Becoming more suspicious Perkins took Williams to the police station where a Superintendent Stockdale, after asking a few questions, suspected that the sailor boy was in fact a girl. This was resolutely denied and so the Superintendent had a woman examine Williams. It was confirmed she was indeed "a pretty looking Welsh girl".

She said her name was Mary Davies, that she was twenty and lived with her father a poor farmer about nine miles from Merthyr. Her brother had left home some time previously and had recently sent her £5 with the request that she join him. Unfortunately she had lost the letter and could not remember the address – even worse she couldn't remember what country he was in. Undeterred she had set out despite the fact that she could not speak a word of English. She decided that she would travel to Bristol and thence to America. Her reason for cross-dressing was that she felt she could travel more safely among sailors as a man than as an unprotected girl.

Word soon spread and both the mayor and Rev. T. Stacey, a local clergyman, visited her at the police station – the later believing that Mary was of a weak mind. She was moved to the Union House, put in feminine clothes, and the vicar took her money for safekeeping until her family could be contacted.[4]

It later turned out that the girl's name was not even Mary Davies. It may well have been falsely given as if it was impossible to find the family the police would have no option but to release her and she could resume her plans. It may be she did not want to bring shame on herself and her family. And her real name may never have been discovered except for a tragedy that was to befall her.

Two months after being unmasked Mary, it was discovered, was really Anne Rees. Her father Rees Rees was not a poor farmer but a gamekeeper at Rhygos. After being taken from the ship, Anne had returned to Merthyr where she had looked for work as a 'tip-girl', those often androgynous women at the mines, but had found nothing and had no money to pay for lodgings. Which raises the question of what happened to her money? Going through what today would be about £400 in two months suggests that the Rev. Stacey was right to worry about her losing it. And a later newspaper article confirmed that Anne was of a 'weak intellect'. She had managed to gain entry to a night lodging-house, a sort of workhouse accommodation costing only a few pence, near the Cyfarthfa iron works. Going to sleep near the fire her clothes caught alight, and after suffering great agony for 20 hours she died.[5]

A similar story concerning an early discovery was that of Anne Cartwright from the Rhos in North Wales. In 1857 she attempted to follow her young man to Australia from Liverpool. Despite being dressed in sailor's attire (although it is not stated how she managed to acquire it) she "prematurely betrayed her sex". She was shipped back to the parental home but tried again. This time she took her brother's clothes, stole 4s 6d but only got as far as Wrexham. She spent her money on drink and was so tipsy she attracted the attention of a PC

Sheen, who locked her up. She told the police that she wanted to go to Australia as a cabin boy having performed several voyages in that capacity. But it seems this was a lie as she certainly was not cut out to impersonate a sailor and was once more sent home.[6]

The two Annes never made it to sea but one woman who allegedly did was Susan Brunin from Newport. Susan's story came to light after she was arrested for being drunk and disorderly in Bristol in 1855. Brought before the magistrates 'the renegade' appeared dressed in a "Guernsey shirt, canvas trousers, braces, blue cap, &c, and her hands being all tarred it was difficult to discover the disguise." She was, said the newspaper, rigged out like a sailor in every respect and she certainly 'personified a smart Jack Tar.'[7]

Susan told the magistrates that she had been passing as a sailor for fifteen months and had been on several foreign voyages. She had recently returned from three months at sea as an able seaman on board the *Eliza* of Newport. Securing another job in the Cardiff docks she was engaged by a captain who was to pay a month in advance. But on finding that she was a female he refused to keep his contract. It seems she had been discovered when, said the *Pembrokeshire Herald*, "she was gallanting another lass about the town, and seemed to act the sailor throughout." It is not possible to make any definitive conclusions about Susan 'gallanting a lass' about town. Some of the most famous female sailors such as Hannah Snell, Mary Anne Talbot and Mary Lacy all pursued women. They may have done so in order to protect their disguise, or they may have been gay or bisexual as we understand those terms today. In their biographies there was an emphasis on the fact that after discovery they became heterosexual – it had all been such a lark.

Susan gave no reasons why she had undertaken such a life. The *Pembrokeshire Herald* mused, "It might have been merely a great desire to obtain more money than she might earn on shore, or a more romantic object." Having been rejected by the captain in Cardiff docks Susan had wandered the streets getting drunk. In court she said nothing would induce her to change what the *Pembrokeshire Herald* called her 'fancy attire', and in return she was given a severe lecture by the magistrates on her improper conduct, advised her to return to her home and to adopt a more decent mode of living. She was then discharged.

Some stories of the female sailors which appeared regularly in the press did not concern anyone actually going to sea. Instead a number of women would impersonate men for prostitution. A man caught having sex with a female prostitute, no matter how she was dressed, would only face the run-of-the-mill fines. However a man caught having sex with another man could face a life-time in prison. Throughout Britain the papers are full of women of a certain 'notoriety' dressing as men. Examples from Wales are once again few, though one such is Catherine Williams, apprehended by the police in 1860. She was brought up at Swansea police-court charged with drunkenness and fighting. When she appeared in court it created great laughter:

> She was attired as a true British tar – a man-of-war's man. Her hair was neatly trimmed and tucked up short on both sides, and she wore a large cloth cap, with blue ribbands (sic) hanging down about a quarter of a yard over her neck. She had on a large sleeved white shirt, trimmed with blue tape, turned down over the shoulders. Her "trousers" (forgive the expression, gentle readers, as it refers to a "lady") were of large dimensions, made of white canvass, whilst her feet were enveloped with patent leather slippers. In this disguise "Miss Owen" appeared before their Worships, who could not forbear a smile, for she appeared as brazened, weather-beaten a jack-tar as ever trod a plank.[8]

The magistrates asked the police how often Catherine had been before the bench and were informed by the Superintendent that it was her twenty-ninth appearance that day – one can only assume a ship had docked! The magistrates sentenced her to twenty-one days imprisonment and she left the court "with all the daring and braggadocio of a veteran tar of the first water."

The most fully documented story about a woman sailor from Wales is that of Alice Amelia McKinley, who was sixteen years old when she ran away to join a ship. She had managed to acquire a berth on a coal supply ship to various European destinations.

On board Amelia shared sleeping quarters with five men. She knew there would be difficulties when the watch turned in and had to be very

Illustration from the *Evening Express* of Miss Mckinley
(The Girl Who Would a Sailor Be)

careful. She would sit on a seat in the fo'c'sle until the men were in their bunks, and then, "I would turn in 'all standing,' as sailors say; that is, with all my clothes on, and when the fo'c'sle lamp was blown out I used to undress quietly in my bunk."[9] There is very little coverage in the media on how the women were able to achieve such a complete disguise. This was at a time when people often owned one set of clothing and would live in it for years. Wearing baggy clothing would conceal breasts and with hard manual labour women's breasts are often small – something also seen in female athletes. And the conditions under which sailors worked meant they were enduring harsh physical labour on a daily basis. They would have been lean and wiry. Some women may have used binding, the winding of cloth around the upper portion to strap down the breasts. Menstruating when subject to hard physical labour will either slow down or stop entirely. Sailors suffered from a variety of diseases and a woman could claim any number of conditions to explain blood or the need to arrange wrappings. The absence of facial hair often raised suspicion as did the light sounding voices and small hands and feet. "Although she did not look like a girl," said a man to whom Amelia applied for a berth, "her voice was very soft for that of a boy, and her laugh was distinctly feminine."

llustrations from the *Evening Express* of Amelia first
in sailor clothes and then in female attire

There is no record of Amelia 'gallanting a lass', in fact quite the opposite. She related a story that when they were docked in Cagliari some of the men brought a very young girl on board clutching the hand of her small brother. A sailor brought her down and pushed her over to Amelia saying, "Here's a sweetheart for you Tommy," at which point Amelia became scared and snapped back, "Send her out of this. For shame! Have you got no conscience?" The sailor roared with laughter, "Conscience," he said, "whoever heard of a sailor with a conscience?" Moved by the plight of the young girl and her brother Amelia gave the pair something to eat and they left.

Amelia's discovery came at her own hand – confessing to an officer that she was a girl, though she gives no reason why she does this. The captain arranged her passage to London where she told her story to the journalists. All she wanted now, she said "and I want it so badly – is to get back to America".

However, as soon as these details began to appear in the newspapers Amelia's story unravelled. Far from being born in America, she was from Newport. Her real name was Amelia Vella and she was the eldest of seven children. Her father, Frank Vella, was from Malta and was described as a donkeyman and a ship's mechanic. Her mother was in the Abergavenny

Asylum. It seemed that Amelia had persistently adopted various aliases and that "her mother has often tried to persuade her not to act so foolishly as to dress in boy's clothes." Amelia told an employer that she wished she was a boy and that she might one day strive to become President of the United States. A fund was raised to send her to America but at Ellis Island she fabricated yet more stories about her American background. Nobody believed her and so she was sent back to Britain.

As was often the case, once their stories had appeared the women disappeared. Nothing more was heard of Amelia and the only appearance in the death records is that an Amelia Vella died in 1906 in Newport – the very town she had been trying to escape.

Public attitudes varied towards these women. When cross-dressing to reach their man they were seen as gallant, loyal and admirable. But those women who became men were puzzled over and their motives questioned. In the eighteenth and nineteenth centuries social convention saw an increased emphasis on the fragility of women and it became increasingly difficult for people to reconcile the two images.

And the question has to be asked if there are hundreds of stories we know about how many more have never come to light? It is not possible to tell how many women were actually transmen, 'butch' lesbians or cisgender heterosexual women. For the most part women, whatever their sexual orientation or gender identity, had to get married. Even when newspapers reported that a female sailor had married it cannot be assumed that it was truly for love. Yet even allowing for their desire to escape harsh environments, the women would have to have been extraordinary to embark on passing themselves off as men. And all of them must be on the gender identity spectrum to be able to first consider, then execute and pass often for many years as men. It meant they had to learn to be men and were comfortable doing so.

9. The Butterfly Dancer

Sherlock Holmes became a hugely popular literary character in the late nineteenth century, so much so that American actor-manager William Gillette collected a number of Conan Doyle's stories into a play, *Sherlock Holmes*. It was a huge hit, and in September 1901 was playing at the Lyceum Theatre, London. At which point a strange 'life imitating art' event took place.

In the audience on 20th September were Henry Paget, the 5th Marquess[1] of Anglesey, and a large group of his friends. After the play they returned to Henry's hotel and were alarmed to find several jewellery boxes broken open and their contents missing. The police were summoned and Chief Detective Inspector Drew immediately raised an alert to trace a missing valet, Frenchman Julien Gault. Henry seemed more excited by the experience than about missing jewels. According to the *Lichfield Mercury* he threw himself into the investigation and "subject to Inspector Drew's approval, it was decided that they should become amateur detectives and assist Scotland Yard in their search ... from early morning till late evening on Thursday, his lordship was exploring with his 'Sherlock Holmes' the mysteries of Soho and other French quarters."

Gault was eventually arrested in Dover attempting to take a boat to France. He claimed that he had gone out for a walk, met a woman called 'Mathilde' and telling her of his recently acquired position with the Marquess she persuaded him to steal the jewels. These were not just a handful of pieces but large numbers worth between £20-50,000, so many in fact that Henry himself could not give the police a complete list. Among them was the Anglesey Pearl, one of the great pearls of history, said to be worth £10,000 (about a million pounds today). Gault, for his part in passing on the jewels to Mathilde was only given £94. Mathilde then disappeared.[2]

Unable to find his jewels Henry turned to one man whom he thought could help − the Sherlock Holmes man himself, Arthur Conan Doyle. Doyle, an avid amateur detective, managed to track the jewels to France and amid a series of storybook events the Anglesey Pearl was recovered, though most of the jewels were not.

The story fascinated the public, but they were even more fascinated by the vivid and eccentric character on centre stage − Henry Cyril

Paget. His love of jewels and ostentatious displays were legendary. And whilst much of the press was sympathetic, notes of ridicule crept in to the coverage. The *North Wales Express* commented "… people are laughing at the idea of a man carrying so many jewels with him in order to adorn his person. With a woman, of course, it would have been altogether different; but a bejewelled man, be he prince or peasant, is looked upon as being troubled with effeminacy."

It was a criticism which was to follow Henry for most of his life.

Paget was born on 16 June 1875 in London, the only son of the 4th Marquess of Anglesey and the great-grandson of the 1st Marquess, also called Henry Paget, a war hero at Waterloo where he lost a leg. Despite the preceding Paget men being great sportsmen and military types, Henry was very different. His mother had committed suicide when he was two. The *West Australian Sunday Times* made the curious statement in 1901 that "his mother, who was a beautiful woman, was so happy with her husband that she committed suicide". In addition, controversy surrounded Henry's birth father who some believed was the French actor Benoît-Constant Coquelin, supposedly one of the greatest theatrical figures of the age. This rumour gained ground when it seemed that Henry was sent to be brought up by Coquelin. However, this is unlikely to be true and it is more feasible that Henry was brought up by his mother's sister, who had close links with Coquelin's family and later married his brother. She brought him up as if he had been her own son, and both she and Coquelin's family would remain close to Henry for the rest of his life.

Henry's father remarried for a third time to an American heiress, and they spent much of their time away. The boy was brought back to live at Plas Newydd in Anglesey in an enormous marble-built mansion standing on the shores of the Menai Strait. He was a lonely child with only a nanny and pets for company. Later he was sent to Eton, before joining the 2nd Volunteer Battalion of Royal Welsh Fusiliers as a lieutenant. Given Henry's sensibilities it seems unlikely he would have enjoyed army life. It was probably a role he was expected to undertake given the family's military background – his father had been an honorary colonel in the same regiment. Henry was not physically suited to army life – he missed his week-long 21st birthday celebrations due to ill health and disliked the British cold weather, preferring to winter in Biarritz and Pau. He was not, said The *North Wales Express*, a "robust young man".

In 1898, when he was twenty-three, his father died. Henry became the 5th Marquess of Anglesey and heir to a fortune. His estates, including Beaudesert in Staffordshire, realised around £110,000 a year (about £11 million in today's money). And Henry started spending. The new Marquess had two great loves in life – jewels and acting. The first indication of his mania was his marriage to his cousin, the society beauty Lilian Florence Maud Chetwynd, in 1898. It was, various newspapers claimed, a marriage of societal convenience in order for them both to access property and money, but Henry still gave his bride marvellous jewels like the contents of Aladdin's cave. He inundated her with every conceivable trinket in every conceivable setting and when she stopped to admire one in a window he went in and bought out the shop. For Lilian, who was a modest and retiring girl, this was all too much.

The union was not successful and barely was the honeymoon over before she walked out.[3] "The closest the marriage ever came to consummation," said one person, "was that he would make her pose naked covered top to bottom in jewels, and she had to sleep wearing the jewels."

After living apart for less than three years Lily sought to have the marriage annulled. The court listened to her case in camera. Henry didn't bother to attend and she was granted an annulment. Viv Gardner, Professor of Theatre Studies at Manchester University and an expert in the life and times of Henry, relates that the Public Records Office records grounds of 'impotence and non-consummation'. In a surprising sequel, six months later Lily asked to rescind the annulment and have it replaced with a separation order in what the judge called a 'remarkable case'. Henry raised her settlement allowance to £10,000 a year.

Meanwhile Henry got on with his acting. At Anglesey Castle (now known as Plas Newydd) he built a small theatre said to be an exact replica of Sarah Bernhardt's in Paris, where at the age of twelve he had made his stage debut.

His choice of plays was eccentric, often re-written by himself, and he would think nothing of joining a tragedy with a pantomime. But the most talked about aspect of all the performances was Henry's costumes. In 1902 in *Little Red Riding Hood* the *Daily Express* said he "...is positively aglow with diamonds and other precious stones, his magnificent dress

being thickly studded with them." His most famous piece was Aladdin in 1902 in which the *Carnarvon and Denbigh Herald* reported that "Lord Anglesey appeared in a superb salmon-coloured dress blazing with brilliants." And it was in this production that he introduced his take on a dance that had been made popular by Loie Fuller. An American pioneer in modern dance Fuller had performed skirt dances at the Folies Bergère in the late 1890s and Henry, always back and forth to Paris, was probably very aware of her. Skirt dances had become quite the vogue and another aristocrat, Charles Francis Seymour, son of the Earl of Yarmouth, was creating a similar sensation in Australia.

In Henry's version of *Aladdin* in an outfit said to have cost £100,000, the *Otago Witness* said "he did a butterfly dance, for which he was arrayed in a voluminous robe of transparent white silk. Through this flimsy drapery his slender jewelled legs fitfully appeared, and as he waved the wings he was enveloped in coloured light thrown up from below the great plate glass upon which he went through his antics." And so Henry gained the nickname by which he is most known – 'The Dancing Marquis'.

In 1903 Henry went on tour with his own production of Oscar Wilde's *An Ideal Husband*, in which he also acted. This was just five years after Wilde had been imprisoned for sodomy – which may have explained the poor audiences. For seven years Henry lived an extraordinary life: travelling, acting and spending freely. Although he had inherited a vast fortune most of it was tied to estates which he was neglecting so his debts began to mount. But there seemed to be nobody

Loie Fuller and her Serpentine Dance which
Henry adapted into his Butterfly Dance

who could urge caution. He was a popular person, particularly as he lavished money on his friends and local businesses, but it was his appearance and manner which was generating more and more comment.

"In appearance," said the *Yorkshire Post*, "there was … an almost total absence of the masculine quality in his character, and he went with easy facility from one extravagance to others greater still." The colonial press were more open and critical of Henry. "He is a thoroughly effeminate-looking young fellow," said the *West Australian Sunday Times* "and he may be seen when in Paris walking around with a toy terrier under his arm, the pet being heavily scented and bedizened with bandages and bows. The fingers of the Marquis fairly blaze with rings." His favourite dogs had jewelled collars and their hair was curled and perfumed.

One writer, T.P. in the New Zealand paper *Otago Witness*, tried to understand Henry. "I am driven," he said, "to the conclusion from much that I have seen that there are men who ought to have been born women, and women who ought to have been born men … Bearing the form of a man, he yet had all the tastes, something even of the appearance, of not only a woman, but, if the phrase be permissible, a very effeminate woman."

Taking the evidence of contemporary writers there is little doubt that Henry must be included in the history of gender identity. His effeminacy alone takes him out of the spheres of heteronormativity.

With regard to his sexual orientation most of the evidence rests in comments made by other people with little reference to original sources. The first reference, by the German physician Magnus Hirschfeld, appears in his *Jahrbuch für sexuelle Zwischenstufen* ('Yearbook of Intermediate Sexual Types' which ran until 1923 – the first journal in the world to deal with sexual variants)[4]. Hirschfeld was an important theorist of sexuality and a prominent advocate of gay rights. He believed homosexuality was natural and thought that scientific understanding of sexuality would promote societal acceptance. His comments about Henry were later used by Iwan Block in his 1964 book *The Sexual Extremities of the World*: "the Marquis of Anglesey ... also seems to have had homosexual tendencies, or at least to have been effeminate to a high degree ... resembled a pampered eccentric woman with all the whims and weaknesses of the latter. He really had the appearance of a pretty women attired in male clothing. Silky locks surrounded a pink face, distinguished by the softness and gentleness of its features."

In 1901 Henry had been named in court proceedings in New York when Charles Frances Seymour brought a libel action against the *Daily Telegraph* for defaming him. The prosecution stated, "We will show you that this man ... disgraced his family name, painted his face, roughed his neck, painted his arms and breast, wore petticoats, and assumed the dress of a female ballet dancer." In Australia, where he had lived, a local paper described Charles as "a 'skirt dancer' and local memory is of him performing his dances in a sequined outfit with butterfly wings."[5] The prosecution argued that Seymour's associates alone proved his guilt – that in Britain he had been friends with Lord Alfred Douglas and the Marquis of Anglesey.

The man most quoted on Henry's effeminacy is Montgomery Hyde, a straight man, who was a great advocator for homosexual rights. He even lost his seat as an MP when he campaigned for the Wolfenden Report to be enacted, and wrote extensively about homosexuality. In 1970 he published the first history on homosexuality in the UK, *The Other Love*, and wrote books on both Oscar Wilde and Lord Alfred Douglas. In *The Other Love* Hyde wrote that Henry was "The most notorious aristocratic homosexual at this period... [his wife] left him on their honeymoon on discovering what his particular propensities were ... Anglesey was an extreme example of the effeminate transvestite type, and was a gifted female impersonator. He was in the habit of roughing and powdering his face in order, so it was said, 'to look paler and more interesting'. When he walked along Piccadilly or the Champs-Elysees, he invariably carried a snow-white, pink-ribboned poodle in his arms, who was just as abundantly scented with patchoile and eau d'Espagne as his master."[6]

Hyde doesn't mention his sources but both Henry and Lily were related to and friendly with various people surrounding both Wilde and Douglas. In Hyde's biography *Lord Alfred Douglas* he describes a meeting between Lily and Douglas' wife: "Olive was having a short holiday with her cousin Lady Anglesey in Dinard ... Lady Anglesey, who was far from being straight-laced – her husband whom she divorced shortly afterwards was a well-known transvestite homosexual."[7]

After Henry's death the new Marchioness destroyed all the documents she could find relating to Henry, and other documents were lost in a later fire,[8] Viv Gardner says because she was so ashamed by his finances, sexuality and theatrical notoriety.[9] But the press had been full of his excessive spending, his theatrical notoriety and his bankruptcy so there would have been few surprises regarding those areas of his life. There is no evidence that Henry had a relationship emotionally or sexually with anyone. Perhaps that evidence was in the destroyed papers. The Marchioness's act rather than protecting Henry's (and the family's) reputation has simply fuelled speculation as to his sexual orientation.

By 1904 Henry's excessive spending had caught up with him and his debts had become so large that he was facing bankruptcy to the tune of £544,000. All his property was sold. It took forty-two days and was one of the largest bankruptcy sales in British history.

The jewellery sale realised only a portion of what Henry had paid for them. A poor business man he would pay over the odds with unscrupulous dealers who would follow him around. And many of the jewels had been set in ways peculiar to Henry for his performances. In order to make them usable the settings had to be broken. The famous £10,000 Anglesey Pearl which Henry had fought so hard to get back after his valet stole it realised only £3,650.

Henry's clothing and accessories were displayed for all to see. As with the jewellery many of the clothes and costumes were hard to sell. They were so elaborate that they had to be broken up. Many of his ornate

gowns were purchased by the most successful female impersonator in British music hall, Bert Errol. When he travelled to the US in 1910 Errol created a sensation by paying $1,000 customs duty on his gowns, most of which he had bought at Henry's sale.[10] Another purchaser, Vesta Tilley, the famous male impersonator, recalled, "... the dudes of Broadway were intrigued with my costume, a pearl grey frock coat suit and silk hat and a vest of delicately flowered silk – one of the dozens which I had bought at the sale of the effects of the late Marquis of Anglesey."[11]

As well as the costumes Henry had over 500 pairs of gloves, dozens of ladies' bathing costumes, dolls, toys, and 150 walking sticks, most jewel encrusted. One had a jewel watch in the handle which also rotated to reveal a miniature of a lady, another held a small electric light and one had a camera. It was a curious collection, as he never used a walking stick. Over a thousand photos of Henry and his friends were sold for £30. Even the garden was raided and his Japanese dwarf trees and orchids were sold along with four cannons, a tame squirrel and lot 96 – an old saucepan.

Even before the sale had started Henry had moved back to France. "My fortunes are only temporary," he cheerfully told a reporter from the *Manchester Courier*, "and can soon be repaired. The sales seem to have gone well, and the removal of some of the furniture is half a blessing in disguise. A good deal of it required replacing." But despite his cheeriness a friend who "was with Lord Anglesey at Lucerne during last summer and since at Monte Carlo" told the *Daily Express* that the Marquis was heartbroken at the collapse of his affairs and the sale of his property. "He lost interest in everything, and suddenly became a sad-eyed, pensive recluse, tired of life."

Never very healthy, and suffering periodic bouts of pneumonia throughout his life, Henry was taken ill in March 1905 and for about a month was confined to his room. Shortly before he had affected a sort of reconciliation with Lily and she nursed him alongside his aunt, Madam Coquelin. However he suddenly lost strength and died at 2.30am on 14 March 1905 – not yet thirty years old.

The coffin travelled from Paris to London and whilst some reports say it was unaccompanied others say there was just one person – possibly because the family did not want to attract attention. Placed on the coffin were two beautiful wreaths and a cross. And as it waited to leave "a lady dressed in mourning passed through the little group of railwaymen and passengers who stood beside the open door and placed a bunch of white flowers on the coffin. She paused a moment to gaze intently at the coffin, and then withdrew". His wife and aunt had remained in France and the woman's identity remained a mystery.

"It was at first contemplated that the body should be interred in the family vault at Lichfield," reported the *Daily Express* "with the late Marquis' ancestors. Difficulties are said to have arisen between members of the family which rendered this course impossible." And so Henry was interred in the family vault at Llanedwen church, close to Plas Newydd, on 23 March 1905.

The family would not permit anyone to attend the funeral except the new Marquis and his brother-in-law. But there seemed genuine regret in the local area where many people were very fond of Henry and shops drew their blinds as a mark of respect. At the grave were a wreath of lilies 'From Lily', and a wreath of violets from Madam Coquelin saying 'We shall meet again-Tante Cheri.'

The *Manchester Courier* wrote "so his death removed one of the most romantic and interesting figures in our time." And like so many people who do not conform to the notions of heteronormative Henry has had his life airbrushed out. He is hardly mentioned at Plas Newydd, his old home.

Jenny Rees when writing a biography of her father Goronwy Rees included a quote from A.J.A Symon. The important thing, he said, was to see people as "rare and curious flowers of character interesting both when they conform and differ from the general standards of law and virtue." Henry was a rare and curious flower and he should be celebrated as such not hidden away, or forbidden, to history.

10. A Valley Song Cut Short

The law against homosexuality in men served no real purpose. It criminalised and stigmatised men who had not harmed anyone and it often ruined and ended lives. Its impact reverberated deeply into families and friends of those caught. Since 1885, when Section 11 of the Criminal Law Amendment Act made 'gross indecency' easier to prosecute, thousands of men had fallen foul of the law. Oscar Wilde had been imprisoned in 1895. The spy Guy Burgess defected to Russia in 1951 leaving behind a public chattering about how much his homosexuality had influenced his choice. A year later Alan Turing was brought to trial for nothing more than confessing he was homosexual. The media tore these men apart, whilst those who were lesbian, gay, bisexual and transgender watched in silence, aware that simply being who they were put them at risk. Some lived as secretly as they could, others as openly as they could get away with. A question that will always remain is how much more could they, and others, have achieved if they had been free to live openly? One person who illustrates this dilemma perfectly is Cliff Gordon.

Gordon was born Clifford Thomas Moses in Llanelly on 11 February 1920. His mother Martha Elizabeth lived alone – there is no record of the father's name – so Cliff was adopted by his uncle Charles Moses. Years later when appearing in *Under Milk Wood* in Swansea Cliff recalled, "My real father came to see me. Most of the cast used to go to the bar behind the Empire (the Criterion) for a drink after the show... I introduced him as 'My illegitimate father'; he protested. I told him that as I had been called a bastard for thirty-seven years it was time he took the blame!"[1]

A year after Cliff was born Martha moved back to her native village of Neyland to marry Ernest Campbell Jones with whom she had five more children. As he grew up Cliff would make the long trek across the Cleddau estuary to attend the Pembroke Dock County Intermediate School, which catered very much for the middle classes. He could not speak Welsh and later wrote, "If I am asked by a cheeky Londoner to speak some Welsh, I gabble the verse of Sospan Fach at speed. This has satisfied every challenger except one little *** who was evacuated to Bala during the war".

Cliff's talent for entertaining was apparent from an early age and at just thirteen he cheekily wrote to famous bandleader Mrs Jack Hylton whilst she was in Cardiff. Mrs Hylton granted him an audition and was so impressed that she quickly found him an engagement. The following year he spent the Easter holiday appearing at no less a venue than the London Palladium. His main talent was impersonation, particularly of film stars. He had seen Mary Brough in the play *Thark* and thought he would imitate her. His first attempt was so successful that he began to imitate other stars.

Once noticed, his career swiftly took an upward trajectory and at eighteen he was appearing regularly on Welsh radio either as 'Cliff Gordon and his Modern Young Friends' or simply 'entertainment by Cliff Gordon'.

At some point Cliff decided to join the army as an entertainer in the Entertainments National Service Associate (ENSA), recently formed in 1939 to provide entertainment for British armed forces during World War II. Grafton Maggs, an internet blogger often writes of his time in the army, recalled meeting Cliff, who he called The Welsh Icarus'. They met in Nathanyat in central Israel: "I looked round to see a most unmilitary looking gentleman standing behind me. He was a plump five foot six, with bandy fat legs ending in ankle socks and strappy sandals. His ill-fitting shirt had never known a batman's iron and calf length shorts, mercifully, concealed the virgin whiteness of his upper legs. Above all this was a beaming moon-face of mobile feature, crowned sparsely with fair wispy hair. His pasty skin was showing early signs of damage inflicted by Eastern Mediterranean sun."[2]

Grafton continued, "Returning from the beach, I was invited to meet the rest of his concert party, which consisted of about eight performers, plus supporting dressers and bagmen. Over tea on the officers' mess verandah, I met the outrageous 'Friz', a languid gentleman, à la Noel Coward, with long hair and a limp wrist, (he frightened me a bit, there weren't many like him in Mumbles)… It was so difficult to keep [Cliff] on one subject! Like a grasshopper he would leap from one topic to another. His wit and humour bubbled out and he, himself, would dissolve into uncontrollable bursts of infectious laughter. He was a very funny and most affable man."

After his stint in ENSA Cliff returned to Britain and while appearing in the forces' show *Sky High* at London's Phoenix Theatre he was arrested and charged with gross indecency. The case, which included the prosecution of over twenty homosexuals, caused a sensation. Cliff was indicted on one charge with thirty-one year old William Neville Holly for acts which had taken place between 1 December 1939 and 31 January 1940 at Abergavenny. He was also charged with gross indecency with a Neville Tipton, but in court the case fell apart and the charges were withdrawn.

During his court appearance Cliff was quite open about his sexuality, as he had been during his army days. The Army's response had been to send him to the military psychologist Mayor Wilde. Wilde gave evidence in court, stating that through him Cliff had been trying to deal with his homosexuality, but as William Cross points out in his book *The Abergavenny Witch Hunt*, Cliff was also a very good actor.[3]

Unlike the other men in the Abergavenny case, who were appearing on a range of charges, Cliff had contacts which he used in an attempt to get himself out of trouble. The theatre manager of the Phoenix wrote that, "his absence would seriously upset the production owing to the shortage of actors", and an anonymous man offered to stand the £2,000 bail. Certainly Cliff's influence and charm seemed to work, and he was cleared of the charges. As he had appeared mainly under his birth name of Clifford Moses the case had little impact on his career, and he returned to work.

By 1943 Cliff was regularly appearing at London's Windmill Theatre, Piccadilly in Mrs Henderson's *Revudeville* renowned for its 'static nudes' – the subject of the 2005 film, *Mrs Henderson Presents* which featured the gay actor and singer Will Young. A review of Cliff's performance in *The Times* described, "A comedian who approaches his material with an admirable lack of fuss and fancy. He relies on little – a French verse is rendered by a whole class of imaginary small boys with accents ranging from Glasgow to California and the effect depends on the change of intonation: the shy young officer straight from training school is conveyed down to the involuntary flush of embarrassment and the nervous pluck at the neck-tie."

Cliff's career, as his reviews show, was going extremely well. B.B.'s Gag Book, of the *Daily Mirror*, noted, "Few men can imitate women well, and few women can imitate men. Gordon can do both with equal success."[4] As a relatively out gay man in the entertainment industry he was able to put his contacts among other gay men to good use, and in 1945 he appeared at the Piccadilly theatre in *Sigh No More* written and produced by Noel Coward. Cliff played the character of Nelson alongside Graham Payne, Coward's long-time lover. The *Yorkshire Post* described Cliff as "an unusual mimic of national types"[5] whilst the *Daily Express* said, "There are some bright unknowns – watch for Cliff Gordon cleverly impersonating."[6]

Despite his growing fame Cliff made no effort to hide his sexuality and could often be quite flamboyant, as he had been with writer Christopher Isherwood. Isherwood wrote about their affair in his autobiography *Lost Years: A Memoir* and described how they had met at a steam bath where "they had exhibitionist sex in front of an excited old man." He invited Cliff to a party describing him as "a cute radio and nightclub entertainer."[7] They met at Cliff's flat to have sex but Cliff, always a hypochondriac, became concerned when he discovered that Isherwood didn't take regular syphilis tests, so he talked him into seeing a doctor.

For the next few years Cliff was flying between Blackpool, for a part in *Jewel*, London for the popular BBC radio show *Up the Pole*, and Brighton. He had put together an 'old-time pierrot show' – *Jewel* – featuring a group of entertainers which the *Daily Express* commended, lamenting "I think it is a pity we are losing the pierrots and the minstrels. A good black-faced minstrel show in the West End this summer would I believe be a monster making hit."[8] The minstrel-type show, despite its highly racist overtones, had been extremely popular during the nineteenth century but had died out until revived by blacked-up performers like Al Jolson in the 1920s and 30s in films such as *The Jazz Singer* and *Mammy*.

As well as putting together his own show in Brighton, Cliff was working on the BBC's Kentucky Minstrels. He shared the *Daily Express'* view that this type of entertainment would translate well on stage and so devised a new show which he called *Memories of Jolson*. Unlike other productions Cliff didn't want white people like Jolson 'blacking-up', instead he wanted to try out a daring new idea – he wanted an all-black cast.

Recruiting for the show, Cliff travelled to Cardiff where he met sixteen-year-old-factory worker Shirley Bassey. She had been singing around the clubs and one night in the Workman's Club in Paradise Place, Cliff asked her to join his cast. Thinking this was just another chat up line Shirley told Cliff he would have to ask her mother, and to her surprise he turned up at her doorstep in Splott the following morning. Shirley's mother was concerned about her young daughter going to London, particularly as she had never been away from home. Cliff reassured her by offering to pay for her daughter's friend Iris to accompany Shirley as chaperone.

Shirley recalled, "He asked me to join the show, but I wasn't interested. Finally I agreed. I left the factory – and immediately regretted it. I was out of work for two months and I didn't seem to be likely to get in to the show after all. Then one morning I was lying in bed when my mother came rushing in. 'Get up!' she said. 'There's a woman downstairs to see you. She wants you to go to London.' Bassey had been called back to a second audition for a solo spot, not the chorus line."[9] The show was a huge success, as was Shirley Bassey.

Cliff had written since an early age and was now more and more successful. He had scripted a series of short TV revues, *Once, Twice and Thice Upon a Time* with Ian Carmichael, and had been working on a play *Choir Practice: A storm in a Welsh teacup* since his time in ENSA. The play had been accepted by the BBC and was broadcast on 7 March 1946, with one of the greatest gay icons in the world in the lead role – Cardiff-born Ivor Novello.[10]

Indeed Novello was so inspired by *Choir Practice* that he began to write his own musical, *Valley of Song*, set in the Welsh valleys just before World War I and following the love between a stuttering choirmaster and his leading soprano. Ivor was the son of Clara Novello, who had a great reputation for her women's choirs and who founded and conducted the Royal Welsh Ladies Choir. Ivor's play was intended to be 'a hymn to his homeland', but he died before he could finish it.[11] It was completed by his long-time collaborator Christopher Hassall, although it wasn't staged until 2014 when it was adapted for London's Finborough theatre.

It could also be said that *Choir Practice* was Cliff's 'hymn to his homeland'. He had always been patriotically Welsh. During his time in ENSA when the Royal Welsh had attended a concert he had uncharacteristically addressed them from the stage, personally thanking them and telling them how proud people back home would be of them. *Choir Practice* drew on all his knowledge of growing up in a small Welsh town to present some wonderful characters. Set in the fictional village of Cwmpant, the story concerns a fierce rivalry in the local choir over a much-coveted role. In 1953 the play was made into a film also entitled *Valley of Song* which, although rehearsed in Wales, was filmed in London. Outdoor locations included Llanfynydd and Dryslwyn in

By kind permission of
STUDIOCANAL Films Ltd

Carmarthenshire, and featured the London Welsh Association Choral Society. A young Kenneth Williams in an early role recalled his short appearance in his diary, "To Elstree for my one line in *Choir Practice*".

The film features a character, Clifford Evans, who returns to Wales from London and is asked to replace the recently deceased choirmaster. Trouble starts when he gives the prime role not to the woman who has sung it for years but a young, prettier and better singer. The village is divided in its loyalties as a result.

Cliff watched the film in a number of places. "I first saw the film version of my own radio play *Choir Practice* in Cardiff, afterwards in Swansea. I thoroughly enjoyed the hearty audience reaction. Watching it in a North London cinema, the reactions were just slightly different, almost a matter of timing, but I found myself almost resenting their laughter, because they didn't know Mams are like that, that Bessie Lewis Milk is real… I wanted to turn round and explain. All quite an illogical reaction, for the film was doing what I wanted it to do… crossing the border."[12]

Reception to the film was generally positive, with Bessie the Milk being the most popular character, and the film was released on DVD in 2013 by Studiocanal. It was released in America as the curiously titled *Men Are Children Twice*, despite the fact the story revolves around two feuding women!

Following the success of his film, Cliff was writing regularly, and he continued to act. In 1954 he appeared in London as Willy Nilly in *Under Milk Wood*. His time there was not always happy and he was beginning to develop a problem.

> "I don't care who says it wasn't so, but that company started out with all the August morning happiness of a Sunday School Outing. It was lovely to be nearly all Welsh or nearly all Welsh together in one company … For quite a long time the atmosphere of a small Welsh village on an outing prevailed along with the superb professionalism of the Welsh actor in England. The trouble was it developed along those lines too. The dressing room became family groups, and not all of them happy ones, and gossip! Even if Dylan hadn't liked the production he would have loved the cast! 'There's a nasty lot live here when you come to think!'
>
> But wara teg, it was the drink … People often ask me why I went round the bend when playing Willy Nilly Postman … well the answer is drink, mostly, which Dylan wouldn't have minded, but also there were a couple of North Walian accents in the cast … irritated me no end!"

When he left the production his part was offered to Kenneth Williams who refused, "on the excuse of lacking an authentic Welsh for the part."

Cliff had always been relaxed about his sexuality and had never tried very hard to hide who he was, but it was beginning to take a toll. He drank heavily, and was constantly concerned about his health and the psychological impact of being homosexual. Surrounding himself with other gay men in the 1950s, despite his openness, was not easy. Guy Burgess had hit the headlines in 1951-52 and in 1953 it all went wrong for Cliff.

He had limped home to Wales and was staying in Churchill Way, in Cardiff. His drinking and financial problems had impacted his career and he was losing some of the reputation he had gained. In November 1953 he had travelled to Newtown, in mid Wales, to meet a group of gay men, but the meeting was broken up by the police and Cliff was arrested. He was charged with attempting to procure 'another male person to commit an improper act'[13] but once again he narrowly escaped a prison sentence and was acquitted in February 1954. This time though the media had reported his stage name and there was no doubt as to his identity.

For several years after his arrest Cliff disappeared from view; certainly his career seemed to be over and there were no mention of him in the media. Elsewhere Dylan Thomas had died in 1953 and his widow Caitlin Thomas was desperate to leave the Welsh village of Laugharne, which she described as a permanently festering wound. In September 1957 she moved to Rome with her children and with Cliff, whom she had probably known since his appearance in *Under Milk Wood*. His role as described by Paul Ferris, in his biography *Caitlin*,[14] was as 'a drinking partner for Thomas'. They all lived in an apartment in the Via Mogadiscio and spent most of their evenings in the Taverna Margutta a hangout for film types. Cliff was by now portly and balding.

Caitlin had begun a relationship with Giuseppe Fazio, described as a fiery Sicilian who was not averse to using his fists. One night, drunk and alone in a lift with him, Cliff made a clumsy attempt to kiss him and Fazio hit him so hard he broke his Cliff's arm. Cliff returned to London.

In September 1959 Cliff made his first media appearance since his arrest, in the journal *Wales*. In an article titled 'Testament', he began, "Wales is not a country but an emotion," adding, "Those who know me, and there are many who regret it, will know I am, as a comedian and writer, a professional Welshman, an alcoholic (who has been on a very uncomfortable wagon since February 11th … my birthday…) author of *Choir Practice* and discoverer of nothing more profound than Shirley Bassey. I am currently 'staying' in Horton Hospital, Epsom. A very nice, albeit English mental hospital."

His only other published writing was a poem in 1960, again for the *Wales* journal. He married Margaret E. Truman in 1961 in Kensington, London. They lived in Battle, Sussex and his mother moved nearby to be close to him. He died at St Helen's Hospital in Hastings on 16 October 1964 aged just 44 years. Cliff was an extremely talented writer, but his successful career collapsed following his court appearance and one small fine for being caught with a man. How much more could he have achieved? Indeed, what more could have been achieved by the thousands of men whose lives were ruined by being publicly punished for their homosexuality.

11. Like a shadow I am

In 2015 TV producer Llinos Wynnen became obsessed by finding a grave. As part of the series *Mamwlad gyda Ffion Hague*, the production team went searching for the resting place of one of Wales' greatest female artists. That the location of Gwen John's grave was unknown, and then found, is indicative of her life. Overshadowed for years by her more famous brother Augustus John, she is now recognised as a great artist in her own right. The belief that she was a recluse or someone who lived a predominantly 'interior life' has been challenged. But perhaps the most neglected aspect of Gwen's life is that of her sexual fluidity. She has predominantly been defined by her relationship with the French sculptor Auguste Rodin, and many commentators have completely ignored her bisexuality – some have skittered past it, and some gatekeepers deny its existence.

One of the difficulties of writing LGBT history is access to and interpretation of material. Depending on prevailing attitudes of the time, many LGBT people have had their lives 'edited'. Maria Tamboukou points this out in her book *Nomadic Narratives*[1], when she refers to the 'researcher's cut' or the problems researchers face in deciding what to include and how to interpret material. Throughout history biographical information has been denied or interpreted to exclude elements of sexual fluidity or gender identity – often by people who have little or no understanding of the subject.

Most of Gwen's life has been re-constructed from the letters she wrote to various people, including 2,000 to Rodin. The letters, written in French, have not been published in full and so any examination of Gwen's life is dependent on researchers, who have examined and interpreted the letters according to the needs of their own studies. Due to societal attitudes to behaviour outside heteronormativity people with sexual or gender fluidity would often disguise themselves and their language. This means that researchers not experienced in a language of muted terms, codes and implications can overlook what their subjects really mean.

Gwendoline Mary John was born on 22 June 1876 in Haverfordwest, the second of four children. Their father was distant and stern whilst their mother was artistic, and it was she who encouraged the children to draw. However she was often ill, and she died when Gwen was eight. The family moved to Tenby the same year, where they were cared for by two aunts. Of her childhood Gwen had little to say other than that nothing of importance happened to her before she was twenty-seven. Once she had left Tenby, she rarely visited.

In 1894 Augustus went to study at the progressive Slade School of Fine Art in London, to be followed by Gwen who remained there from 1895 to 1898. It was a period regarded as a golden age of the Slade particularly as it was the only British art school which admitted women on the same terms as men. This was a time of great change in the way women perceived themselves and wanted to be perceived by men. The New Woman was breaking conventions in attitudes, behaviour, dress and sexuality. Gwen, intelligent and an avid reader, was living in a period of flux but rather than embrace it she preferred to work alone in her room. Throughout her life she defied convention and lived as she chose.

At about this time Gwen developed a passion for a woman whose identity is unknown. In his autobiography, *Chiaroscuro*,[2] Augustus writes "She had a great friend at the Slade, a certain girl student whom I will call Elinor. Elinor had formed a close attachment to an outsider. This young man was a curious fellow, giving himself the airs of a superman with pretensions to near immorality, but apparently only occupied for the present in some form of business. Gwen decided that this affair must be stopped: so, after failing to persuade her friend to break it off, and announced an ultimatum – surrender or suicide. I strongly disapproved of all this: Elinor's disposal of her affections was, in this case, possibly regrettable, but, in my opinion, none of our business. The atmosphere of our group now became almost unbearable, with its frightful tension, its terrifying excursions and alarms. Had my sister gone mad? At one moment Ambrose McEvoy thought so, and, distraught himself, rushed to tell me the dire news: but Gwen was only in a state of spiritual exaltation, and laughed at my distress; Elinor, her former love for Gwen now turned to hate, remained obdurate."[3]

In her biography of Gwen, Susan Chitty speculates that 'Elinor' may have been Grace Westray[4], a fellow Slade student who shared a flat with Gwen, Augustus and their sister Winifred. Certainly it was someone who was close to the group, as Augustus draws attention to the 'frightful tension' within it. Gwen's feelings for 'Elinor' must have been extreme, i.e. outside romantic friendship, for her to threaten to commit suicide. The situation was resolved when Augustus threatened fisticuffs and the man retreated to his wife. But Elinor's former love for Gwen had turned to hate.

When she was twenty-two Gwen, in the company of two friends including Ida Nettleship (who later married Augustus in 1901), went to Paris for six months. The city during the late nineteenth and early twentieth centuries was regarded as a mecca for artists and people flocked there. Everywhere were artists, models, writers, poets, teachers, students and salons. Gwen, who had long admired the art of James Abbott Whistler, spent time at his school and he was to prove a big influence on her art. When she returned to London Gwen painted her first self-portrait, influenced by Whistler's self-portrait *Gold and Brown*. Reflective of the time of the New Woman, this was a portrait of a confident almost defiant Gwen.

The next four years were unhappy ones of which Gwen spoke little. She was in love with Ambrose McEvoy, a friend of Augustus, and the three shared a flat – but the relationship was not to last. When Ambrose

Self-portrait (1902)

married in 1901 Augustus wrote "sister Gwen upset", and she cried inconsolably. Unable to continue living in the flat with McEvoy she ended in the bizarre situation of living for a time with his parents. From that point she was fiercely independent.

The following year Gwen and her friend Dorelia McNeil set off to walk to Rome, to study there. Dorelia was extremely beautiful and people of both sexes fell in love with her. Gwen had met her at a party but once introduced to the group it was Augustus, despite being married to Ida, who fell in love with her. Thoroughly disapproving of their travel plans he attempted to dissuade them but both women were determined to leave. At a time when women were still chaperoned theirs was a daring move. They left in the summer and for a month slept rough, singing and drawing in cafes for a meal. When they reached Toulouse they stopped and became 'bourgeois' by renting a room – a luxury compared to sleeping rough.

Although not as conventionally beautiful as Dorelia, Gwen too had admirers and throughout her life both men and women were attracted to her. Chitty says, "That Gwen John was attractive to women is certain. They even stopped her in the street and made suggestions to her." At Toulouse she developed a passion for a married girl who then followed them to Paris. However Gwen refused to see her. Dorelia told Augustus' biographer Michael Holroyd that Gwen was "always attracted to the wrong people for their beauty alone. But her work was more important than anyone." Shortly after the departure of the Toulouse girl a Miss Hart, a "loud and leathery lesbian from London", moved into the room next to Gwen and Dorelia.

Deciding that Rome was too far, Gwen and Dorelia opted for Paris, but when Dorelia left to return to England Gwen was deeply upset. Ida wrote to her offering comfort, and hinting that perhaps Gwen's difficult character may have played a part, that she overpowered Dorelia who thought her bossy, and made her do most of the carrying of their art supplies.

Alone in Paris, Gwen followed her brother's suggestion to meet people through letters of introduction. One of these was Auguste Rodin. Aged 63, Rodin was at the height of his fame and his *The Thinker* and *The Kiss* are among the most recognised sculptures in the world. People flocked to see him and women were fascinated by him.

Despite the fact that he thought her thin (he preferred well-built women between thirty and forty) they began an affair. For over fourteen years from 1904 to 1917 Gwen loved Rodin with an obsession which dominated her life. She planned her day around his occasional visits, preferring to stay alone in her room rather than miss the chance he might call. She pined for him, wrote her 2,000 letters to him, sometimes stood outside his house watching for him, and regarded herself as his 'true wife'. He in turn had a wife and he had affairs. Whilst he cared for Gwen, supported her financially at times, and worried over her state of health and mental wellbeing, he never gave as much importance to the relationship as Gwen did.

Rodin was fascinated by sex and used his models and mistresses to explore female sexuality in over 7,000 drawings, which included erotic poses, and women masturbating or caressing one another.[5] Although he published them widely many thought them shocking. One of his assistants was a Finnish sculptor Hilda Flodin with whom Rodin also had an affair. She confessed to Gwen she had lesbian tendencies and asked her not to tell him – but Gwen did. Later Rodin wanted to have sex with Gwen in front of Flodin, afterwards drawing the two women together in erotic poses. Gwen found it tantalising. She and Flodin continued after Rodin had left but she told him that it was not the same as being with him; it was 'quelque chose' or 'a little thing'.

During the pre-war years the challenging of societal boundaries was common and Gwen was certainly no stranger to sexual fluidity. Her brother's marriage to Ida had not been a happy one and Augustus had an affair with Dorelia. However, she too was dissatisfied and left to become involved with another man. It was at this point that Ida fell in love with Dorelia. She wrote that she longed for Dorelia's 'burning hot, not to say scalding' body next to her in bed. 'With her I feel like a champagne bottle that wants to be opened'[6], she wrote to her husband. It was left to Gwen to convince Dorelia to return to both Augustus and Ida, and the three of them, with a flock of children, moved into a flat in Paris.

In 1908 Gwen modelled for the German painter Ottilie Roederstein[7] whom she called the 'l'homme-femme', "who wore a collar and tie, had a male corporation and barked masculine enquiries like 'Hope you're not too cold, my dear!'"[8] They had a slight falling out once when Ottilie cancelled Gwen's modelling appointment, and the

'man-woman' arrived with a bunch of flowers and five francs to 'demontage' (dismantle) her[9]. Ida Gerhardi[10], a friend of Roederstein's, fell in love with Gwen and frequently invited her to her studio, but Gwen disliked Gerhardi's attempts to kiss her and her constant references to her naked body.

In the early part of her relationship with Rodin, Gwen was sexually demanding and would write explicitly about their sex in her letters. But he tired easily and so she would feel guilty. By 1907 his interest in her was waning yet in 1911 she moved to Meudon, a suburb of Paris, to be close to his house. He had other women and despite popping by occasionally to see her, sending her money and writing a few letters, he remained distant but affectionate. He tried to tell her to live for happiness rather than moments of intense pleasure. Without access to him she resorted to writing him letters telling him of her day, of the people she met, of her beloved cats, and pondering on religion. His letters in reply were short but affectionate. He ordered her to eat more, exercise more, paint and draw more. She treasured every letter he sent. Rodin died in 1917, when Gwen was forty-one, and whilst his death affected her deeply they had not seen each other for some time and her letters had been fewer.

Throughout her life Gwen lived according to her passions, and appears to have also suffered from depression or anxiety. She cried a lot as a child and had a melancholy streak. In 1910 her sister Winifred wrote to her warning that unless she controlled her nerves she would become like 'Aunt Rose', who allowed herself to be governed by hers.[11] Once she started painting she would often not stop for hours, and would forget to eat, sleep and bathe. Both Augustus and Rodin worried about her and disapproved of the long obsessive hours she spent painting. For most of her life the majority of her friends were women and most of her paintings are of women. Her closest male friend, the poet and novelist Rainer Maria Rilke, was probably homosexual.

In 1926, aged fifty, Gwen had her last passionate attachment. She had met Véra Oumançoff, the sister-in-law of the philosopher Jacques Maritain with whom Gwen had become friendly. Gwen, who had become more religious, had been seeking spiritual guidance over her grief for the poet Rilke, who had died earlier that year. Gwen had become a Catholic but even this she did unconventionally, often sketching during sermons to the horror of Véra who admonished her and told her to concentrate on her prayers.

Before long Gwen had developed an obsession with this plump, motherly woman, "fair like a Russian peasant and wore her hair in plaits round her head."[12] Augustus describes her thus: "Véra appears to have been what we call a 'sensible girl' and seeks to curb her admirer's extravagances. She might as well have tried to restrain a whirlwind". Gwen's obsession was beginning to take a familiar path. She would follow Véra home after Mass every morning, taking gifts of drawings, until eventually she was requested to restrict her visits to once a week, on a Monday, and to cease the torrent of impassioned letters. But even the Monday visits discomforted Véra as Gwen would simply sit and stare at her, saying that she loved her so much that "she dared not look in her eyes." On other non-visiting days Gwen could often be found staring through the railings of Vera's garden.

As she had with Rodin, Gwen wrote extensively but replies were few, for either Véra did not write very often or Gwen did not keep her letters in the way that she kept Rodin's. The collection at the National Library of Wales contains only nine letters from Véra, written between summer of 1927 and May 1928. Even so they are revealing – in only her second letter irritation begins to creep in: "Do you really need to write to me every day? I don't think so – and I even think that it is bad for your soul – for you are too attached to a creature, without ever knowing it, so to speak. I am well aware that you have great sensitivity, but you must direct it towards Our Lord, towards the Blessed Virgin".

Véra's subsequent letters are more formal and contain more hints of irritation. She admonishes Gwen for being too sentimental and for waiting for Véra outside her home. Eventually Gwen was restricted to writing once a week, usually on a Monday, which she did from January 1928 to July 1929, often including a drawing or watercolour. Véra paid them little attention. "If you don't like them tell me," Gwen wrote, "and I'll change them as I would my clothes if you disliked them". The drawings, a hundred or so, were tossed into a cupboard where they remained until they were discovered after Véra's death in 1959. Their friendship lasted four years, and ended in 1930 when Véra's family declared they were restricting visitors to concentrate on prayer.

Gwen spent the last seven years of her life in isolation. She ceased painting altogether after 1933 and turned to gardening. One day in September 1939 she left Paris for Dieppe with nothing but a copy of her will and burial instructions. She died in the public hospital and was buried in an unknown grave.

Ffion Hague from Mamwlad gyda Ffion Hague.
By kind permission of ©Llinos Wynne

In 2015 the TV documentary team discovered Gwen's grave in Dieppe's Janval Cemetery. She had been buried under the name of Mary John – Mary was her middle name. Now a slate, commissioned by Tinopolis and S4C, records the birth place and death of Gwen in French. It is also inscribed: "Mae pobl fel cysgodion i mi ac fel cysgod ydwyf innau" (People are like shadows to me and like a shadow I am to them) a sentence Gwen once wrote to Rodin.

Gwen is like a shadow – her existence hidden by larger subjects, her brother, her lover, her isolation. She was devoured by passions for painting, for her cats and her love for both men and women, which could be "outrageous and irrational"[13]. She is difficult to categorise and is summed up in her desire to "be alone, be remote, be away from the world." Location was never that important to her. Her life in Paris was dominated by her proximity to Rodin and she moved to be near him. She showed little interest in Wales, in Britain, France or even in World War I which raged around her. "It becomes, finally, irrelevant to attach Gwen to any particular country or nation," wrote Lloyd-Morgan. A similar statement could be made about Gwen's sexual fluidity. Gwen, perhaps more than many others, exemplifies that instability of sexual orientation or gender identity – an instability which cannot always be so easily catalogued into definitive histories. In an ideal world it would be irrelevant to attach Gwen to any sexual orientation. In an ideal world any sexual orientation or gender identity would be irrelevant.

12. There are no rules

In 1937 a Welshman moved to pink-coloured house in Suffolk and opened an art school with his partner. The school would come to greatly influence not only artists, many of whom became famous in their own right, but also horticulturists. The Welshman was Cedric Lockwood Morris from Sketty, Swansea. He was a member of one of the great local industrial families – one which descended maternally from Owain Gwynedd, the twelve century prince of North Wales. Like many families of wealth it had its characters. They included the bank manager who conveniently rearranged the figures in profit and loss columns and was imprisoned for two years. And the woman-chasing ancestor whose sickly wife was confined upstairs whilst downstairs he kept a mistress. When the wife died the mistress went to her funeral dressed in every piece of the dead woman's jewellery.

Cedric, as his partner Arthur Lett-Haines later put it, "was born, of phenomenal vitality, on December 10th 1899."[1] His parents were Sir George Lockwood Morris and Wilhelmina Cory. George was the great-grandson of John Morris, who had founded the Swansea suburb Morriston. He also played rugby for Swansea and was the first Swansea player to represent Wales. Wilhelmina also came from an influential industrial family, the Corys of Swansea, and there had been various marriages between the Morrises and the Corys. She and George had three children, Muriel who died in her teens, Cedric and Nancy. Just three months before he died George inherited the Morris baronetcy from a distant cousin.

Art played an important part in the Morris family. Cedric's great-aunt Margaret Morris married the art collector and dealer Noel Desenfans. Using her marriage dowry she became one of the three founders of the Dulwich Picture Galley, the oldest public art gallery in England – and was painted by Sir Joshua Reynolds. Cedric's mother had studied painting but Cedric did not immediately take to art. As a young man he seemed unsure of what he wanted to do. After being educated at Eastbourne and Godalming he failed the entrance exams for the army. "Bored and nonconformist in his father's household," Lett later said of him, "he made off to Canada. There he worked as a hired man on ranches in Ontario where the farmers seem rather to have taken advantage of his unusual energy and his naif [sic] ignorance of standard wages in the New World ... Eighteen months later, he seems to have been studying singing at the Royal College of Music under Signor Vigetti, whose attempts at raising his light baritone to a tenor were unsuccessful".

Giving up on the singing, Cedric travelled to Paris to study art in April 1914, where he enrolled at the Académie Delecluse. However at the outbreak of World War I he returned home and enlisted in the Artists Rifles,a regiment of the British Army Reserves. The Rifles had originally been formed in 1859 and consisted of painters, musicians, actors, architects and other creative professions. As they were about to leave for France Cedric was declared medically unfit for military action and was sent instead to Berkshire, to train war horses.

He was discharged from the army in 1917 and moved to Newlyn in Cornwall where he became the friend of a struggling artist from New Zealand called Frances Hodgkins. In November 1918 he went to London for Armistice Day, and met and fell in love with the man who was to be his partner for the next sixty years.

Arthur Lett, born in 1894 in London, was one of three children of architect Charles Lett and Frances Laura Esme. After their divorce his mother married S. Sidney Haines, so Arthur changed his surname to Lett-Haines. He too enlisted, and served in the Royal Field Artillery. He became a Second Lieutenant and was wounded fighting in Mesopotamia.

In 1916 Arthur, or Lett as he was commonly called, married Gertrude Aimee Lincoln, the granddaughter of Abraham Lincoln. Soon after the two men met and fell in love Cedric moved in with Lett and his second wife. The three planned to move to America but in the end Aimee went by herself.

The two men went instead to Newlyn and afterwards to Paris in 1920, becoming part of the artistic community which included Marcel Duchamp, Man Ray, Nancy Cunard and Ernest Hemmingway among others. Kathleen Hale, with whom Lett had a long affair, recalled, "I remember them coming gracefully towards us along the Boulevard like gazelles, both in light-coloured socks, the two of them extremely handsome and elegant."[2] Returning to London in 1926 they set up an enormous studio in Great Ormond Street where, quite open about their relationship, they hosted legendary bohemian parties attended by many gay and bisexual people.

By the late 1920s Cedric had become an enormous success as an artist. His second exhibition in London featured a series of nudes, many of which his grandmother disapproved of and at the exhibition turned them to face the wall. Cedric was also receiving commissions such as poster designer for Shell and BP. Indeed so well was his career advancing and so poor were his promotion and administration abilities that Lett put his own career on hold to promote that of his partner.

They both joined a number of organisations, such as the newly formed London Artists Association which helped young artists with promotion and financial support. They were also members of the Seven & Five Society (seven painters and five sculptors), another new project to promote Modernist art. The Society staged the first exhibition of abstract art in Britain. Cedric and Lett became part of an elite London circle which included D.H. Lawrence, the Sitwells, Wyndham Lewis (who was often criticised for his hostile portrayals of homosexuals, Jews and other minorities) and Ben and Winifred Nicholson.

Certain members of the Seven & Five became disillusioned with the way the society was being run. When Ben Nicholson became chairman he introduced a rule that exhibitions could only show abstract work. Cedric, who was painting flowers, animals and portraits, was effectively barred from exhibiting and was the first of several artists to leave.

Disillusioned with much of the London art world and its rules, Cedric and Lett decamped to the countryside, to the pink-coloured farmhouse called Pound Farm, in Higham, Suffolk. In nearby Dedham they set up a modern art school. At Pound Farm Cedric was able to pursue his other passion – the painting, growing and breeding of flowers.

Within a year they had sixty students at the school and Pound Farm had become a magnet for students, artists, and visitors to the spectacular garden that Cedric had designed, and for the legendary parties they held. In 1932 Vivien Gribble, the wealthy owner of the farm and a wood engraver and student of Cedric's, died and left the property to him. Seven years later young student Lucian Freud, grandson of the psychoanalyst, may have burnt the place down by leaving out a cigarette. Alfred Munnings, the artist and president of the Royal Academy of Arts, lived locally and had a passionate hatred of Modernism. He had his chauffer drive around the smouldering ruins as he cheered loudly the destruction of what he saw as an odious development in art. Unperturbed, Cedric suggested the students paint the ruins.

The school re-opened at Benton End, where it became a hothouse of contemporary talent for the next forty years. Cedric and Lett did not teach using traditional methods. Instead they believed in a free rein approach, which they had experienced in the French schools. Instruction was kept to a minimum with, as one student put it, more a 'sitting at the feet of the master' approach. They believed artists should paint influenced by their feelings rather than rely on academic learning. Part of the success of Benton End was the contrast between its founders and between the different kinds of art they practised. Lett was a painter and sculptor who experimented in different media, but generally was a surrealist. Cedric painted portraits, landscapes and still lives of flowers and birds aflame with colour, in a more a Post-Impressionist style. He was passionate about colour and many of the artists who stayed at Benton End show the same vitality in their work. Lett once said that apart from Matisse Cedric was the finest colourist of that century. His teaching for both painting and horticulture was that the only rule is that there are no rules.

Shortly afterwards the writer Ronald Blythe was introduced to Cedric: "I was initiated into a realm of flowers, botanical and art students, earthy-fingered grandees and a great many giggly asides which I didn't quite get. He had just inherited his father's baronetcy and this seemed to add to the comedy. The gardeners wove their way round easels propped up in the long grass and the artists, of all ages, painted peering visitors and dense foliage in the exuberant Morris manner. The doors and window-frames of the ancient house glared Newlyn blue and there was a whiff of garlic and wine in the air from distant kitchens. The atmosphere was well out of this world so far as I had previously witnessed and tasted it. It was robust and coarse, and exquisite and tentative all at once. Rough and ready and fine mannered. Also faintly dangerous."[3]

It was dangerous because it was a place where anyone's sexuality was accepted at a time when homosexuality was still against the law. Just a few years later, in 1940, the scandal in Abergavenny (which included Cliff Gordon) saw a number of men imprisoned. But most at Benton End knew about their relationship and regarded them as an old married couple. They had a stormy but successful relationship despite their both having affairs with other people, Cedric with the painter John Aldridge and the American artist Paul Odo Cross, the latter causing tension between Cedric and Lett. Lett was more bisexual than homosexual and mainly had affairs with women, such as Stella Hamilton. Probably his most long-term affair was with Kathleen Hale. Known mainly for her children's books *Orlando the Marmalade Cat*, she drew inspiration for many of the stories and the illustrations from life at Benton End. She was for a while secretary and lover of Augustus John, of whom she made a portrait. Describing their affair in her autobiography, she wrote of how important Augustus and Dorelia were to her. "I was smitten," she told the *Independent*. "I'm not a lesbian but I really was in love with Dorelia, I think. She was very funny, so beautiful and naive."[4]

In his biography of Cedric's great admirer Lucian Freud, Geordie Greig wrote, "It was a refreshingly uninhibited time for the students at Cedric Morris's … 'everyone was homosexual or lesbian at the school, or so it seemed'."[5] Among them was Frances Mary Hodgkins, now regarded as one of New Zealand's most prestigious and influential painters. She had a series of affairs with women and was a close friend of Cedric and Lett. They also included Denis Wirth-Miller and his long-term partner Richard Chopping, who designed some of the most famous dust jackets for the James Bond novels. Richard, influenced by Cedric, became a botanical and zoological painter. Richard and Denis were the first couple to register a civil partnership in Colchester.

Cedric spent as much time with his garden as he did with his students. So attached was he to his garden that Lett was more jealous of it than any of Cedric's lovers. Cedric bred new varieties of flowers, many of which were named after him or Benton – including the Papaver orientale 'Cedric Morris', a pink oriental poppy. But he is probably best known for his award winning iris collections, which included the first pink specimen bred in Britain. They held Iris Parties in June when hundreds were in bloom; famous gardeners visited, like Vita Sackville-West and David Horner the life-long partner of Osbert Sitwell. Cedric was very fond of Vita and described her as "a great lady who never lost her integrity". He was upset when her son published *Portrait of a Marriage*, a biography of both his parents' bisexuality, and including Vita's relationship with Virginia Woolf. Plantswoman Beth

Chatto was also a former pupil of Cedric's and many of his plants can still be bought today from her garden centre.

Students were often expected to do the gardening and housework, as well as painting. They called Lett 'Father', and it was he who took care of the community, of the administration and of cooking two meals a day for all the students. Invariably with a drink in hand he produced large, delicious meals even during war-time rationing, by plundering the garden and hedgerows to make soups and casseroles laced with ash from his cigarettes. Having given up his own career to support Cedric he came to hate his partner's passion for horticulture, and cooking became his creative outlet. Bernard Brown, a local boy and student who went on to become a lawyer recalled, "All this took place at eating and drinking times in the brick-floored kitchen. Lett Haines (the locals swore he was 'Heinz') was the presiding genius. A big totally bald pink man, he sported a slashing (sabre duel?) scar which ran from crown to forehead ... Lett Haines was the first man I had seen in an apron and the only one before I left Suffolk."[6]

The house was never that clean or tidy and was filled with pictures, the smell of flowers, numerous people discussing art and plants, marmalade cats, formidable women, wine and exotic birds. Lett's kitchen, his personal domain, was chaotic but he created delicious food and drink. He rarely ate with the students, preferring to take a sandwich to his bedroom which doubled as his studio. However he was also the story-teller of the house, telling scandalous tales about himself or of his and Cedric's travels and encounters, occasionally corrected by Cedric. His stories were designed to shock and many of the naïve young students did not always follow his innuendos. "Lett talked through a big wicked smile like the wolf-grandmother in Little Red Riding Hood. With his large grand and rearing, scarred bald dome, a legacy from the Western Front, and his mocking courtesy, he made no bones about dominating the scene."[7]

Bernard Brown recalled, "Words cut out from newspapers and cinema posters, then put together in sentences, decorated the walls. Their messages eluded me, but doubtless they were very funny and in keeping with the generally fey atmosphere of the place. There were big heavy-framed paintings upon most walls and many more stacked along the main hallway and in the studio. Two galleries at the front of the house were covered in them. There was a huge nude of a lady from

Raydon. I had often seen her biking to Hadleigh and it was years before I could pluck up the courage to enter the shop where she served."[8]

Cedric, on the other hand, was extremely disciplined and hardworking on both his paintings and gardening; he had nothing to do with the house. He was an elegant figure in his corduroy trousers, Welsh linen shirt and soft silk scarf, but with dirt and paint covered fingers. He could hardly boil an egg and rarely wrote a letter. When he sold a painting Lett would have to check if he actually took the money. It was often stuffed forgotten into a pocket. Lett rarely went outside and, on a doctor advising him to get more fresh air, he went into the garden once. He complained that Cedric was a contrary and stubborn dreamer who wouldn't help around the place. He would have loved to have painted more but catering for the students and the hordes of visitors took up most of his time. Cedric and Lett were like an old married couple, but there were occasions when their relationship was strained. Then Lett would avoid sitting at the table if Cedric was there, and they would have stormy rows as the students sat quietly by. Or other times when one or the other would stomp off and not speak to each other for weeks. But it worked – for sixty years it worked.

Each had different groups of friends. Cedric was exclusive about his choice and demanded loyalty whereas Lett was more open and easy going. Kathleen Hale became close to Cedric, who invited her to paint with him "which was a great honour, for it was not in his nature to share his work-time with anyone."[9] But when she moved from Cedric's camp to Lett's she earned Cedric's lasting disapproval. "Whenever we met face to face, his would assume the expression of a disgusted camel." When Cedric was helping Denise Broadley, Lett occasionally wandered in and a furious Cedric would send him away which in turn infuriated Lett. Maggi Hamblin who is openly, as she puts it, 'lesbionic,' said "they were total opposites. Cedric would be out at 5am collecting wild flowers, whilst Lett would appear at midday holding a dry martini."[10]

The power of their personalities and their dedication to art won over many people. Both had a wicked sense of humour, although Cedric did not suffer fools gladly. He disliked the hordes of women who arrived to view his garden and often walked off, having lost patience with them. One particular woman he disliked so much that he presented her with a plant called *Dracunculus vulgaris*. He neglected to tell her as she got

into her car to drive home on a hot day that it is one of the worst
smelling flowers in the world.

Cedric was also an avid animal lover and the house was a menagerie.
Cats ran all over the place and were fed by Cedric at midnight. He had
a long running feud with a local gamekeeper who would shoot at his
and other people's cats and dogs – a feud only ending when the man
tripped over his own shotgun and killed himself.

Despite spending most of his life in England Cedric considered
himself Welsh, and he proved an important influence on Welsh art. He
returned often to south Wales, and the suffering of the people in the
valleys during the Depression influenced him greatly. He painted
Caeharris Post Office and *Dowlais from the Cinder Tips, Caeharris* during
his time there. In the years after the First World War Welsh art was not
widely appreciated. Little was exhibited in London, with the exception
of artists like Sir Goscombe John, David Jones and Augustus John, and
there was an equal lack of appreciation at home.[11] Cedric organized an
Exhibition of Contemporary Welsh Art in 1935 in Cardiff, which led to
the founding of the Contemporary Art Society for Wales. In a radio
interview about the exhibition he called for a community in art to be
developed, a Welsh magazine and the organisation for exhibitions. That
same year the South Wales Group was founded on very similar lines
and Cedric became a member. He was also closely involved with the
Merthyr Tydfil Educational Settlement at Gwaunfarren House which
had been set up in 1937, providing education and welfare services to
people suffering in the Depression. The Educational Settlement was
also a focus for Esther Grainger, Heinz Koppel, Glyn Morgan and
Arthur Giardelli[12].

Cedric taught at an art centre set up by the philanthropist Mary
Horsfall in Dowlais. He knew Heinz Koppel, a German Jewish émigré
who had fled Germany in 1933. Ten years later, through Cedric's
influence, Heinz was teaching art at the Merthyr Tydfil Education
Settlement. This later grew into the Merthyr Tydfil Arts Centre, with
Koppel as principal.

Cedric also encouraged Welsh artists to become students at Benton
End. Glyn Morgan from Pontypridd was taught by Ceri Richards at
the Cardiff College of Art and was introduced by him to the works of
Picasso and Augustus John. Whilst on a visit to Cardiff Museum he
first saw a painting by Cedric Morris which was to influence him for

the rest of his life. Cedric judged a show at Pontypridd in which the seventeen year-old Glyn had entered two pictures. Cedric thought his work had promise and invited him to join the school at Benton End, which he did in 1944 and said it was "just a lovely place to be."[13] For the next thirty-eight years he would return as often as he could, and his art echoes the vibrancy and colours present in Cedric's work.

The Second World War saw the numbers of students fade, and the bohemian reputation of Benton End gave rise to rumours about what went on at the house. There was talk of sheltering spies and storing ammunition, which weren't helped by Cedric and Lett's lax attitude towards the black-out. Locals believed they were signalling to enemy planes. Things reached a head when a damaged plane jettisoned its bombs on the old Mill House a mile from Benton End. Ah, said a local, one of them arty types had painted the Mill just a fortnight ago. Before long a rumour was running rife that the artists had been painting local scenes to send to Germany.[14]

By the 1960s the school had more or less ceased to function. Lett had more time for his own work and produced a number of small sculptures made from animal bones left over from his cooking, which he called his 'Humbles'. By the mid-1970s Cedric's eyesight was failing and he had almost given up painting. He desperately wanted to visit Wales again and a friend, John Morley, planned a visit to the Gower, but it never came about. The school officially closed when Lett died in 1978 but Cedric continued to live there. As he grew old he cursed God, "whom he still took to be some ghastly Sunday misery from Glamorgan, for 'insulting' him with old age."[15]

Cedric died in 1984. His obituary in *The Times* stated that "he was unmarried". Like so many forbidden lives the people they loved were simply airbrushed out. Cedric and Lett were like thousands of people who lived married lives, but didn't have the certificate to prove it.

13. A tangle in my life

In the Introduction to *Conundrum*, Jan Morris said the book described "a tangle in my life, and parts of it have been painful to write". She added, "I offer it diffidently, like a confidence: in love to my family, in explanation to my friends, and in sympathy to all my comrades, anywhere in the world, who are suffering still in the same solitary and unsought cause."

That solitary and unsought cause was transgender issues, and *Conundrum* was one of the first autobiographies in the world to discuss a personal gender reassignment. There had been books before about gender diversity, some as early as the nineteenth century. Several had appeared in the 1950s with probably the most famous being written by American trans woman Christine Jorgensen. She had told her story to the media in 1953 and published her autobiography in 1967. Flurries of books appeared in the 50s and 60s but most were American. The first major UK work was by Roberta Cowell appeared in 1954. Cowell had been a World War II fighter pilot and racing driver, and was the first known British trans woman to have sex reassignment surgery. Yet despite a number of high publicity cases like April Ashley's in 1960s public knowledge of gender diversity was poor and discrimination was high so it took great courage for Jan to publish her story – particularly as she was already a well-known writer.

The opening lines of *Conundrum* have since become famous: "I was three or perhaps four years old when I realized that I have been born into the wrong body, and should really be a girl. I remember the moment well, and it is the earliest memory of my life." Despite criticism at the time that a child of three or four could not possibly know, and that this was retrospection, her statement is supported by studies into gender dysphoria in children.

In the book Jan outlines her early life as James Humphrey Morris born at Clevedon, Somerset to a Welsh father and an English mother. She was, she said, a happy but lonely child gazing through a telescope to the blue mass of the Welsh mountains which were "far more exciting" to her than the local Somerset landscape. Throughout many of her works Jan speaks of her separateness and of feeling a constant stranger. At the Catherine Choir School in Oxford Jan would attend prayers at the cathedral, inserting before the final 'Amen' "and please,

God, make me a girl" – a request extended to every breaking of a wishbone, every shooting star or coin in a fountain. As she grew older she felt as though she was in a masquerade. Many have quizzed her for answers and reasons for being transgender – was it her childhood, was it her parents, was she gay, where did it all begin? Answers she has none and consigns it all to a riddle.

After Oxford University Jan joined the 9th Lancers just as World War II was ending. Despite the fact that soldiering attracted her and she enjoyed her time there, she still felt like a woman masquerading as a man. And sex had no great appeal to her. Whilst she enjoyed the company of women she did not feel particularly attracted to them, though she found happiness in marriage. Her wife Elizabeth knew from the start that Jan was transgender, and was supportive. It is a marriage of which Jan is immensely proud; they had five children, one of whom died aged two months.

Determined not to do anything whilst having a family Jan put her dreams on hold. However during those years she fell more and more into depression and self-repugnance. She began to hate the strain of living in a false world. So she resigned from everything she associated with masculinity. At the time she was one of the most successful journalists of the 1960s having built a career on breaking the news of the conquest of Everest on the day the Queen was crowned. Her book *Coronation Everest* (1958) was a bestseller and she is now the last surviving member of that Everest team. But all her success as a journalist had been as a man, and this was not her. There seemed no choice but to leave all this behind for something more true to her. She became instead an independent and much-loved writer achieving enormous success with books such as the *Pax Britannica* trilogy about the British Empire. She was one of the first writers to break through the restrictions of historical writing as an academic subject, into popular history. She had written sixteen enormously popular books and so the decision to transition was taken knowing that it would excite great public curiosity and discrimination. The writing of *Pax Britannica* was begun as a man and finished as a woman.

With Elizabeth's help she took the first steps to achieving her great wish. For Jan and many others gender is not about sex – the measurement of a body by counting the number of breasts, genitals, x's and y's. It was the form that was to be changed not the person. She suffered from no gender confusion – a term so many have tried to force onto transgender people. For Jan there was never any doubt about her gender: "Nothing in the world would make me abandon my gender, concealed from everyone though it remained." When asked by psychiatrists if she felt guilty in changing her body she replied that she was aiming at an 'inner reconciliation'.

The first book on the subject which Jan read and was influenced by (as were many others) was *Man Into Woman*, the haunting story of Lili Elbe, made into the film *The Danish Girl* (2015). The story gave Jan hope and determined her on a step towards surgery. She would, she said, rather die young than live a long life of falsehood. She had taken a long and weary journey through doctor's surgeries, psychiatrics and sexologists, most of whom thought that she was looking for a 'cure' – but no psychiatrist has ever 'cured' a transgender person or a homosexual. Many tried to convince her that she was a transvestite or a homosexual. Medicine in the 1950 was not equipped to cope with transgender issues although there had been inroads made by a number of people including John Randell, the specialist in transgender surgery. Jan made her way to Charing Cross (where all transgender people had to go for consultation on gender dysphoria) and was told that she and Elizabeth would have to get divorced. She refused: "After a lifetime of fighting my own battles I did not feel in a mood to offer my destiny like a sacrifice upon the benches of Her Majesty's judges. Who knew what degradations we might both endure? What business was it of theirs, anyway? No, I resolved, I would make the rules now. We would end our marriage in our own time, lovingly, and I would go for my surgery, as I had gone for so many consolations and distractions before, to foreign parts beyond the law."

Transgender people unable to acquire surgery under the strict criteria of Charing Cross often resorted to finding help elsewhere in the world. Some would deliberately mutilate themselves in order to force a surgeon's hand, some went to unscrupulous or inexperienced surgeons who too often maimed them, some bankrupted themselves, some died. Some who had not undergone the usual requisite living as the opposite sex for years embraced surgery only to find that life did not improve. Those without money were left to suffer alone. There are no official figures regarding the number of trans people in the UK just as there are no official figures for LGB people. The UK census does not include questions about sexual orientation or gender identity, although from 2011 civil partnerships are included. However the figure most used is around 1% of the population is transgender which would give a Welsh population of around 30,000 people.

Jan eventually found her way to Dr Harry Benjamin in New York, who had a growing reputation in the understanding of transgender issues. It was he who coined the word 'transsexual'. He made a number of recommendations to Jan, who began taking hormone tablets made from "the urine of pregnant mares". She took them for eight years, supplemented by artificial female hormones, calculating that between 1964 and 1972 she had swallowed at least 12,000 pills and 50,000 milligrams of 'female matter', turning her into 'something perilously close to a hermaphrodite'. She wrote "if I were trapped in that cage again nothing would keep me from my goal, however fearful its prospects, however hopeless the odds. I would search the earth for surgeons, I would bribe barbers or abortionists, I would take a knife and do it myself, without fear, without qualms, without a second thought."

There followed several years of androgynous appearance. Family and friends seeing different genders at different times as slowly the outer female began to match the inner. And she was given a passport with no sex defined on it, to the 'mystification of foreign officials'. She began experimenting by walking about Oxford, where she had a flat, wearing make-up and a long dress. It was not exciting, she said, it was a huge relief, and fun.

In 1972 in Morocco, and at the age of forty-six, James became Jan and she felt 'deliciously *clean*'. Whilst the operation is outlined in *Conundrum* much of the angst and risks were left out – if she experienced thoughts of suicide, depression and self-harm so common to others, then they are absent. The surgery itself was dangerous and doctors warned that a gender reassignment could have profound and lasting changes not only on her personality but on her writing. Indeed many have claimed they have seen a change in her writing.

Conundrum was the first book published under her new name. It appeared in 1974, a year after homosexuality had been removed from *Diagnostic and Statistical Manual of Mental Disorders*. Two decades later the *Daily Express* said it "did much for public understanding."[1] But it was a difficult book to write. "I don't know if I was right to write it.

There are lots of things against it," she told *The Times*. "If I hadn't written it, I would always have had it at the back of my mind, I suppose. But it's an interesting subject, and it would have been rather unnatural not to."[2]

Back home in amongst the Welsh "with that accomplishment of performance which is the national birthright, [they] simply pretended not to notice, spoke to me as they always did, asked after the children, and by the skill of their prose put me at my ease, and in their debt." Elsewhere things were not so straightforward. Former male colleagues flustered over whether to greet her with a kiss as they did with other women. Should they pull out a chair for her? And they stumbled over the he-she, him-her, James-Jan.[3] In the *Independent* Jan related an amusing story of when she met the Queen. "Do you remember," she asked, "when they climbed Everest for the first time, and the news came to you on the day before your coronation?" Of course replied the Queen, to which Jan said "I was the person who brought the news back from Everest so that it got to you on time." A very bemused monarch was left to wonder how a woman had achieved such a feat. "I felt sorry for her," said Jan "because she always has people to explain things, and there was nobody around to put her straight. She suddenly found herself in totally unknown territory."[4]

Reading any work about Jan illustrates the confusion people have about transgender matters. Writers confusingly and arbitrarily switch back and forth from 'he' to 'she' despite including the ubiquitous quote of Jan saying that from three or four she knew she was a girl.

With Jan's new identity came the problem of her being in an illegal same-sex marriage. Eventually she and Elizabeth had to divorce. And there was another conundrum as to what they called each other. They settled on sister-in-law as Jan did not want to deny any kinship with her children. In 2008 they entered a civil partnership in Pwllheli on 14 May, in the presence of a couple who invited them to tea at their house afterwards. Nothing, she said, had changed their marriage.

To many her sexual orientation seems complex – a heterosexual marriage which turned into a same-sex marriage. Surely, people argue, if she knew all her life she was a woman this made her a lesbian? Her feelings towards men are contradictory, she says. The homo-erotic touches and engagements at school did not appeal to her and of her elite upbringing she claimed that "the whole of the English upper-class life ... was shot through with bisexual instinct." Yet her attraction to men surfaces in her work, her biographies of John Arbuthnot Fisher and the American president Lincoln contain musing on their sexual complexities. And she speaks of wanting to be loved by Fisher. After her gender reassignment a London taxi driver gave her a kiss on the cheek and she loved it. Elsewhere she has spoken of being attracted to the idea of being cherished by a man. Being "Lieutenant to a really great man – that's my idea of happiness," she told the *Independent*.

"As to sex," she once said, "I cannot recommend too highly the advantages of androgyny ... at a time of sexual indeterminacy, I found myself entertained as never before or since, because I discovered that both men and women, far from being repelled by my equivocal state, were intrigued and even attracted by it." And when her sexual indeterminacy had been settled she rather missed the 'sense of ubiquitous passport' her androgyny gave her. But "the ultimate object of sex is not physical after all, but spiritual ... the sealing of profounder unions."

In the 1960s, Plaid Cymru's general secretary J.E. Jones wrote to Jan to suggest that she stop writing about Wales as an outsider and make herself part of it. Jan admits she was flattered and moved to Wales, saying later "if I have fulfilled myself anywhere, I have fulfilled myself in Welshness." She was initiated into the Gorsedd of Bards 1993, taking the name Jan Trefan, and describes the acceptance as one of the proudest moments in her life. She is a Welsh nationalist and says "I call myself Anglo-Welsh, but I have always preferred the Welsh side of me to the English."

Since *Conundrum* Jan has rarely spoken in detail about her gender reassignment and being transgender. Many LGBT people do not come out or speak frequently as to their sexual orientation or gender identity because it does not define them. They are first and foremost a writer, AM or MP, sports personality, actor, etc who just happen to be gay. The public tend to be more fascinated by someone's sexual orientation or gender identity than the individual themselves, so much so that Jan once commented, "I do not doubt that when I go, the event will be commemorated with the small back-page headline 'Sex Change Author Dies'."

In 2008 Jan was voted the fifteenth greatest British writer since the war having written over fifty books (most of which have never been out of print) and hundreds of articles. When she came to re-edit *Venice*, the most successful book of her early career, Jan could not find a way into James – it was he who now occupied a foreign land to which she no longer had access.

Jan remains a very private person and *Conundrum* is really the only glimpse into her personal life. And yet it dominates everything she does. "I've come to recognize that what I am is the result of the experience itself. The tangle that was there is something that has gone subliminally through all my work."[5] Almost every mention of her includes what she calls the 'Conundrum Factor' the inescapable curious fact that she changed gender.

Jan does not join LGBT activism and does not speak extensively about being transgender. We should not expect or require her to do so. By writing *Conundrum* she added to LGBT history and for that she has gratitude and respect. Sexual orientation has come a long way in that people can be musicians, actors, writers, etc who also happen to be gay. But no transgender person can yet happen to be – it's all still so new. Like tick box exercises the first woman Prime Minister, the first woman astronaut, the first woman nominated to be President in America (even if most of the front pages carried pictures of Bill Clinton!), are milestones which have to be endured so that we can move to a time when sexual orientation and gender identity happen to be, and are not the main event. Young people, she notes, mostly accept her story without question. It is those of her own age and older who still cringe or look aghast. Transgender people of Jan's age are few but their stories must be collected to illustrate the wide diversity of society in all eras.

In 1989 Jan wrote *Pleasures of a Tangled Life,* a book in which she aimed to discuss the happy side of life. The sexual confusion of *Conundrum* having been settled, she would "dismiss the tangled past, celebrate the unencumbered present." She added, "there was a time when, new to life as a woman, I tried to forget that I had ever lived as a man, but it had grown on me over the years that this was not only intellectually dishonest, but actually rather dull of me ... the tangle was part of me, whether I liked it or not."[6]

On writing more about transgender issues she said "perhaps I'm not a big enough writer to tackle that." What of the conundrum itself of how and why James first came into being and not Jan? Does she understand it at all? "Sometimes" she says, "down by the river I almost think I have: but then the light changes, the wind shifts, a cloud moves across the sun, and the meaning of it all once again escapes me."

14. The Veronal Mystery

The first inquest into the death of Eric Trevanion was held at his flat. Eric had died on 11 September 1912 supposedly of a drug overdose, and it was assumed to be very much an open and shut case. Yet not everyone was convinced. Eric's mother harboured suspicions, and made them clear at the inquest. It was perhaps a case of murder, she said. But when she said those words Eric's close friend Albert leapt to his feet and shouted "Does Mrs Trevanion accuse me of murdering her son?" It seemed ridiculous to think so, and she was persuaded to drop her objections.

Mrs Trevanion's unease persisted and she went to the police. Whatever she said convinced them to reconsider the case and for two weeks the police carried out extensive interviews. What they learnt led to the exhumation of Eric's body. And the results were startling.

Chemical analysis showed at least 150 grains of the drug Verona a powerful barbiturate. As they had not dissolved they must have been taken within an hour of Eric losing consciousness. Usually, 30-50 grains was a fatal dose. There was no indication of suicide – Eric was quite normal, fairly cheerful on the day and perfectly sober. So was Mrs Trevanion right – was this perhaps a case of murder?[1]

Eric was born into a wealthy family, the youngest of three sons. His parents Hugh Arundell-Trevanion and Florence Eva had already caused a media sensation themselves. They had married in 1882 but Hugh turned out to be a violent husband. Just a week before Eric had been born he had pulled his wife out of bed, knocked her down and cut her left eye open. And after another violent kicking Florence finally left him. Shortly afterwards she found he had been having an affair but even so they reconciled and made a fresh start. When he beat her again he was arrested, charged with assault and spent six weeks in jail doing hard labour. On release he simply resumed his life as a barrister, to the disgust of many. Hugh and Florence divorced, and he married his mistress.

However Florence was concerned that her sons would be denied a proper place in society and surprisingly suggested they re-marry only three months after Hugh's second wife died. The press, fascinated by the novelty of a couple re-marrying, particularly given his cruelty, salaciously covered the story. Things did not improve and their second attempt turned out to be as disastrous as the first. They divorced for a second time.

This was the tumultuous relationship into which Eric was born in 1883. He grew up the sickly but pampered child of wealth and privilege, but never really fitted in. He suffered an accident when he was three years old which resulted in periodic convulsions, and he never went to school but was taught by private tutors and usually wintered abroad. He lived apart from his family for most of his childhood and his constant ill-health caused a great deal of sleeplessness. Eric decided to spend his life travelling the world, a plan made much easier by the fact that on his coming of age Eric inherited a fortune – somewhere between £80,000 and £100,000 (about £2 million today). It was on these travels that Eric first met Albert.

Albert Edward Roe was almost the complete opposite of Eric. He was born and brought up in Swansea, South Wales, where his father kept a public house. A strong, muscular man, Albert also wanted to travel and asked his father to get him an apprenticeship at sea. A hard worker, he climbed steadily through the ranks until in 1906 he was appointed fourth officer on board the just completed *Orotava*, a ship owned by the Royal Mail Steam Packet Company carrying mail to Australia.

As part of his duties Albert was required to patrol the sleeping quarters each night to ensure that everything was in order. One night about a week out at sea he heard something which caught his attention: low sobs coming from one of the cabins. So he knocked and being admitted found Eric sitting alone on the floor moaning and crying, his head resting on the bunk. Somewhat alarmed, Albert asked him what the matter was and between his tears Eric told him of how depressed and lonely he felt. He was completely neglected, he said, by his travelling companions, his younger brother Charles Cecil and his brother's friend. They had agreed to accompany Eric on one of his trips to Ceylon but had paid him little attention and shunned his company.

Over the following days a friendship grew between Eric and Albert, and the lonely twenty-three year-old began to rely on the thirty-eight year-old man. He sought out Albert's company whenever he could and when Albert and other officers sat on deck Eric would join them, although he appeared lonely and somewhat pathetic to them. Over the

Albert Roe (illustration from the
Cambrian Daily Leader)

Eric Trevanion (illustration from the
Cambrian Daily Leader)

next few years Eric would follow Albert either on his travels or wait at
the dock for him to return.

They were an incongruous pair. Eric was "shy, delicate, averse from
sports, and fond of indoor life, rather a dandy, tall, slim and pale with
almost girlishly small hands and feet" whilst Albert was "robust, a
well-built man, with a clean-shaven face and thick black hair, keenly
interested in many forms of sport and a devoted motorist." But Eric
had become obsessed with his friend and it seemed that the older man
was the only person who could influence him. So much so that Eric's
family started to reach out to him to see if he could help stop Eric
taking drugs. Crippled by sleeplessness Eric had become dependent on
Veronal and alcohol, but there was little Albert could do.

In 1908 Albert was taken ill with blood poisoning and as he
recuperated in Swansea Eric often visited him. He stayed either at the
Singleton or the Cameron Hotel. "I remember him well, a hotel staff
member told the *Cambrian Daily Leader.* "Mr Trevanion was very
affectionate in his ways; in fact, in this respect he was more like a lady.
During his stay here he occupied room No 219. I went up to him on

one occasion, and was surprised to see the quantity of powders, puffs and cosmetics he had lying about. It was just like a small chemist's shop. Mr Trevanion appeared to be of a generous disposition, and was seemingly not a man who drank much; in fact, I should say quite the contrary. He wore a watch fastened round his wrist, and several rings; indeed his fingers were almost covered in them."

As Albert was unable to return to sea due to ill health, Eric offered him a job as his companion and they moved to Brighton. It was as he was busy with the alterations to their flat that Eric died. During the second inquest details of their life together began to emerge.

Eric's friends were all of his own sex. At the inquest Albert was asked if Eric was partial to female society. Not really was his reply, but there was only one lady whom he liked. Instead he clung to Albert. "The two men were scarcely ever apart," said a Brighton acquaintance. "Mr Trevanion seemed to think a tremendous lot of his friend, and always wanted to be with him. In his company, he would seem so far as his ill health would permit, to enjoy life, but in Mr Roe's absence he would become almost spiritless." Whenever Albert returned to Swansea for a few days to visit his family Eric would write and telephone and "was never satisfied until he had got an assurance that his friend was on the way back to the flat."

Albert assured the court that the relationship was entirely platonic – although they slept in the same room and the same bed. Eric was nervous of sleeping on his own and in the past both the man-servant and the chauffer had to spend the night in his bed to allay his nerves – according to their testimony. In court the prosecution tried to show this was not quite as innocent as it seemed and asked Albert about arrangements when staying in hotels abroad. He testified that they always asked for twin beds but that sometimes they could not get them. However it seemed that whilst staying at the Paris Hotel at Lugano, when shown a room with two beds in it Albert had wanted a little matrimonielle (marriage bed). Albert denied it. The man servant at the inquest also seemed very reluctant to confirm that Albert and Eric shared a room and a bed. "Always?" insisted the judge. "Yes, sir," was the reply.

Certainly there was a strong suspicion of 'unnatural vice' throughout the inquest. The foreman of the jury asked Eric's doctor if he was addicted to such practices but the doctor replied, "No. I am quite sure he was not." But Eric's autopsy revealed signs which suggested otherwise. The coroner stated that the skin around the anus was unusually loose, indicative of a "habit far worse than that of drug-taking". The autopsy cards (which have been preserved in the Wellcome Archive) have written at the top "sexual pervert".

There were several exchanges about Eric's appearance and mannerisms. He was nearly six feet in height, slender to the point of fragility, his hair was fair with a reddish tinge, face pale and eyes sunken. He was very noticeable as he went about with dyed hair, painted face, bangles on his wrists, and high heels. Neighbours thought he suffered from heart weakness. "The least exertion fatigued him and he had to be assisted into the lift when he descended to the motor-car in which he and Mr Roe took almost daily drives."

The coroner said Eric wore a plain gold ring on his ring finger and when a juror asked "Like a wedding ring?" the answer was yes. There were a series of questions at the inquest: "Were his dress and manners more like a female than a male?" "Did he try to pass himself off as a female?" "Was the deceased, to your knowledge, addicted to any immoral practices whatever?"

As their relationship had progressed Albert seemed to tire of Eric. A heavy drug user for many years. Eric had suffered three near-death experiences by overdosing. He swore he had not been trying to commit suicide – that he had done it deliberately to frighten Albert. Due to his excessive drug taking and resistance to them Eric had a peculiar idea that he could control his intake of what to others would be an enormous amount of drugs. Doctors warned him to cut down but he never did.

After the third attempt Albert stormed to the doctor, "if Eric recovers from this as he has recovered from the last two attempts, I cannot stand it any longer. I shall refuse to live with him, and his own people will have to look after him. It is the third time, and I cannot stand the anxiety any longer."

Events reached a climax on the night of 11 September 1912. Eric and Albert had dined together, though Eric ate very little. According to Albert the young man was sullen and demanded that Albert let him have more of his own way with regard to the amount of alcohol he drank. To which Albert replied, "I want something more to live with than the furniture in the house!" After the meal they had coffee and

Eric went to the bedroom where his man-servant opened a bottle of hock for him. Later, Albert looked in on him and apparently they were chatting about ordinary things when suddenly Eric said, "I've taken an overdose. Ring Dr Baines", which were the last words he spoke.

What happened next was subjected to intense scrutiny at the inquest. The first consideration was whether Eric had committed suicide or had attempted another deliberate overdose. One thing was certain, Eric must have been aware of how many drugs he was taking.

Veronal had been created in 1903 and was freely available over the counter. Its use was predominantly for those who had trouble sleeping. Ten to fifteen grains was the recommended dose whilst up to 30 grains were used without ill effect in patients with mental health problems or those who were difficult. However 30-50 grains often proved fatal. Prolonged used built up a tolerance and so higher and higher doses had to be taken to get the desired effect. Fatal doses were not uncommon. Veronal had an extremely bitter taste and was often taken dissolved in strong tasting liquids such as coffee or wine. To have taken 150 grains would have meant opening twenty-one sachets and pouring them into a lot of liquid. Eric had taken a bottle of hock with him to bed but the bottle was removed by the man-servant after he died and could not be examined. It would have required about five bottles to dissolve the 150 grains.

A nurse who had been employed to take care of Eric was asked if she thought he would commit suicide, to which she answered "I don't think he ever took his life. He was too fond of living." She told the coroner that Eric was very unhappy and when asked why she wrote her answer on pieces of paper. The prosecution said it was "undesirable they should be read out in public" and was inadmissible under the hearsay law." Everyone who saw Eric on the day he died said he was very cheerful, though Albert said he was depressed and not very communicative at dinner. The coroner asked Albert if he had ever threatened Eric with exposure that would cause him anxiety, but Albert denied it. He also asked if Albert had threatened to leave him several times and Albert admitted he had but had never really contemplated doing so.

Throughout the inquest a number of events occurred which raised suspicion. Albert was accused of throwing something in a fire, there were missing drug wrappers, the timeline seemed odd, Albert had not wanted an inquest and Eric's mother was not notified until some sixteen hours after he lapsed into unconsciousness. When Eric's brothers, Claude and Cecil, arrived they suggested everything should be removed and made tidy. The man-servant and his wife presented confused and contradictory testimony. Eric's nurse related a conversation she had with the wife saying now that Albert had the money he would probably turn them out. To which the wife replied "that they were not going unless they got a good lump sum, or unless they were well paid." The reason why they might have been paid off was not made clear.

Probably the issue which created most suspicion was what had happened to Eric's money. He had employed Albert as his companion at a very high wage and had regularly transferred money into his account. Of the £100,000 he had inherited only about half was left and most of that was in Albert's bank. Other actions by Albert also raised suspicion, such as locking all Eric's rings into a vault in his name. His argument was that he wanted Eric to stop wearing such showy jewellery. Eric's will left everything to Albert. According to various witnesses Eric was completely under Albert's control and would do whatever he was told.

For a long time Eric had been estranged from his family, particularly his mother. He bore her so much animosity that Eric, when leaving directions for his funeral, wrote "I wish that the ashes of my lifelong friend, Albert Edward Roe, if his body is cremated, shall be placed in an urn in the same mausoleum as that which contains my ashes, and that both urns shall be above the level of the ground and I prohibit you or your successors in title from allowing any member of my family to be buried or their ashes places in such mausoleum or in the ground belonging thereto."

However, subsequently Eric had reached out to his mother but had not told Albert. For months prior to his death he had been writing to her, addressing her as 'Dear Mother' and ending "with best love from your affectionate son." The prosecution asked Albert that even when Eric was on the point of death why he had not sent for the family. To which Albert lamely replied that he knew that there were difficulties between them. When Eric's mother was finally informed of her son's overdose she and Albert had several words. Despite claiming at the inquest he knew nothing about being left everything in the will,

Florence told them that Albert had said to her that "everything was in his name; the flat and the furniture, and all the heirlooms were in his name. I said why, and he said, "To kick you out if there is any fuss with you." He had also discussed the will with his lawyer and admitted they were expecting trouble over it. So he had lied about not knowing of the will.

The press, followed the case closely, had a great deal of suspicion of Albert. They suspected him of making Eric leave everything to him. And at the time of the inquest he was often seen laughing and joking. He spent a lot of time in Swansea where he was employed as a colliery agent, and was often seen with "an intimate personal friend in the person of Mr Andrew Paton, the well-known local golf and billiard player."

Albert's family had also received a number of extraordinary anonymous letters which the newspaper the *Leader* said it had read but was not in a position to make them public. To make matters worse it seemed that Albert had been planning on palming Eric off onto the local doctor. There had been an arrangement that Eric would be cared for either at his flat or the doctor's home. In return the doctor would be paid £1,000 a year. Albert, who would then have had complete control over Eric's money, was planning to move back to Swansea and marry.

As the second inquest came to an end the judge began his summing up, and was clear about his feelings for Albert:

> By Trevanion's death Roe gained a fortune and freedom, and a very considerable fortune without restriction of any kind as to its use. Apart from the fortune, he would be gaining absolute release from the duties, whatever they were, of acting as companion and bedfellow to a delicate and eccentric young man. He would at once become free and enjoy £10,000; perhaps marry, and make a career for himself …
>
> Imagine the life he was actually leading as companion to this effeminate and ridiculous young man, with his incurable addiction to drugs and drink, so that death would be a heavenly relief.
>
> … is it likely that Roe knew nothing about the will? He lived on extremely intimate terms with the deceased, who

spoke freely of his money affairs and his family quarrels, and certainly told Dr Sandifer and Dr Baines what he had done. It is likely, do you think, that Roe knew nothing about the will ...

...considering the almost insane infatuation of the boy for his companion, but it has an ugly look, and can Roe complain if he is regarded by the friends of Trevanion and others as an unscrupulous adventurer, capable of doing anything to secure the fortune of the boy by what means no one can say."

The judge spoke of the confusion over the actual taking of the drugs. It would have been impossible to dissolve 150 grains in the hock and "it would be impossible for a person to administer veronal in the form of cachets without the knowledge of the person to whom it was administered." Trevanion could not have failed to notice unless he was too muddled with drink. "Whether Roe might have not persuaded or encouraged the deceased to take an extra-large dose, not letting him know, of course, how large a dose it was, by way of calming him and securing a good night's sleep after the agitating events of the evening ... It is conceivable that a second half bottle of hock, and possibly other drinks – there were whiskey and sherry, I think, drinks not spoken to by Roe – may have made Trevanion in such a muddled condition not to notice what Roe was doing. It may have done. It is also possible that Trevanion might have requested Roe to make him a good strong sleeping draught, but these are conjectures unsupported by any positive evidence at all."

In the end the jury returned to say that death was due to an overdose of Veronal but how or by whom this had been administered there was no evidence. The jury added a rider that Veronal and its derivatives should be placed on the poison schedule. Just a few months after Eric's death, and as a direct result of the case, the sale of Veronal became restricted to registered chemists only and had to carry the label 'poison'.

Even before the echoes of the inquiry had even begun to fade the will was disputed. Rumours began later in the year that Albert had been negotiating with the family for a settlement. It was said that he received a 'substantial sum', settled apparently on the condition "that certain allegations on the pleadings made against Mr Roe should be unconditionally withdrawn." Four months later Albert married Margaret, widow of the late W.H. Derrick, sweet manufacturer of Swansea.

The open verdict of the inquiry left more questions than answers. Did Albert become nervous about Eric's reconnection with his family who would undoubtedly try to stop the will? Or did Eric, getting wind of the plan to have the doctor take care of him, decide to commit suicide? Did he, as he had done before, simply try to scare Albert and it got out of hand? Or was Eric, having gone through his fortune, about to ask Albert for his money back? Or was it as Mrs Trevanion believed – a case of murder?

One of the interesting questions this case raises is had it involved a woman and an older man, might it have been treated differently? Had the older man kept all her jewellery and fortune and then tried to have her locked up by a doctor whilst he went off to marry someone else been enough to go to trial for murder? Throughout the inquest the nature of Eric and Albert's relationship was questioned but then brushed aside. Something that would not have happened had it been a man and woman involved. This Edwardian sensibility may have protected Albert from going on trial for murder.

15. A Wonder of Nature

Just above the beach in the village of Manorbier sits a castle. Now a ruin, it was the seat of the Anglo-Norman family of de Barri. And here in c. 1146 that Gerald de Barri was born. He was the grandson of Nest, regarded as one of the most beautiful women in Britain. Nest was to have a profound impact on the world as her descendants include all Tudor and Stuart monarchs, as well as John F. Kennedy, Diana, Princess of Wales and, ultimately, Prince William – Britain's future king.

Gerald was destined to become one of the best-known Welsh writers in the world under his nom de plume Giraldus Cambrensis (Gerald of Wales). His works are still in print 900 years later. Gerald was, by his own description, a very handsome man, a brilliant conversationalist and had a fascination for everything around him. He was always scribbling and noting every little thing. There are twenty-two known works by him, although three are lost. They included biographies of saints, books on the church, two books on Ireland and two books on Wales: *Itinerarium Cambriae* (Journey Through Wales, 1191) and *Descriptio Cambriae* (Description of Wales, 1194). *Journey Through Wales* was the result of Gerald's travels through the country to preach the Cross – urging people to join the Crusades. Gerald himself set out for the Crusades but on the death of King Henry II was sent back to Britain.

In 1185 Gerald had become a royal clerk to Henry II and was ordered to accompany Prince John on a trip to Ireland. This was Gerald's second trip, having visited family there two years earlier. The culmination of both trips was one of his most famous works, *Topographia Hiberniae* (Topography of Ireland, 1188) – admittedly less a topographic work and more a history, and a highly prejudiced history at that.

The book, written in Latin, is full of descriptions of the landscape, people and their history, and contains interesting accounts. In part two, 'Of the Wonders and Miracles of Ireland', he describes two women. Of the first he wrote

> Duvenald, king of Limerick, had a woman with a beard
> down to her navel, and, also, a crest like a colt of a year old,

which reached from the top of her neck down her backbone, and was covered with hair. The woman, thus remarkable for two monstrous deformities, was, however, not an hermaphrodite, but in other respects had the parts of a woman; and she constantly attended the court, an object of ridicule as well as of wonder. The fact of her spine being covered with hair neither determined her gender to be male or female; and in wearing a long beard she followed the customs of her country, though it was unnatural in her.

Of the second he wrote,

Also, within our time, a woman was seen attending the court in Connaught, who partook of the nature of both sexes, and was a hermaphrodite. On the right side of her face she had a long and thick beard, which covered both sides of her lips to the middle of her chin, like a man; on the left, her lips and chin were smooth and hairless, like a woman.

The image of the bearded woman was apparently overseen by Gerald himself and to emphasise that she is a woman she is seen spinning with a distaff and spindle. @ National Library Ireland.

It is doubtful if Gerald actually met the women, as he did not travel extensively in Ireland. Instead it is quite probable he was simply repeating stories he had been told.

The natural causes for hirsutism (opposed to deliberate shaving) are varied but one of the most common is Polycystic Ovary Syndrome, a common condition affecting women's ovaries. One of the features of the condition is a high level of androgens, the compound in the body which defines male characteristics (the word androgen comes from the Greek *andro* meaning masculine). Numerous examples of hirsute women can be seen in historical records, and some of the earliest were perceived as supernatural or 'other', such as witches. In Shakespeare's *Macbeth* published in 1623 are lines describing the three witches in the play:

> you should be Women,
> And yet your beards forbid me to interpret
> That you are so. (1. 3. 37-45)

Interestingly very few productions of *Macbeth* include bearded witches.

Bearded women were often thought (wrongly) to be hermaphrodites. In the fifth century a well-known Roman writer, Macrobius Ambrosius Theodosius, wrote in a compilation of religious and antiquarian lore, *Saturnalia,* "There's also a statue of Venus on Cyprus, that's bearded, shaped and dressed like a woman, with sceptre and male genitals, and they conceive her as both male and female. Aristophanes calls her Aphroditus, and Laevius says: Worshiping, then, the nurturing god Venus, whether she is male or female, just as the Moon is a nurturing goddess. In his *Atthis* Philochorus, too, states that she is the Moon and that men sacrifice to her in women's dress, women in men's, because she is held to be both male and female."

Bearded women have long fascinated society – in 1859 John Pavin Phillips from Haverfordwest wrote to the magazine *Notes and Queries*: "Bearded Women – Some fifteen or sixteen years ago I remember a hairy woman being exhibited in London. She had a flowing beard and moustache, of a soft and silky texture, but in all other respects was perfectly feminine. She was a young married woman, and was the mother of children ... Are there any other records of a similar lusus naturae?"

His request saw a flurry of replies detailing women throughout the ages and across the world. As a doctor Andrew Wilson pointed out in the *Cardiff Times* "… Such individuals are not very uncommon. There was a case reported in 1852 by Dr Chowne of a bearded lade who was a patient at Charing Cross Hospital. Her whiskers and beard were 'four' inches long. Her sister exhibited a like development. 'Krao', who was exhibited in London some years ago, had a hairy face. A whole Burmese family described by Captain Yule in 1855 showed an excessive growth of hair on the female sex, and Julia Pastrana, the Spanish dancer, was noted for this peculiarity." And the *Evening Express* in 1893 noted, "Breconshire boasts possession of a very fine sample of the bearded woman" but gives no further details.

Throughout history bearded women have for the most part been treated harshly, from being burnt at the stake as witches to being a staple feature in the Victorian 'freak' shows. Do they fare any better today? 'Bearded lady reveals she now loves her unshaven look after years of bullying: "I wanted to kill myself"' screamed a *Daily Mirror* article in March 2015. Harnaam Kaur, just one of a number of modern women, had a beard growing at just eleven years old. But by her mid-twenties she decided to embrace the way she looks and joined an anti-bullying charity. It seems society hasn't yet got over its fascination.

The other reason Gerald of Wales is famous in the context of sexual orientation and gender identity history is a passage which also appears in the *Topographia Hibernica*. In 1994 the American academic John Boswell included it in his book *The Marriage of Likeness: Same Sex Unions in Pre Modern Europe* – a volume which created a storm of controversy.

Boswell was a specialist in the history of homosexuality, particularly in relation to Christianity, and had written three previous books on the subject. In *The Marriage of Likeness*[1] he argued that in medieval Christian Europe unions between same-sex couples were commonly accepted. He preferred the term 'same-sex unions' due to the fact that marriage had changed drastically throughout the history of the church. "The meaning and purpose of marriage," he wrote was "profoundly different from its modern counterpart", citing examples showing how romantic love, an integral part of modern couples, was rarely a consideration in the past. Marriage for the most part was about property, power and children.

Only months after Boswell's book was published it had gone through four printings and sold in excess of 31,000 copies, far more than most books on medieval history. Christian reviewers were on the whole negative whilst others praised Boswell's complex research for opening up the subject for discussion. Many, however, questioned his accuracy in translating and interpreting the wide range of specialist texts. A number of critics dammed the book before it had been published, giving an indication of the sort of reviews it would receive, no matter how accurate.

In his work Boswell used a large range of examples from history to argue that there were many different kinds of recognised unions men could be involved in around the world. (It was mainly men due to the dominance of writing by and for men.) Many of the discussions regarded the meaning of the Adelphopoiesis relationships.

Adelphopoiesis or adelphopoiia from the Greek meaning 'brother-making' refers to a ceremony uniting two people in a

church-recognised friendship. The meaning and purpose of the
Adelphopoiesis relationship in religion continues to be hotly debated.
The church maintains it is a celebration of friendship with no sexual
component. Others argue that any same-sex relationship which is
openly celebrated crosses the boundaries of heteronormal behaviour
which could, and did, lead to deeper affections and love.

Evidence of these types of ceremonies can be found in various forms
of Christianity up to the eighteenth century. One of the most discussed
couples was the saints Sergius and Bacchus. The two saints were fourth
century high-ranking Roman soldiers who, when suspected of being
Christians, were tested by being ordered to worship at a pagan temple.
When they persistently refused they were chained, dressed in female
attire, and paraded around the town. Bacchus was beaten to death but
the next day his spirit appeared to Sergius urging him to be strong and
reassuring him that they would be together forever. The following day
Sergius was tortured to death. There is considerable doubt as to the
truth of the story, but they became popular saints and were venerated
widely. Boswell argued that the relationship between Sergius and
Bacchus contained a romantic element due to the earliest text
containing the word *erastai*. In Greek *erastai* is the plural of *erastēs*
which referred to a pederastic relationship between an older man and
a younger man. Despite much criticism of Boswell's translations and
interpretations, Sergius and Bacchus have become very popular in gay
culture.

Similar criticism surrounded Boswell's translation of Gerald of
Wales. The passage only takes up one of 390 pages in Boswell's book
but the point is the same for all the examples he gives – trying to make
sense of a medieval ceremony. The extract appears in the third book of
Topographia Hiberniae, 'Of the Inhabitants of Ireland' No XXII, and
Boswell's translation is:

> A proof of the iniquity (of the Irish) and a novel form of
> marriage.
>
> Among many other examples of their wicked ways, this
> one is particularly instructive: under the pretext of piety
> and peace they come together in some holy place with the
> man they want to join. First they are united in pacts of
> kinship, then they carry each other three times around the

church. Then, entering the church, before the altar, in the presence of the relics of saints and with many oaths, and finally with a celebration of the Mass and the prayers of priests, they are permanently united as if in some marriage. At the end, as further confirmation of the friendship and a conclusion of the proceedings, each drinks the other's blood, which is willing shed for this. [This, however, they retain from the rites of pagans, who customarily use blood in the sealing of oaths.]

Alternative suggestions and translations have interpreted the piece with a completely different emphasis. Some of these interpretations Boswell referred to as "artful mistranslation and a general unwillingness to recognize something as ostensibly improbable as a same sex reading."

The most widely available translation of *Topographia Hiberniae* was the Penguin Classics edition of 1969 by John O'Meara. He believed the passage said:

A proof of their wickedness and a new way of making a treaty. Among many other tricks devised in their guile, there is this one which serves as a particularly good proof of their treachery. Under the guise of religion and peace they assemble at some holy place with him whom they wish to kill. First they make a treaty on the basis of their common fathers. Then in turn they go around the church three times. They enter the church, and swearing a great variety of oaths before relics of saints placed on the altar, at last with the celebration of Mass and the prayers of the priests they made an indissoluble treaty as if it were a kind of betrothal. For the greater confirmation of their friendship and completion of their settlement, each in conclusion drinks the blood of the other which has willingly been drawn especially for the purpose.

It was this translation which was republished in 1982.[2] An 1876 edition by John S. Brewer and James F. Dimock give the piece more or less the same meaning as John O'Meara.

Boswell was accused of translating Gerald with an agenda, that he wanted it to read like a homosexual marriage. But if Boswell can be accused of having an agenda so can the others. In 1876 the death penalty for homosexuality had been removed only fifteen years earlier. The penalty for homosexuality was ten years to life so it is unlikely Brewer and Dimock would have wanted to publish anything positive. When O'Meara published his version in 1969, homosexuality had only been partially decriminalised two years previously. Men could still be sent to jail and public opinion was predominantly negative. Again it is unlikely O'Meara would publish a positive piece on homosexuality. Also, if the piece was truly about a treaty why in certain cases, as reported by Dimock in 1867, was the page defaced in one version and cut out of another?

Very few translations have appeared since Boswell. A 2000 translation in the Medieval Latin Series from Cambridge, Canada conforms to the treaty version. So in order to seek some elucidation, in this modern age of equality, this author decided to see if any clarity could be shed on the translation.

The title of the piece in the original Latin is *De argumento nequitiae, at novo desponsationis genere*, and the word that has caused so much controversy is *desponsationis*. Throw the word into Google and the results will show that most definitions are betrothal, engagement or marriage. A similar search on the singular term *desponsare* shows the same results. In Portuguese and Spanish *desposar,* from the Latin root, also refers to marriage. As does the English word *spouse* meaning betrothed.

However, far down at the bottom of the lists of definitions the words 'contract', 'treaty', 'pledge' and 'promise' appear. It is obviously these last definitions that early translators have concentrated on, ignoring the most popular definitions which are always listed first in any dictionary. Not being a Latin scholar I sought expert advice from the National Library Wales, the National Library of Ireland and the British Library. The last two hold original copies of *Topographia Hibernica.* Wales and Ireland felt it might be more appropriate to approach academics but the British Library replied with information taken from R.E. Latham's *Revised Medieval Latin Word-List: from British and Irish sources* (1965). They said *desponsationis* "gives the meaning espousal, betrothal or marriage" and added "betrothal was as legally binding as marriage", which raises interesting points. If the British Library in 2015 are quoting from a 1965 reference then John O'Meara in his 1969 translation appears to have ignored the leading definitions. For, as the British Library points out, a treaty, promise or contract of marriage was as good as marriage. Professor Bjorn Weiler in the Department of History and Welsh History at Aberystwyth University and who teaches on Gerald of Wales described the use of the word 'treaty' as 'bland', implying it lacks the strong characteristics of the leading definitions.

The other area of contention is around the Latin word *oppetere* or *appetere*. Boswell argued that it meant 'to join' but the other translations had insisted it meant 'to kill'. In the variety of Latin dictionaries available online the most common definition is to 'grasp', 'seek for', and 'reach after'. No definitions offered 'to kill'.

During the discussions around civil partnerships and same-sex marriage Boswell's book found new audiences and new discussions about his findings were undertaken. The purpose behind the ceremonies described in the book may never be fully known to us. Many ancient texts were destroyed due to societal pressure not to accept anything outside heteronormality. All we can really say is that human emotions are too complex to be so easily explained away.

Boswell died from AIDS complications in the year his book was published and so we are denied his responses to critics. However I think it is now time to revisit the extract and have a balanced and fair discussion about the most accurate, and unbiased, translation.

16. And the pray was granted

In 1906 Francis Knight died. Francis was just a baby, and in the early twentieth century when infant mortality was high the death was not unusual. What made this death different was that Francis was a hermaphrodite.

The Knight family lived in Penylan Road, Newport where the father Henry was a commercial traveller. The mother described the child as delicate from birth and "was so formed that it was impossible to tell whether it was a boy or girl." The post-mortem found death was to be due to a blood clot in the aorta. The coroner decided that Francis was a girl.[1]

Reports of hermaphrodites appeared regularly in the British press although Welsh examples from the nineteenth century are few. From Llanfynydd, Pembrokeshire came the story of Sarah and her shoemaker husband Evan Jones. On the 28 October 1951 Sarah had given birth to "a perfect hermaphrodite" and the "registrar is consequently puzzled how to register it". The report went on to say that "The medical faculty have as yet failed to solve the problem submitted to them in this case", and assured their readers, "had not this fact been communicated to us from a source which we have every right to rely upon, we should have been inclined to doubt its authenticity, but there is no reason to doubt the correctness of our information."[2] It is not known what happened to the baby.

One of the earliest mentions of hermaphrodites in Welsh history occurs in the laws of Hywel Dda. Hywel ruled most of Wales in the tenth century and during Lent in 940 he held a grand national council at Y Tŷ Gwyn ar Daf[3], also known as Whitland Abbey. One role of the council was to compile and enact a code of laws. He "summoned to him from every commote of his kingdom six men who were practised in authority and jurisprudence … and the king selected from that assembly the twelve most skilled laymen of his men and the one most skilled scholar who was called Master Blegywryd, to form and interpret for him and for his kingdom, laws and usages …"[4]. In the laws the definition of hermaphrodites is discussed:

> XXXVI O deruyd geni dyn ac aclodeu gór a rei góreic
> ganthaó, ac yn petrus o ba vn yd aruerho; rei adyweit panyó

heróyd y móyaf yd aruerho y kerda y vreint; os o bop un yd
aruerha ynteu, kyfreith adyweit dylyu o honaó kerdet órth
y breint uchaf, sef yó hónnó breint gór: ac or beichogir ef,
dylyu ohonaó kaffel treftat y gór ae beichocco; os ynteu a
veichocca góreic, kaffel or mab y dref tat ynteu.

36. If a person be born with the members of a man and
those of a woman, and it be doubtful of which it may make
use; some say, that according to such as it principally may
use, its privilege is to rank; but, if it make use of each, the
law says, that it is to rank with the highest privilege, and that
is the privilege of a man: and, if it should become pregnant,
the offspring is to have the patrimony of the man who
caused the pregnancy; but, if it should make a woman
pregnant, the son is then to obtain its patrimony.[5]

Essentially this means that if 'it' principally had sex as a man then 'it'
was a man and if 'it' had sex as a woman then she was a woman. If 'it'
had sex as both a man and a woman then 'it' was to take the highest
rank, which was that of a man. If 'it' became pregnant then the
offspring took the patronage of the father and if 'it' made a woman
pregnant then the son was to the take name of 'it'.

This is in keeping with other laws of the time. Peter Cantor (d.
1192), the French Catholic theologian, when addressing sodomy in the
De vitio sodomitico, wrote "the church allows the hermaphrodite to use
the organ by which s/he is most aroused. But should s/he fail with one
organ the use of the other can never be permitted and s/he must remain
perpetually celibate to avoid any similarity to the role inversion of
sodomy, which is detested by God."[6]

The word hermaphrodite is a combination of the names Hermes
and Aphrodite. Their son, Hermaphroditus was a minor god, the child
of Hermes the Greek messenger to the gods, and Aphrodite, the
goddess of love. As a young man Hermaphroditus was travelling when
he came across a water nymph called Salmacis. On seeing the boy she
was overcome with lust and tried to seduce him, but he rejected her.
Salmacis left and Hermaphroditus undressed and entered the pool to
bathe. But the nymph, who had been in hiding, leapt on the boy and
wrapped herself around him. As he struggled she called to the gods

The Borghese Hermaphroditus

asking for them never to part – granting her wish the gods made them one. Hermaphroditus then also prayed to the gods asking that anyone else who entered the waters should be made the same way and the prayer was granted.

Depictions of Hermaphroditus are usually of a beautiful female with male genitalia. One of the most famous the Borghese Hermaphroditus, or *Sleeping Hermaphroditus*, in the Louvre, Paris. It is a second century AD Roman copy of the Greek statue by Polycles (155 BC). Because of the sexual duality Hermaphroditus is considered a symbol of marriage – of the sacred union between men and women.

More prosaically, a modern word, intersex, is an umbrella term used to define "people who are born with sex characteristics (including genitals, gonads and chromosome patterns) that do not fit typical binary notions of male or female bodies."[7] Numbers of intersex people vary depending on which definition is used and which condition is being referenced – there are seventeen or so sexual variations. In addition to the seventeen variations, you would have to question as to what is, and isn't, strictly male and female. Do women with an excess of androgens in their body and so produce beards count as intersex or women who just happen to have more androgens than other women? What if there is no external ambiguity? Does an anomaly in chromosomes count as intersex?

This anomaly in chromosomes caused John Randell, the transgender specialist at Charing Cross, to raise suspicions about Wallis Simpson – the woman who caused the abdication crisis of Edward VIII. Randell had been given details from a colleague who suspected that Wallis was intersex. And Michael Bloch, in his biography of Simpson, concluded she had Androgen Insensitivity Syndrome or AIS, a mild form of intersexuality. A woman born with AIS often has the XY chromosome of a male although all outward appearances are female. Without medical evidence no conclusion can be reached about Wallis Simpson.

Counting all the variations together, the now disbanded Intersex Society of North America put the figure of intersex people at 1 in 1,500-2,000 births – which would give a Welsh population of around 1,500-2,000 people. However, in the last few years there has been a higher number of people self-defining as transgender and so the figure is likely to be higher.

Throughout history society has been fascinated by individuals who are outside the typical binary notions of male or female. Gerald of Wales mentioned one in his *Topography of Ireland* (1188). In Hereford on the Welsh border the Cathedral's Mappa Mundi (drawn around 1300) features a hermaphrodite. The figure appears in Africa with the description 'a race of dual sex born with many strange instincts'.

William Jones[8], an Anglo-Welsh philologist knew over twenty-eight languages and wrote extensively on Indo-European languages. He lived in India for much of his life, where he was a judge. He was one of the first English language scholars to collect and explain laws in India, and believed it was his life's mission to share what he had learnt with the Western world. In 1792 he published *Al Sirájiyyah: The Mohammedan Law of Inheritance*, in which he writes according to one chronicler:

> To the hermaphrodite, whose sex is quite doubtful, is allotted the smaller of the two shares, I mean the worse of two conditions ... when a man leaves a son, and a daughter, and an hermaphrodite, then the hermaphrodite has the share of the daughter.

To other writers they argued that the son should have one share, the daughter half a share, and the hermaphrodite three fourths of a share since if the hermaphrodite was a male they would be entitled to one share and half if a female and so had to take half the sum of the two portions. There followed a selection of claims on how much a hermaphrodite could inherit. Inheritance for hermaphrodites varied from country to country. It often depended on a range of conditions such as how they had sex, how they urinated or if they gave birth.

The word hermaphrodite was also used extensively as a catch-all for something not understood, something out of the ordinary or ineffectual, or of sexless people. Newspaper reports would speak of 'hermaphrodite governments' or of people as 'moral hermaphrodites'. The *Evening Express*, which reported on the Home Rule struggle in Ireland quoted Neville Chamberlain as he spoke of the Liberal League.

HALF AND HALF.

"I can't make you out. Sometimes you appear really manly, and sometimes you are quite effeminate. How do you manage it?"
"It's hereditary, I suppose. One half of my ancestors were males and the other half females."

They had he said "the sterling vigour of the male and all the winning attractiveness of the female," and advised them to stamp hermaphrodite on their notepaper.

Something similar occurred in literature. In Mary Morgan's book *A Tour to Milford Haven in the year 1791,* she writes "I walked some way down on the beach, and on looking towards the sea, I saw, at a considerable distance, three people seemingly walking in it; but upon approaching them, I found they were three females in bathing dresses, sporting like Nereids in the water, and with as little apprehension. They were hand in hand, moving in somewhat of a minuet step and attitude, and at intervals curtseying to let the sea wash over them. Thus they continued holding fast together, till they bathed their full. Had there been two only I should have believed they were Salmacis and Hermaphroditus."

Mary's description is startling and surprising – implying that the two women are actually a man and a woman. The common conception of Salmacis and Hermaphroditus together is one of struggle and violence as Salmacis essentially rapes Hermaphroditus. Mary does not qualify her statement and we are left to wonder what it was about the two women on the beach which caused her to make this statement.

Throughout the fighting years for women's suffrage, suffragettes would often be referred to as hermaphrodites by the press in an attempt to de-sex them, make them look 'other' and not part of 'normal' society.

The blurring of gender was an established part of ancient mythology. The twelfth century Welsh *Mabinogion* is amongst the earliest prose literature of Britain and is based on earlier traditional oral stories. Many countries have mythologies or religious narratives which include same-sex relationships or gender blurring. Many of these countries had their myths sanitised by Christian re-writing. In the Fourth Book of the Mabinogion Gwydion helps his brother Gilfaethwy rape their aunt Goewin. When their uncle Math learns of this he changes his nephews into a series of animals. Each year for three years they produce an offspring which is sent to Math who turns them into a male child. It's a strange story, incorporating different sexual orientations and genders – both brothers undergo periods of being female and giving birth. At the end of the third year Math releases them from his spell.

Gender blending can be found in other Welsh myths. The hare is an animal which was mysterious to people and were thought to be of double-sex or hermaphrodite. In old Welsh laws animals were given certain values which varied according to their age and condition or gender. However for the hare there was only one value because it was believed that the animal changed its gender from month to month. Hermaphroditism does occur in animals, and a report in 1858 illustrated such a case. A fishmonger gutting a salmon which appeared to all aspects on the outside to be a male discovered on the inside that the fish had both milt (sperm) and roe (eggs).[9]

In the 1863 a Welsh farmer asked a question on the Agriculture page of *The Welshman* on the subject of freemartins, a type of hermaphrodite from mixed-sex twin cattle. The farmer, who owned a valuable breed of cattle, wanted to know if a freemartin should be raised for breeding purposes. For the freemartin twin, to all exterior appearance looks female, but has masculine behaviour and is infertile. The answer was that freemartins were almost invariably hermaphrodite and as such would not breed. Modern tests have shown that they have both male and female chromosomes. All freemartins have a male twin and it is believed that at some point in the womb the female absorbs male chromosomes through the placenta. The most noted examples from Roman times onwards have been in cattle, goats, pigs and sheep – the *Welsh Journal of Agriculture* of 1928 records a rare example in a lamb. The term was adopted by a number of science-fiction writers to portray sterilised females such as in Aldous Huxley's *Brave New World*, genetically-engineered pseudo-females in Robert A. Heinlein's *Beyond the Horizon,* and a woman who questions her sexuality in *Footfall* by Larry Niven and Jerry Pournelle.

Other supernatural types from Wales are those of witches. In 1878 a series of letters appeared in the *Western Mail* debating the nature of Welsh witches. A writer called Sais Cymreig from Roath was considering the phrase 'Cefn-y-Wrach' as applied to the Penarth shoal which is in the shape of hunched old woman. The writer argues that the suffix 'ach' was used to denote something small, of no account, such as problach (common people), dynionach (people of little account) and corach (dwarf). Therefore 'gwrach' is taken from *gwr* for man and *ach* for small – a small man. Yet this male term was applied to witches, which strictly speaking should have the feminine suffix 'en' so 'gwarchen' for a small woman. The word gwrach has been attached to many place names such as Pant-y-Wrach, Bryn-y-Wrach, Cae-y-Wrach.

J.A. Morris from Sketty Park responded by dissecting the word 'gwr' for man and, according to him, 'ach' meaning a woman (although 'ach' is more associated with 'disgusting' such as ach-y-fi). Witches were generally supposed to be of the epicene gender "and hags, which that word signifies as well, were always supposed to have lost all their feminine beauty, and to have taken up some of the attributes of men, such as moustachios and other equally virile appendages. Here, therefore, there is no change of a single letter in the Welsh word, and makes it mean a 'man woman' or a 'woman man'.

In Webster's dictionary the word 'hag', Morris points out, derives from German meaning a hedge or bush. The modern Online Etymology Dictionary bears this out, stating that both Old Norse and Old High German used words 'hedge-rider' meaning someone who straddles the hedge or the boundary between two worlds. He also suggests that hag may derive from the Welsh word 'hagr' meaning ugly, unseemly or deformed and akin to the Cornish word 'hagar' for witch.[10]

Twenty years later Morien, the well-known Welsh journalist, was also drawn into the discussions around the definition of 'gwrach'. He argued *gwr* was 'manly or virile' and *ach* meaning characteristic. To him, then, *gwrach* meant someone of manly characteristics such as an Amazon.

Gwrach y Rhibyn (hag of the dribble) is a Welsh spirit usually deemed to be female – a hideous hag who approaches people about to die and calls them by name. Although female in appearance and legend, she will cry out "Fy ngŵr, fy ngŵr" or 'my husband, my husband'. Sometimes she will adopt a male voice and cry "Fy ngwraig! Fy ngwraig", 'my wife, my wife' or call for her child "Fy mhlentyn" or 'my little child', "fy mhlentyn bach." She has been known to appear in male form.

Mythology aside, the medical community often regarded hermaphrodism as something that could be 'solved' or 'cured' by corrective surgery or by picking in which gender to raise a child. These decisions were made very early on in the individual's life and hardly ever took into account what damage they might later cause. Quite often people, when they attain, adulthood, did not identify with the gender they had been assigned which could lead to confusion, depression, shame, and in some cases suicide.

In 1998 an article appeared in *The Observer*[11] on an intersex person, Linda Roberts. The headline read 'In Ancient Greece, she'd have been a god. In Wales, they spit on her' and detailed Roberts's life in North Wales were she received a huge amount of discrimination and hate. In the article Linda relates how on her deathbed her mother told her how the midwife had said, "Mrs Roberts, you have a perfectly healthy baby. Would you like to register it as a boy or a girl?" She was brought up as a boy because her father wanted a son. When Linda tried to argue she was a girl her father beat her.

In 1997 Linda moved to North Wales, to the remote village of Penrhyndeudraeth in Snowdonia. However there was to be no welcome in the hills. A group of around thirty people were intent on driving her out as they perceived her as a man dressed as a woman and defined her as a 'pervert'. She was spat at, had stones thrown at her and her windows smashed. In the year the article was published she had been assaulted, kicked, stamped on and had bones broken. The police, far from helpful, responded with "What do you expect, a person like you moving to a village like this?"

The expected notion that boys will be boys and girls will be girls is being challenged throughout the world. More and more organisations and individuals have to deal with the fact that defining sex and gender in binary notions does not work anymore. One area where discussions are particularly prevalent around intersex is sport. How do women's sports cope with those who have elevated but naturally occurring testosterone in the body? Women like the South African runner Caster Semenya, who in 2009 was subject to humiliating gender testing caused great media speculation. The International Association of Athletics Federation claimed that tests had to be made to ensure that a rare medical condition did not give her an unfair advantage. The tests were handled extremely badly and completely insensitively, and transgressed Caster's human rights. In a later interview Caster said, "God made me the way I am and I accept myself." She was cleared of any 'unfair advantage' and is now one of the world's best runners, winning gold at the 2016 Olympics.

17. I have a certain amount of regrettable notoriety

In 2015 *The Danish Girl*, a film about a transgender woman was released. It told the story of Lili Elbe, a male-to-female transsexual of the 1930s. And despite historical inaccuracies and criticism of a cisgender[1] actor (Eddie Redmayne) playing a transwoman it was very successful. It has an audience score on Rotten Tomatoes of 73%.[2] Lili was one of the very first people to undergo gender reassignment and since then a number of operations have been carried out in various countries. In the UK, the first place to have a dedicated clinic was in Charing Cross Hospital, London; it was the brainchild of Dr John Randell.

John Randell was born on August 25 1918, in Penarth. He was, he said "Educated badly at a private school and much better at the Welsh National School of Medicine"[3] where he qualified as a doctor in 1941. He worked briefly at the Cefn-Coed psychiatric hospital in Swansea and Sully Hospital in the Vale of Glamorgan before serving as a Surgeon Lieutenant from 1942-6 in the Royal Naval Volunteer Reserve. He then spent some time at Guys, St George's and St Thomas' hospitals in London until in 1950 he was appointed Senior Psychiatrist at Charing Cross Hospital.

The post-war years in Britain had seen a huge rise in discussions around homosexuality particularly with regard to crime and psychology, with people trying to 'understand' and deal with the issue. The prevailing view of psychiatry at the time was that homosexuality was an addiction which could be 'cured' through a variety of ways such as therapy, chemical castration (as practised on Alan Turing) or electric shock treatment. Whilst many did not believe it to be a naturally occurring condition, they did believe it should not be as harshly treated as the law demanded. Desmond Curran, one of the most distinguished clinical physicians of his generation, and a committee member of the Wolfenden Commission, wrote in his Foreword to Randell's book, *Sexual Variations*, "What should be regarded as 'normal' sexual activity? Should the criteria for normality be what is statistically average, or an approximation to an 'ideal' standard?" Like so many others, including Randell, Curran believed that "One must admit at once that there is very little scope for altering an established patter of sexual behaviour."

Care and Welfare Library   consultant medical editor A R K Mitchell

Sexual Variations

John Randell

Foreword by
Professor Desmond Curran CBE FRCP
The Chancellor's Medical Visitor

Randell had published *Sexual Variations* in 1973, in which he outlined a number of sexual practices. Aware that some of the 'variations' might shock some readers he reminded them, "To some degree sexual acts which are to be tolerated as acceptable (even in the privacy of the conjugal bedroom) depend on the moral climate and level of permissiveness in the society in which they take place. Different cultures have different standards: English rejection as sinful of deep kissing – known as the 'French Kiss,' was common thirty years ago; now it is regular practice. So, too, are variations in sexual positions during coition. Kissing acts extending to the sexual organs of the partners were, and by some still are, regarded as perversions."

Randell conformed to the medical views that there was little scientific evidence to support natural homosexuality. He preferred to believe that sexual orientation was due primarily to family and societal pressures, and that sexual attraction could be conditioned, as Pavlov's dogs could be trained to salivate on hearing the ringing of a feeding bell. "We are the subjects of our conditioning," he said, and if a person could be conditioned into something then they could also be 'deconditioned'. He claimed that reorientation could change 25-30% of individuals, but only if they were 'motivated'. We now know that these 'aversion' or 'conversion' therapies rarely worked. People learned how to mask their responses, and many therapies caused long term problems, including suicide.

Randell was also against locking up either male or female homosexuals as this simply placed them in an environment suited to their sexual needs and would 'reinforce the orientation'. "If a sexual act is no threat," he wrote "to property, the Queen's Peace, to life and limb, the right to choose or reject, it should not be proscribed just because it is not rigidly conformist". The ideal, he thought, was to offer psychiatric help.

Randell's greatest influence came through his work with transsexual people. At Charing Cross he had worked with the South African born Lennox Ross Broster, one of the first surgeons to routinely operate on intersex (previously called hermaphrodite) patients in the 1930s and 40s. His most famous patient was the Olympian Mark Weston.

Having gained experience with Broster, in 1959 Randell wrote a paper on his own patients, 'Transvestitism and Trans-sexualism: A Study of 50 Cases'[4] which comprised of thirty-seven males and thirteen females. At this time the term transvestite was generally used for all non-surgery individuals, whilst transsexual was used for those who either wanted to or had changed anatomical sex.

Despite early attempts to undertake sex reassignment operations it was not until the 1950s that techniques were being perfected, particularly by the famous surgeon Georges Burou, a French gynaecologist. He had established his Clinique de Parc in Casablanca, Morocco, where he treated over 3,000 people up to 1973, including April Ashley in 1960 and Jan Morris in 1972.

Initially Randell was not in favour of surgery and of the fifty patients covered in his paper only two he felt were suitable as they were "so manifestly lacking in masculine traits and so feminine in appearance, manner and speech that this step is logical." During 1960s Randell was seeing fifty cases a year but less than 10% of his patients had surgery and only a third of the male-to-females (mtf) had vaginoplasty. In 1960

Randell completed his MD thesis *Cross Dressing and the Desire to Change Sex* at the University of Wales. This was the first higher degree thesis on transgender people in the world.

Things were beginning to change. Patients were returning from abroad, particularly from the Clinique de Parc, with favourable reports, and Randell's own patient list was growing rapidly. The tabloid media was showing interest and throughout the 1960s a number of cases were covered. The *Sunday Pictorial* had been the first newspaper in Britain to give the subject serious attention when it serialised Christine Jorgensen's life story in 1953. The first television coverage took place on the BBC *Horizon* programme, 'Sex-Change?' in 1966, which drew attention to the fact that five Russians had withdrawn from the European athletics championships rather than take a sex test. Concerns had been growing since Mark Weston's case whether "some of the more extraordinary feminine records have not essentially been achieved by men." It is a concern which still raises its ugly head even today.

To cater for this growing demand for his services Randell set up the Gender Identity Clinic at Charing Cross in 1966. The importance of this clinic cannot be understated; many felt enormous relief that there was now a place where they could finally be recognised. "At last I felt everything would be understood," said one patient. "Everyone is in the same boat at Charing Cross, and this has made me feel more calm and relaxed." Another said, "I am not so depressed now or suicidal... The most helpful thing about the clinic is the recognition that there is something here that matters, we are not just pretending."[5]

In July 1969 Randell helped organise and then appeared in the First International Symposium on Gender Identity in London,[6] reading his paper 'Indications for Sex Reassignment Surgery'. The delegates came mainly from the UK and the USA, which had six gender-identity clinics. Due to the rising interest in the media the symposium was widely reported and journalists turned to the experts to explain what was going on. *The Times* heralded "1,000 sex changes in twenty years", so Randell explained that he had seen about 183 patients in the past 20 years of whom forty-seven had had sex change operations. "As a rule," he said, "there is a definite upgrading of social adjustment after the operation". He went on, "Transvestism, the desire to dress in the clothes of the opposite sex, was well known, and could be helped by psychological treatment, but trans-sexualism, where certain individuals, male or female, desired to change their sex, was a relatively unexplored field of medicine."

By the late sixties Randell had become convinced that surgery in many cases was more suitable for some patients. He insisted on studying them for at least a year and that patients live in the new sex role for at least six, and preferably twelve, months prior to surgery. His reasons were that there should be "unequivocal demonstration that they are markedly better adjusted in the role they desire than the role they have left". He summarised, "It is up to you to prove that you are a suitable candidate for surgery". He also devised an idiosyncratic criterion to decide who could have surgery. Patients should be free of any serious mental disorder, reasonably intelligent, single and most importantly they should be able to pass in public in the gender they chose. He believed that transwomen should be ladylike and as conventionally pretty as possible, and that they should wear skirts below the knee. They should conform to ideal womanhood – an ideal that few women in the 70s were adhering to. And once they had transitioned individuals had to appear heterosexual. Jan Morris did not fit Randell's criteria as she continued to live with her wife. Anyone not accepting Randell's rules would be declared a transvestite and therefore not suitable for surgery.

In 1970 Randell came to prominence in one of the most famous transgender cases in British legal history – Corbett v Corbett. In September 1963 April Ashley and Arthur Corbett were married in Gibraltar. Arthur knew that April had undergone a gender reassignment three years earlier at the Clinique de Parc. They had been together for just fourteen days before they got married – and it had not worked out. April sued for maintenance and Arthur countered by applying to annul the marriage based on either the fact that April was a man or that the marriage had not been consummated. This was at a time when marriages could not be annulled by mutual consent and had to have a 'reason'. The case caused legal confusion as there was little precedent, and so began an extended legal discussion on the nature of defining transsexualism.

An unusually large number of doctors gave evidence. Each side called three medical experts and whilst they broadly agreed, they differed in their inferences and conclusions. Randell appeared for

Arthur. During the court case almost every part of April's body, both internally and externally, was discussed. In a testimony praised by the judge, Randell stated that April was "properly classified as a male homosexual transsexulist", whilst other court doctors preferred the description castrated male. The verdict of the judge was that the marriage was void due to the fact that April was a man. Consummation, had the marriage already not been voided, could not have happened because "using the completely artificially constructed cavity could never constitute true intercourse"[7].

The judge further ruled that in determining a person's sex for the purposes of marriage the determining factors were biological. The gonadal, chromosomal and genitals determined a person's sex. The entry on a person's birth certificate was also taken as prima facie evidence of that person's sex. It was this judgement that was used as a benchmark to decide all future cases until the Gender Recognition Act of 2004.

During the 1970s Randell was becoming the go-to doctor for information on transgender issues. In 1976 he told the *Daily Express* "I have a certain amount of regrettable notoriety because sex-change has been said to be unethical by other members of the profession."[8] Despite being quite liberal-minded, many of Randell's views reflected current thinking. He defined transgender people as either homosexual or 'obsessive compulsive' and had limited sympathy for claims that their sex had been mistaken at birth. He was at the vanguard of a growing interest and awareness of transgender people but there was limited sympathetic treatment from the general medical profession.

By the late 70s Randell still clung to the views he had held in the 1950s, that family played a part in determining gender dysphoria: "It's possible for an abnormal learning pattern to be imposed early on in childhood, probably before two years old. The desire of parents for a child of the opposite sex is something of a factor. A boy child may be treated as a girl or feminised to some degree in upbringing." In what would be considered an astonishing categorisation today he went on: "Mothers of male transexuals are often disturbed themselves. They tend to keep the child in close physical contact. The child is then unable to consider himself as being separate from mother." His analysis of transmen was equally bad. "Gender confusion often dates back to the fourth year for girls. They are tomboys scorning dolls and domestic interests and their family histories often show a cruel or absent father." And he summed up by saying "My own view is that every individual has a mental organisation of his or her own at birth. But that some have learned patterns of the opposite sex."

Randell never saw trans people as anything other than the gender they were born in. He would always refer to patients, including post-operatives, by their birth gender and would tell an mtf 'you'll always be a man'. One of his most well-known patients, Mark Rees, wrote in his biography *Dear Sir or Madam: The Autobiography of a Female-to-male Transsexual*, "he continued referring to me in the female pronoun even years after I had become Mark. Although willing to give me the treatment he made it clear that in his eyes I was a female and a lesbian. It angered me but I didn't realize that help could have been available from elsewhere so I tolerated his behaviour. At this stage I saw him as my salvation."[9]

Yet there were hints of forward thinking. In *Sexual Variations* he wrote, "It has been suggested by my colleague, Professor Sloper, that chemical factors manufactured in the brain – the so called 'release factors' – can influence thought and behaviour, and that some are appropriate to maleness and some to femaleness. How these operate is not clear but it does point to the possibility of 'male' and 'female' brains." This was later borne out by a study in 2013 by the University of Barcelona which used MRI scans examine the brains of 24 ftm and 18 mtf before and after treatment with cross-sex hormones. The results showed that "even before treatment the brain structures of the trans people were more similar in some respects to the brains of their experienced gender than those of their natal gender."[10] Antonio Guillamon, who led the project, said, "Trans people have brains that are different from males and females, a unique kind of brain. It is simplistic to say that a female-to-male transgender person is a female trapped in a male body. It's not because they have a male brain but a transsexual brain." With the caveat that behaviour and experience also shape brain anatomy it is impossible to know if these differences exist at birth. However a 2010 study of 121 transgender people found that 38% knew they had gender variance by the age of five[11] which would imply it is present at an early age in some trans brains. This is borne out by Randell's experience, "most say that for as long as they can recall, often as early as five or six years of age, they have felt different from other boys, that they have envied the life patterns of girls, their clothes ... and the games and occupations of females."

For all his pioneering work in transgender studies and surgery, Randell was not always an easy man. Patients often spoke of his rudeness and God-like control. A common strategy when people went to see him was to try and persuade men to take female hormones and consider gender reassignment to dissuade them from cross-dressing, which he saw as an obsessive-compulsive disorder.[12] However, others got on well with him, and understood that some of his behaviour was a reflection of the negative press attention.

In 1979 the TV documentary *A Change of Sex* followed Julia Grant as she pursued a gender reassignment. Randell, her consultant, did not appear on screen fully, with the camera shooting over his shoulder only his voice could be heard. In one scene Julia informs him that she had a breast augmentation to which he sternly replies, "I take exception to that." When Julia pointed out that it was her personal choice he snapped, "It isn't a personal choice," and admonished her for overstepping the mark, before concluding "I don't like it."

The *Daily Telegraph* was shocked by Randell's attitude. "What stood out among some rather mundane sequences, and indeed could be said to justify last night's episode, was the extraordinary attitude of the medical profession as exemplified by the Invisible Doctor. This was Julia's NHS psychiatrist, who appeared to wield absolute power over her future progress towards the female state. Told that she had gone to a private surgeon for the breast operation, he frothed at the mouth, or he would have done if he'd been on camera."[13]

The programme produced a backlash – it damaged the reputation of the Gender Identity Clinic and cast Randell as an arrogant, cold and demanding man. The comedy show *A League of Gentlemen* (1999-2002) quoted Randell directly for their despotic Dr Ira Carlton. Some commentators have suggested that Randell's manner was deliberate, a means of testing those who would be forced to face discrimination in the future. If they couldn't handle a rude doctor how would they cope with a society that could be so much worse?

By 1980, approximately 100 of the 670 ftms Randell had seen had undergone surgery and 250 of the 1,768 mtfs[14] but this still only amounted to only 15% of his patients. Randell was performing one sex-change operation a month with an eighteen month backlog. The

News of the World claimed he and his surgeon Peter Phillip were making London the 'sex-change capital of the world'.

Shortly afterwards, on 30 April 1982, Randell died of a heart attack, aged sixty-three. Despite his flaws he was a pioneer in an area which was ignored or vilified by others. He helped many transgender people and his Gender Identity Clinic is today recognised as a centre of excellence. After many years of campaigning, in August 2017, thirty-five years after Randell's death, the Welsh Government announced that Wales is to have its first gender identity clinic, in Cardiff. From March 2018 there will also exist a network of general practitioners across Wales with specialist interest in gender identity health care. The move was endorsed by the All Wales Gender Identity Partnership Group, which includes representatives from the transgender community, and service users.

18. Dear Ernest … we disagree with you

In 2003 Daniel Twomey[1] published a paper on 'British Psychoanalytical Attitudes Towards Homosexuality' in which he outlined the difficulties facing LGBT people when seeking therapy. He quoted figures from a separate 2001 survey which found that of 218 members of the British Confederation of Psychotherapists who completed the survey, 64% believed that a gay or lesbian client's "sexual orientation was central to their difficulties". Twomey also stated that as far as he could find there were no 'out' gay psychoanalysts in Britain. "I was unable to find any British psychoanalyst who was of the theoretical belief that homosexuality could be a normal, healthy end-point of psychosexual development. These attitudes among psychoanalytically-oriented psychotherapists could be traced back to Ernest Jones, the psychiatrist who founded the British Institute of Psychoanalysis in 1919."[2]

Alfred Ernest Jones was a Welsh doctor. Born on 1 January 1879 in Gowerton, an industrial village on the outskirts of Swansea, he was the son of a colliery engineer. A brilliant scholar, he won many prizes and scholarships, first at Swansea Grammar School, then Llandovery College, Cardiff University and University College London. He was a passionate reader of widely varying subjects and believed science could save the world.

Whilst at UCL a colleague mentioned to him someone who was causing a stir with his novel ideas of psychiatry. Jones remembered "the deep impression of there being a man in Vienna who actually listened with attention to every word his patients said to him...a revolutionary difference from the attitude of previous physicians."[3] This was, more than at any other point, the moment when psychoanalysis in Britain began.

The man in Vienna was, of course, Sigmund Freud. Throughout the late nineteenth century Freud developed a new method of treating people. He believed that they could be cured of anxiety disorders through the revealing and analysis of unconscious thoughts such as dreams. Simply put, by talking freely the patient will eventually reveal the subconscious factors which underlie their problems and so can alter their attitudes or behaviour, or both.

Jones, appalled at the treatment of the mentally ill, was experimenting with hypnosis when he became aware of Freud's work and viewed it as a better method. In 1906 he was working as an inspector of schools for mentally handicapped children when he attempted some research into childhood sexuality. This idea was too much for Edwardian Britain. Society understood little about repressed memories and early sexual influences on behaviour. So Jones was arrested for improper conduct, sent to trial but acquitted. In 1908 he again tried to demonstrate that repressed sexual memories were the underlying cause of the hysterical paralysis in a young girl's arm. Once again he was accused of improper conduct, and was forced to resign. His reputation in Britain was at a low point. So he moved to Canada.

Some years earlier Jones met Carl Jung and had helped in the planning of the first Psychoanalytical Congress in Salzburg in 1908, at which he met Freud for the first time. For the rest of his life Jones would be devoted to Freud, becoming the most important advocate of Freudian analysis in the English-speaking world. Whilst living in Canada he co-founded the American Psychopathological Association in 1910 and the following year the American Psychoanalytic Association. He then moved back to Britain.

Meanwhile, in Vienna tensions had been growing between the two great proponents of psychoanalysis – Freud and Jung. Jones proposed a secret committee of those dedicated to safeguarding the legacy of psychoanalysis and Freud agreed. Jung became isolated. With a little manoeuvring Jones effectively took control of the International Psychoanalytic Association, so becoming the most powerful man in the world of analysis. He then set about forming the British Psychoanalytical Society, in 1919. His writings and lectures were the first in the English language by a practicing psychoanalyst, and it was mainly through his work that the British Medical Association officially recognised psychoanalysis in 1929.

In the 1920s, however, psychiatry was not widely trusted. There were a number of charlatans at work, many making huge amounts of money on quack diagnoses and giving qualified analysts a bad reputation. One of these self-styled therapists raped a patient, and another seduced several women. A case was brought against one of these men, and Jones became embroiled. The defendant falsely claimed that his expertise had been gained though a correspondence course with Jones. Lord Alfred Douglas (Oscar Wilde's 'Bosie') then became involved. He had converted to Catholicism and become leader of a

Purity League. At this time a number of societies had formed to campaign for high standards of 'purity' in society – at least according to their definitions. Douglas had sworn against psychoanalysis, and Jones in particular.[4] The book that had been published was a minor work on psychology, and one which Jones considered rubbish, but due to the inclusion of sexual analysis Douglas had taken offence. Despite his low opinion of the book Jones was concerned that success for Douglas might set a precedent. In a letter to the secret committee he wrote, "Douglas swears he will uproot Ps.A. in England and will make all publication impossible."[5] Douglas did win and all copies of the book were destroyed, but it did not set the precedent that Jones had feared.

In 1927 Jones read a paper at the 10th International Congress of Psycho-Analysis in which he wrote of "the unusual experience, a couple of years ago, of having to analyse at the same time five cases of homosexuality in women." He wrote to Freud: "An actively homosexual girl came to be analysed in December. Now her feminine partner who lives with her has come also... so you may imagine that the analytical work is especially interesting."[6]

In the paper he placed homosexual women into two groups. The first who "retain their interest in men, but who set their hearts on being accepted by men as one of themselves. To this group belongs the familiar types of women who ceaselessly complain of the unfairness of women's lot and their unjust ill-treatment by men." The second group he described as "those who have little or no interest in men, but whose libido centres on woman. Analysis shows that this interest in women is a vicarious way of enjoying femininity; they merely employ other women to exhibit it for them."[7]

One of the most famous women he analysed was the painter Dora Carrington. Jones wrote about Dora using an alias which fooled no-one. At the time she was having an affair with Henrietta Bingham, the daughter of the American ambassador, which it seemed everybody knew about. When Henrietta ended the relationship Dora was 'crushed', according to James Strachey. He wrote to his wife that "Jones lectured about Henrietta, and explained that the real reason why she threw over Carrington was because she [Carrington] wasn't a virgin."[8] One of the other women whom Jones was analysing was Mina Kirstein, also bisexual, who also had an affair with Henrietta.

James Strachey had trained with Freud and had become one of the first British psychoanalysts. He recalled, "I was, launched on the treatment of patients, with no experience, with no supervision, with nothing to help me but some two years of analysis with Freud."[9] He was bisexual himself – having had an unrequited love for the poet Rupert Brooke as well as affairs with the mountaineer George Mallory and the economist John Maynard Keynes. In 1920 he married Alix Sargant-Florence, with whom he translated Freud's works into English. He had fallen in love with Alix because he said she resembled a 'melancholic boy'.

James' brother was the writer Lytton Strachey, with whom Dora Carrington had a long and complicated relationship. They lived together for fifteen years and both had same-sex relationships. She had an androgynous appearance with short hair long before it became popular, but she was troubled by her sexuality. Writing to a friend, she speculated on the differences between loving women and loving men, and "that she felt no shame at the ecstasy she found with Henrietta but thought if she was completely 'sapphic' such relationships would be less problematic."[10]

Despite Jones referring to the women as 'homosexual' most were at least actively bisexual. Freud himself believed that people were fundamentally born bisexual but naturally evolved into heterosexuality. He thought that sex included complex psychological inputs which gave rise to a range of possible sexualities. However like many at the time he conformed to the idea that homosexuality was arrested development, and it was the repression of homosexual desire which caused neurosis. His famous letter of 1935 to a mother about her homosexual son outlined his beliefs: "Homosexuality is assuredly no advantage, but it is nothing to be ashamed of, no vice, no degradation, it cannot be classified as an illness; we consider it to be a variation of the sexual function produced by a certain arrest of sexual development. Many highly respectable individuals of ancient and modern times have been homosexuals, several of the greatest men among them (Plato, Michelangelo, Leonardo da Vinci, etc). It is a great injustice to persecute homosexuality as a crime and cruelty too."[11]

Freud's theories however were not supported by many of the psychologists of the day. Jones disliked homosexuality but even his views of it as arrested development were not as extreme as others. Ronald Fairbain, a Scottish psychiatrist, thought that not only should homosexual people be denied counselling but that the men should be removed from society and put into camps.[12]

In 1921 Jones received an enquiry from the Dutch Psychoanalytical Association whether a homosexual man should be admitted to train as an analyst. Jones wrote to Freud informing him that as head of the International Psychoanalytic Association he had rejected the applicant but opened up the question of prospective members. His argument was that anyone who persevered in their pathological orientation meant they could not be analysed therefore could not analyse others. Freud consulted one of his closest colleagues, Otto Rank, and wrote back "Your query dear Ernest concerning prospective membership of homosexuals has been considered by us and we disagree with you. In effect we cannot exclude such persons without other sufficient reasons, as we cannot agree with their legal prosecution. We feel that a decision in such cases should depend upon a thorough examination of the other qualities of the candidate."[13]

Had Freud's advice been taken the relationship between LGBT people and counselling may have developed along more liberal lines. However, Jones rejected it and homosexuals were excluded from becoming psychoanalysts. Many other leading psychoanalysts also rejected Freud's liberalism. Jones said "before the eyes of the world homosexuality is disgusting and a crime, if it were committed by one of our members it would bring a serious disrepute."[14]

There is an argument however that they could not have accepted an openly homosexual person to train because it was against the law. By merely admitting they were homosexual they would be guilty of criminal behaviour. Indeed the man about whom the original query rose was in fact jailed shortly afterwards.[15] What closeted men and women, such as James Strachey thought, is not recorded as they had no vote on the matter.

Over the next fifty years the refusal to accept homosexuals was strengthened by the influence of the American association which Jones had helped create. He also had the backing of Freud's daughter Anna, who "played an important role in misappropriating her father's theses, campaigning against any possible access of homosexuals to analytic training. With the support of Jones and the North American societies of the IPA, she had considerable influence in this area."[16] Anna was vehemently against homosexuals becoming analysts – a stance which

Sigmund Freud, Stanley Hall, Carl Gustav Jung, Abraham Arden Brill, Ernest Jones (centre back) and Sándor Ferenczi, in 1909 (*Wellcome Library, London*)

both then and now raises a few eyebrows given her relationship with Dorothy Burlingham, with whom she lived for many years. There is no evidence to confirm that the relationship was or was not one which we would today recognise as lesbian but it certainly was not a heteronormal one.

However the attitudes of the psychoanalysts, whilst not wanting homosexuals amongst their own ranks were, like Freud's, quite liberal towards ordinary homosexual people. This can be clearly seen in the important role they were to play in the history of sexual orientation when they were invited to submit testimony to the Wolfenden Report. By this time Jones had retired and was to die in 1958, the year following the publication of the report. However, the general testimony presented to the Wolfenden Committee reflected the ideology that he and others had constructed.

Most of the studies on homosexuality by these leading

psychoanalysts took place at the Institute for the Study and Treatment of Delinquency at the Portman Clinic – of which Jones had been vice president. Its work was to promote the idea that treatment was better than prison. It was to the Portman that many convicted homosexuals were sent by the courts for treatment. The Portman's psychoanalysts gave their opinions in a combined Joint Committee report, alongside another report from the British Psychological Society.

Pyschoanalysts such as Edward Glover, William Gillespie, Wilfred Bion and Hanna Segal had an important role in submitting evidence to the Wolfenden Commission. Edward Glover, who became second only to Jones in power in the British Society, believed that homosexuality was a perversion. Over the years he changed his position and was the first to write an account of the impact of psychoanalysis on homosexuality. He submitted his own report 'The Problem of Homosexuality' to the Wolfenden Committee, recommending legal reform – arguing that if sexual offences did not infringe the rights of others they should be removed from the criminal convictions.

Hanna Segal, who became president of the British Psychoanalytical Society and vice-president of the International Psychoanalytical Association, was opposed to homosexuals becoming parents, which she saw as an attack on heterosexual couples. In an interview in 1990 she recalled, "I was part of the working party from the Psycho-Analytical Society that gave evidence to the Wolfenden Commission and I think we had quite an influence on liberalising the laws…. I would not call it normality because it is a developmental arrest. But I would not legislate against it. For example, I would not legislate against obsessions unless their obsessionality damaged other people – but that doesn't mean that I consider it constructive."[17] Other members such as William Gillespie, despite discarding all Freud's bisexuality theories wrote about his patients in a sympathetic way. Mervin Glasser, who was an adviser for the British Board of Film Classification, maintained that women became lesbians "because of the persistence of the attempt to deny what they believe to be their anatomical inferiority"[18].

In America things were not much better. Karl Menniger, an American psychologist wrote in the introduction to the American edition of Wolfenden that "homosexuality …. constitutes evidence of immature sexuality and either arrested psychological development or regression. Whatever it be called by the public, there is no question in the minds of psychiatrists regarding the abnormality of such behavior."[19]

The psychiatric profession in the UK as a whole, whilst promoting homosexuality as a perversion, as pathological and as arrested development, did believe that adults should not be criminalised. A almost all recommended to Wolfenden a partial decriminalisation. The conclusion of the Portman Clinic submission stating, "there is no answer to homosexuality save tolerance on the part of the intolerant anti-homosexual groups in the community"[20].

Despite their liberal attitude towards partial decriminalisation, the beliefs of the psychoanalysts were to dominate the history of sexual orientation. Chris Waters, professor of Modern European History[21], argued that developments in psychoanalysis in the 1920s and 30s informed policy for the next few decades and played an important role in the making of the modern homosexual.[22] It was not until 1973 that the American Psychiatric Association removed some definitions of homosexuality from the *Diagnostic and Statistical Manual of Mental Disorders*. It was not until 1986 that all definitions were removed. Only in 1992 did the World Health Organisation remove homosexuality from its list of mental disorders.

Ernest Jones had an enormous influence on psychiatry, not just on its policies and attitudes but because he also saved Freud's life. At the time of the outbreak of World War II he put himself at considerable risk travelling to Vienna to rescue Freud, Anna and others of Freud's circle from the persecution of Jewish people by the Nazis. He later wrote a three volume work on Freud which became the standard reference guide.

Leo Abse referred to Ernest as "one of the most distinguished Welsh thinkers of the past century"[23]. He was patriotically Welsh and became a member of the Welsh Nationalist Party, Plaid Cymru. He also had a particular love of the Gower Peninsula and was instrumental in securing its status in 1956 as the first place in the UK to be designated an Area of Outstanding Natural Beauty. In 1924 he had been excited about a Welsh poem that included traits of psychoanalysis. The poem 'Atgof' (Memory) by Edward Prosser Rhys had won the National Eisteddfod at Pontypool. However it had caused great disquiet due to its homosexual content. Professor W.J. Gruffydd had mentioned psychoanalysis in his adjudication and described the poem as "one great lyric on the essence of Personality in its relation to life."[24] T.G. Davies in his biography of Jones laments that Jones, as a non-Welsh speaker, would not have been able to understand Saunders Lewis' biography on William Williams Pantycelyn, a seminal work in the understanding of this great Welsh writer. In Pantcelyn's 6,000 line poem 'Bywyd a Marwolaeth Theomemphus', 'The Life and Death of Theomemphus' written in 1764, Lewis shows how he anticipated Freudian understanding of the psycho-sexual dynamics of human consciousness.

Jones died in London on 11 February 1958. His *Times* obituary stated "death … has removed from the world of psychoanalysis its most eminent figure since the death of Freud."[25] His ashes were scattered in the grave of the oldest of his four children in the churchyard of St Cadoc's, at Cheriton on the Gower Peninsula.

Ernest Jones had an influential role in the development of psychoanalysis and LGBT history. According to Jones' biographer, Brenda Maddox he had a tendency to run both the International Psychoanalytical Association and the British Pyscho-Analytical Society as his own personal fiefdoms[26] and earned himself a reputation as a dictator. He would not even allow members of the Society to lecture on psychoanalytical subjects without first receiving his permission.[27] Would things have been different if he had allowed openly homosexual people to practice? Perhaps they could have directed more studies of healthy, happy homosexuals or bisexuals rather than those who had either sought or been compelled to undergo treatment.

Today things are getting better. In the late 1990s the therapist Dominic Davies, whilst living in Australia, co-edited three volumes of *Pink Therapy*, a series of extremely influential books due to their affirmative psychology. Returning to Britain in 1999 he established the Pink Therapy clinic in London, which provides therapy and training in sexual orientation and gender identity. Alex Drummond, a psychotherapist and transactivist[28] in Wales said "What Dominic did was to write from a perspective that took a gay affirmative stance – to offer a model that would allow therapists to validate and work constructively with clients to help them overcome internalised shame from years of exposure to homophobia". Through this, Alex said, people could "find self-acceptance – by validating same sex attraction as a healthy but different outcome to the heteronormative expectation of dominant psychology up to then". This was something of which Alex was only too aware – "In my own training in the late 90s we didn't touch on sexuality or gender. So I qualified as a therapist still indoctrinated in the historic pathologising models of sexuality and gender. It was only post-qualification that I came to find out about pink therapy and through training with them was able to deconstruct a lot of the toxic ideology that was the legacy of twentieth century psychology/psychiatry."[29]

19. A most intimate friend

In 1953 an MP who described himself as "an Englishman with an Irish name sitting for a Welsh seat"[1] wrote a letter. From his cliff-top home on Strumble Head looking out across the Atlantic, Desmond Donnelly wrote to the Home Secretary asking him to consider the issue of homosexuality. He wanted it added to the 1926 Royal Commission on Lunacy and Mental Disorder. A month later Conservative MP Sir Robert Boothby went a step further, asking for a new Royal Commission to examine "the treatment of … homosexuals … in the light of modern scientific knowledge …"[2]

Boothby had previously made a speech to the Hardwick Society and his comments had been widely reported by the press. He wrote to Sir David Maxwell-Fyfe, the Home Secretary, asking him to also consider the situation of homosexuality. Maxwell-Fyfe famously replied, "I am not going down in history as the man who made homosexuality legal." However Boothby persisted, and Maxwell-Fyfe asked him to write a memorandum on the subject. And it certainly was a hot topic. The annual number of prosecutions against homosexual men had risen from 622 in 1931 to 6,644 in 1955.[3] There were much publicised physical attacks on homosexuals. Men fleeing McCarthyism in America, which equated spying with homosexuality, were being harassed by MI5 when they arrived in the UK.[4] By 1954 over 1,000 men were in prison.

In April that year Donnelly kept up the pressure by addressing the House of Commons. In his speech he outlined the current laws – the Offences Against the Person Act, 1861, and the Criminal Law (Amendment) Act, 1885. The majority of cases concerning homosexuality had been brought under section 11 of the 1885 Act, a section which had been tagged on to another Act. A bill had been brought forward to make provision for the protection of women and girls. It had moved to the committee stage when the homophobic MP Henry Labouchere asked to insert a clause which ultimately became Section 11 of the Act. Section 11 made all homosexual activity a crime. Previously the law had only concerned itself with public indecency and the corruption of youth, and tended to ignore consenting adults in private. The only other amendment was that the maximum punishment should increase from 12 to 24 months. And so with no discussion and no agreement, a bill was passed which ruined many men's lives – and which became known as the Blackmailers' Charter.

Donnelly laid out his arguments why homosexuality should be decriminalised. Blackmailers were becoming rich, prisoners supposedly were indoctrinated, and homosexuals became indoctrinated with criminal techniques. He added "I think it is quite unusual for the law to interfere in what is essentially a moral issue." Reading from the Church of England Moral Welfare Society pamphlet he quoted, "In no other department of life does the State hold itself competent to interfere with the private actions of consenting adults." He concluded, "To stand by at this moment and do nothing about this matter is a grave indictment of our existing society."

In response Maxwell-Fyfe decided 'with reluctance' to refer the matter to a committee. They were to consider and recommend changes to laws relating to prostitution and homosexual offences and were to look at how those who had been convicted were being treated. The committee of fifteen people was chaired by John Wolfenden, the Vice-Chancellor of the University of Reading. It included, "representatives of the legal profession, medicine, government, education and religion; attempts at some kind of balance from England, Scotland and Wales; and three token women, mainly to contribute to the prostitution side of the mandate."[5] On its formation Wolfenden said to Boothby, "I have only one grudge against you. You have ensured that, for the rest of my life, my name will be associated with homosexuality."[6]

The 'balance' of the committee, however, was tilted firmly in England's favour with ten members. Scotland had four and Wales just one. The Welsh man was Goronwy Rees, born on 29 November 1909 at Aberystwyth, later educated at Cardiff High School for Boys. He did not speak English until he was 11. He won three scholarships to Oxford and in his autobiography *A Chapter of Accidents*, he outlined his views on and experiences of homosexuality there. It was a time exemplified by Evelyn Waugh's *Brideshead Revisited* with its simmering homoerotic tensions.

Rees believed that homosexual men were simply continuing behaviour they had learnt at school and were living in a state of conditioned infantilism, which was the prevailing view shared by many others, including Leo Abse and John Randell, who also believed adult homosexuals were infantilised. At Oxford Rees said, "It pervaded the entire life of the university, giving it a peculiar colour and flavour of its own, which accentuated even further the differences between life within and without its walls; it was as if some thousands of young men lived under conditions which, in one important respect at least, approximated to those of the nursery."[7]

Boothby reflected a similar attitude in his autobiography, "... Oxford immediately after the First World War was, basically, a homosexual society. By this I do not mean that all the undergraduates slept with each other. I simply mean that ... girls never impinged upon our lives at all ... our extraordinary education system, unique in the world, under which, in the so-called upper and middle classes, the sexes were completely segregated from the age of ten to twenty-two ... As for the homosexual phase, most of the undergraduates got through it; but about ten per cent didn't."[8] Rees claimed he was one of those who didn't, although his daughter wrote in her biography of him that he had fallen in love with "a very beautiful and wild young man" in his second year.[9] Perhaps it is this love Rees described in his novel *The Summer Flood* about an undergraduate returning from Oxford to stay with his family on the Cardiganshire coast and falling in love with a cousin. It includes a "very emotional section on a homosexual affair".

Marxism also swept Oxbridge in the early 30s. Many saw its utopian ideals as counter for the country's state of depression and traditional old boy networking. Rees wrote, "undergraduates woke to the fact that even in Britain there were three million men and their families who were near the starvation line."[10] He admitted he had a "romantic and sentimental view of the Communists cause." But most abandoned the ideology of communism when it didn't live up to expectations. Russia, the mother of Marxism, conducted a series of show trials of dissidents, starved the Ukraine and committed other atrocities. When it made a pact with the Nazis many in the West felt betrayed.

In 1934, whilst visiting Cambridge, Rees met Guy Burgess.[11] He had already heard of the undergraduate rumoured to be the most brilliant of his day, and when they met Burgess made it quite clear he was a homosexual and a communist. Despite making 'tentative amorous advances' he 'cheerfully desisted' when Rees told him he was one of those who didn't. "He would have done the same to any young man," Rees said, "because sex to him was both compulsion and a game which it was almost a duty to practice."[12] However according to a contemporary, A.L. Rowse, Rees was not so sanguine about it and had made a complaint about the pass. Rowse simply told him to keep out of Burgess' way.[13]

The two men went on to become very good friends. They were so close in fact that Burgess confided to Rees that he was a Russian spy. Rees didn't believe him, or so he claimed. He thought Burgess completely untrustworthy and unreliable, put the whole thing aside and forgot about it. Years later Rees would try to distance himself from the revelation.

After leaving university Rees worked as a journalist for the *Manchester Guardian* and in 1936 was assistant editor of *The Spectator*, before joining the Royal Artillery during World War II. After the war he resumed his career as a journalist before becoming principal of Aberystwyth University in 1953.

The following year the Wolfenden Commission was under way. In his autobiography Wolfenden recounts the manner in which he was appointed chairman of the committee. A phone call followed by a chance meeting resulted in an offer from the Home Office a week later. The members of the committee were chosen in a similar manner.[14] Here were two men – Wolfenden and Maxwell-Fyfe – who simply 'agreed' on a course of action, unthinkable today. Had there been a transparent process it would surely have revealed that Wolfenden's own son was openly homosexual. Jeremy, also at Oxford, had lived quite a dissolute lifestyle and having studied journalism opted for a career in Russia despite advice against this for fear he would be blackmailed over his homosexuality. His father was aware of his sexuality: when he was appointed chairman he wrote to Jeremy: "I have only two requests to make of you at the moment. 1) That we stay out of each other's way for the time being; 2) That you wear rather less makeup."[15]

John Wolfenden is usually presented as someone raised with the pre-war beliefs of nineteenth century England, staunchly conservative and believing that most of the public were unaware of what homosexuality was exactly. The same attitude prevailed in the government, which chose not to make the report a Royal Commission, which would require all evidence to be published. Instead it was designated a Departmental Committee where, if necessary, evidence could be withheld.

The committee met for sixty-two days, of which thirty-two involved interviewing witnesses. Over two hundred people either appeared before the committee or submitted written testimony, but only three homosexual men appeared and only two made written submissions. There was no real enthusiasm by Wolfenden or the committee to talk to the men about whom the report was being written. They preferred to rely on the evidence presented by the police, health professionals and religious bodies – despite the high level of homophobia to be found in these bodies. The evidence was also predominantly London-centric: the Chief Constable of Glamorgan stated that prostitution and homosexuality were marginal in the provinces.[16]

Four self-identified men offered to appear before the Committee the response was lukewarm. One, Peter Wildeblood[17], a journalist on the *Daily Mail*, had recently been in prison and Wolfenden was not keen to talk to a convicted offender. Goronwy Rees however endorsed Wildeblood's 'very interesting statement' and asked for the testimony to be sent to all members ahead of meeting Wildeblood. The other men were Patrick Trevor-Roper, a Harley Street consultant, Carl Winter, the director of the Fitzwilliam Museum, and the author Angus Wilson (who dropped out due to other commitments). Trevor-Roper and Angus Wilson contacted Goronwy Rees to suggest speaking to the committee. Rees, "by far the most lateral thinking and perceptive member of the committee"[18] knew both of the men slightly. Wolfenden agreed to meet to, as the secretary W. Conwy Roberts put it, "see what a few [homosexuals] look like". Rees himself had complained that few members on the committee had ever encountered a homosexual 'in a social way.'[19] It was he who suggested Wolfenden get to know the men over dinner rather than through the formality of being a witness – an ordeal resembling a magistrate's court. When the three men arrived at the Home Office it was Rees who according to Trevor-Roper "gave us a very warm and encouraging entrance, saying that … he is entirely on our side."[20]

At an awkward dinner they eventually discussed the subject in hand, and Wolfenden made it clear that he was only interested in speaking to 'chaps like us' – chaps who were well educated, professional men who conducted themselves discreetly and in private. They were not interested in speaking to screaming queens, promiscuous or 'trade' men, effeminate and bisexuals or ordinary common men.

As the Wolfenden committee progressed it was suddenly hit by an enormous scandal. In 1956 the Sunday newspaper *The People* published a series of shocking articles about Guy Burgess. They were not signed but the writer described himself as a "most intimate friend, a man in a high academic position". The articles described Burgess as corrupt, a spy, a blackmailer, a drunk and in great detail described his sordid sex life. The public was horrified and demanded to know how anyone who could call themselves an intimate friend could be so spiteful. But the thinly disguised identity meant that many people already knew the writer's identity. Michael Berry, editor-in-chief of the Telegraph newspapers, and rumoured to have been one of Burgess' lovers, was so incensed by the articles that in March 1956 the *Daily Telegraph* revealed that the author was Goronwy Rees.

Several years earlier Burgess, with Donald Maclean, had defected to Russia as part of what later become known as the Cambridge Spy Ring. Members also included Kim Philby and Anthony Blunt. Rees later admitted that Burgess had identified Blunt to him as a spy, but again claimed he did not believe him.

Following their defection Rees had written an account of his friendship with Burgess and approached an agent to have it published which it was – in *The People*. Rees, rather disingenuously, tried to distance himself from the articles saying they "were to be based on the material contained in my manuscript but were to be written by a member of *The People*'s staff, in a style which they felt would be more acceptable to their readers than my own, and would therefore appear anonymously." However *The People* denied this and claimed that the original articles included reams of detailed homosexual promiscuity that the paper simply couldn't print.

One of the reasons Rees gave for writing the book was that he wanted to distance himself from Burgess. Yet he admitted that he had known Burgess for twenty-four years, that they constantly visited each other's houses, that they had the same friends and went to the same parties. There was also the problem that Burgess had told Rees that he had kept every letter ever sent to him. Jenny Rees, in the biography of her father, speculates that perhaps Burgess did have something that Rees was anxious not to be revealed. By portraying him as evil, anything Burgess then said could be seen as evil. Isaiah Berlin told Jenny Rees, "It was a kind of insurance policy. I think it was because he was afraid, he was afraid of Burgess spreading disinformation and telling terrible stories about him and everyone else and had to get in first ... I think Goronwy thought that anything could happen and he panicked. Goronwy was easily panickable." Hugh Trevor-Roper believed that Rees thought the Security Services tainted and therefore it would be no use talking directly to them. They would only notice him through the pages of a newspaper.[21]

The articles were to have a much wider impact than Rees merely trashing Burgess. He implied more spies lurked in the corridors of power and "his articles kaleidoscope together the public sphere of high politics with private vice, and they hinted that these connections were endemic among leading figures in Westminster and Whitehall."[22] Rees "had breached the 'complicated moral code' through which the upper class was bound together".

Meanwhile Wolfenden was on holiday at the King Arthur Hotel, Reynoldston in the Gower, when *The People* articles broke. Furious, he dashed off a letter from his hotel room outlining his concerns about Rees' relationship with Burgess and the impact it would have on the findings of the committee. "It would be regrettably easy," he said, "for the 'Telegraph' – or anybody else – to say, 'What would you expect, with this man as a member of the committee?'." Quietly Rees was removed.

A few months later he was called before the university president to explain himself. They met over lunch and discussed the matter. Rees' tenure as principal of Aberystwyth University had been dogged with controversy. His unconventional social behaviour and his determination to turn the university into his vision of modernity meant he was not always diplomatic and had begun to make enemies. Rees refused to resign, and was backed by enormous support from the students, who liked his progressive ways. But many of the staff thought him unworthy of his post and threatened to resign unless there was an inquiry. In October 1956 the Willink Report into Rees's position opened, and concluded the following February. It was highly critical. One of the questions that dominated was whether he had written the Burgess articles merely for monetary reasons, as he was known to be in debt. Burgess himself, when told about the articles, thought Rees did it for the money. But the Report found that financial motives were not the reason. The Willink committee were uneasy about Rees' association with people like Burgess and his knowledge and the wiliness to write about it brought the university into disrepute. Rees, unwilling to accept the conclusion, resigned.

On a number of occasions Rees had attempted to report that Blunt was the fifth Cambridge spy but no-one believed him. Instead there were several accusations that Rees himself had been a spy and that he had passed on information to Burgess. Donald Maclean had said of Rees "you used to be one of us, but you ratted". Rees claimed that Maclean meant he was a communist not a spy. Vasili Mitrokhin, a former member of the KGB, also claimed that Burgess attempted to have Rees assassinated because he knew too much. Despite persistent rumours many believed that Rees was never in a powerful enough position to supply useful information. However he did know many influential people and had a keen analytical mind that could assist Burgess in political hearsay.

In 1991, a senior archivist at the KGB, Mitrokhin defected to Britain bringing with him around 25,000 pages of files. In one Rees was identified by the code name Gross. It revealed that Rees had indeed been recruited by Burgess – it seems he did after all have something to fear from the spy. In 1937 Burgess had been impressed with Rees' socialist review of the book *Grey Children: A Study in Humbug and Misery* about life in Merthyr Tydfil, and had recruited him. But Rees' communist sympathies, like many who originally signed up, were more ideological than political. In his few years of contact with the Russians he passed on no information of any importance that is known of. Disillusioned with Russia over their pact with the Nazis, he had no further involvement.

As Rees lay dying of cancer Blunt was finally revealed as the fifth spy. Andrew Boyle had published his book *The Climate of Treason*, and had finally unmasked him. Rees was delighted. Blunt was stripped of his knighthood, lost his position and standing, and died alone three years later.

After *The People* articles Rees became persona non grata and his family suffered years of unemployment and hardships. He was finally saved by another gay man, Stephen Spender, whom he had met shortly after the end of World War II. Spender got Rees a job on the Anglo-American literary magazine *Encounter*, which he had co-founded, and Rees swore eternal gratitude.[23] However when

Spender later found out that the journal was receiving covert funding from the CIA he felt betrayed and resigned. Rees sided with the magazine and remained. Spender described his behaviour as appalling.

Goronwy Rees died of cancer on 12 December 1979 at Charing Cross Hospital in London. His daughter said he "was a brilliant man, and he would have had a brilliant life but for a catastrophe. Instead he made a mistake, one whopper of a mistake, and paid for it for the rest of his life."

Did the removal of the "most lateral thinking and perceptive member of the committee" make life any different for homosexual people? By the time of his departure the conclusions were already been drawn up and Wolfenden himself had undergone something of a conversion with regard to homosexuality.[24] Possibly Rees may have pushed for a more liberal outcome. Whether he would have, or could have, been more influential we can never know.

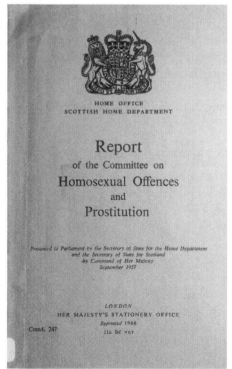

The Wolfenden Report

20. I was concerned with liberty

The Wolfenden Report was published on 4 September 1957 and was an instant bestseller – a rarity for any government report. The committee had made recommendations on both prostitution and homosexuality. All those on prostitution were enacted, but the recommendations on homosexuality were not.

The Report suggested thirty-one changes to the law. They ranged from a ban on prosecuting acts older than twelve months[1] and that those who reported blackmail, excepting serious cases, should not face prosecution themselves. Various terms of imprisonment were proposed and changes made with regard to armed services and conditions in prisons. The main recommendation was that men who were in the privacy of a home where nobody else was present, and who were both over twenty-one, would not be prosecuted. Most of the committee with the exception of James Adair, a Scottish solicitor, did not think the recommendations went far enough and some that the prison sentences were too severe.[2]

Despite the popularity of the report and a flurry of interest from the media nothing else happened. Three months later Lord Longford, the social reformer, brought up the subject in Parliament.[3] "One day," he said "this change will be wrung from us ... let us take advantage ... while it is still in our power to do the civilised thing."[4] Seventeen peers supported him in calling for reform but the Home Secretary, Sir David Maxwell-Fyfe, argued that society would be against it – and suggested more investigations into public opinion. The man who had reluctantly agreed to the inquiry was now stalling its recommendations.

Wolfenden himself believed the delay was for political reasons. He felt that the majority of the British people, as well as the House of Commons, agreed with the recommendations but the Government, with eighteen months of its term left, did not want to alienate some of its supporters.[5]

Meanwhile in Somerset a Dr Robert Douglas Reid, a former headmaster who had been convicted of importuning in 1937, condemned the lack of progress. He began a letter writing campaign including one to *The Spectator* published on 3 January 1958. "Even though the government," he wrote "for reasons which they are not prepared to give, are to throw over the recommendations of the

Wolfenden Committee, one would still have expected the police authorities to pay some attention to them." The report had made no impact on the police and courts, and prosecutions continued unabated. "The police," Reid continued, "go round from house to house, bringing ruin in their train, always attacking the youngest men first, extracting information with lengthy questioning and specious promises of light sentences as they proceed from clue to clue, i.e. from home to home, often up to twenty." He ended, "we desperately need some society to afford support and comfort to the victims and their families."

Dr Reid's letter was quickly followed by support from notables such as E.M. Forster, Sir Robert Boothby, and Peter Wildeblood. But one letter was to change everything. It came from A.E. Dyson of University College of North Wales in Bangor.

Anthony Edward Dyson was born in London on November 28, 1928. He came from a lower middle class background and was a bright child who won a scholarship to the Sloane Grammar School in Chelsea. Tony was excused from conscription and National Service due to a heart murmur and spent two years working for the Ministry of Food. He then went to Pembroke College, Cambridge in 1949 and took a double first. In 1955 he was appointed Assistant Lecturer in English Literature at the University in Bangor.

Tony went on to write a number of well-respected books of literary criticism often with Brian Cox, whom he had met at Cambridge. Together they wrote *Modern Poetry,* which was a popular standard text book for many years. At the end of the 1950s they started the journal *Critical Quarterly,* which provided a focus for literary criticism and original poetry. Many famous poets contributed including Ted Hughes, Thom Gunn, Philip Larkin and Sylvia Plath – who won her first poetry competition with them. The journal is still in existence today.

When he was a teenager Tony realised he was gay. He thought discrimination against gay people was the same as racism or anti-Semitism and he was disturbed by the constant police activity against homosexuals. He too had written a response in *The Spectator* following Dr Reid's letter that the recommendations in Wolfenden should be enacted. He ended, "Is it not time, therefore, that those who feel strongly on this issue should work together and attempt to make more widely known the compulsive moral and rational reasons in favour of a change of law?"

Before the month was out Tony had taken his own advice and proceeded to write to as many people as he could. He approached those he knew through his literary work but also contacted MPs, Archbishops, celebrities and academics. Using his own time and money he wrote hundreds of letters asking for signatories to an open letter to *The Times*. Peter Wildeblood helped with journalistic contacts and the writer E.M. Forster approved the wording.

Tony wrote on the University of North Wales headed paper. He made a bold statement of exactly who and where he was. As a gay man this was a risk. "It is difficult," said a *Times* journalist writing Tony's obituary "to comprehend the danger of living as a homosexual before the law was reformed in 1967, with the ever-present threat of criminal proceeding or blackmail. Dyson's careful and courageous handling of the campaign during these years was instrumental in ensuring that it did not arouse animosity and become counter-productive."[6]

Letters flooded back to North Wales from the great and the good. The replies were varied but many reflected the views of the conductor Sir Malcolm Sargent, "to make the offence legal is more or less telling youth that it is no bad thing." Many ignored Tony's letter but after hundreds sent he was left with thirty-two famous signatories – and his own. On March 7, 1958 their letter appeared in *The Times*:

Homosexual Acts

Call to Reform Law

To the Editor of the Times

Sir, We, the undersigned, would like to express our general agreement with the recommendations of the Wolfenden Report that homosexual acts committed in private between consenting adults should no longer be a criminal offence.

The present law is clearly no longer representative of either Christian or liberal opinion in this country, and now that there are widespread doubts about both its justice and its efficacy, we believe that its continued enforcement will do more harm than good to the health of the community as a whole.

The case for reform has already been accepted by most of the responsible papers and journals, by two Archbishops, the Church Assembly, a Roman Catholic committee, a number of non-conformist spokesmen, and many other organs of informed public opinion.

In view of this, and of the conclusions which the Wolfenden Committee itself agreed upon after a prolonged study of the evidence, we should like to see the Government introduce legislation to give effect to the proposed reform at an early date; and are confident that if it does so it will deserve the widest support from humane men of all parties. Yours, &c.

It was signed by N.G. Annan, Clement Attlee, A.J. Ayer, Isaiah Berlin, the Bishop of Birmingham, Robert Boothby, C.M. Bowra, C.D. Broad, David Cecil, L. John Collins, Alex Comfort, A.E. Dyson, Robert Exon, Geoffrey Faber, Jacquetta Hawkes, Trevor Huddleston, Julian Huxley, Cecil Day Lewis, W.R. Niblett, J.B. Priestley, Bertrand Russell, Donald Soper, Stephen Spender, Mary Stocks, A.J.P. Taylor, E.M.W. Tillyard, Alec R. Vidler, Kenneth Walker, Leslie Weatherhead, C.V. Wedgwood, Angus Wilson, John Wilson and Barbara Wootton.

The letter generated a number of responses. One simply quoted from the Bible referencing Sodom and Gomorrah, which a subsequent correspondent called 'hardly a sane response', and another pointed out that homosexuality is not even mentioned in that story. One correspondent took issue with the mention of support by the Church Assembly. It pointed out that its resolution had been passed by a majority of 17 when only 293 members of the 730 attended. Elsewhere members of the House of Lords, Thomas Carliol, Christopher Roffen, Lord Lawson and Earl Winteron, pointed out that as Wolfenden stated that only a minority of men were prosecuted for offences in private it would mean there would be little impact on the law. Instead they claimed it 'would divide the nation' and 'bring a most unsavoury subject' into undesirable prominence. And, perhaps worst of all, it would "encourage the weak, the ignorant, and the vicious to think that there was no harm in indulging in a practice which the law no longer treated as an offence". D.A. Rhymes, from All Saints' Vicarage in London, responded that their logic didn't make sense and suggested instead that all adultery and fornication should be criminalised. Wilfred Kitching, a general in the Salvation Army, weighed in saying that he did

not think imprisonment was effective. Just over a month later a group
of married women wrote "we believe the Government statement that
public opinion is not ready for a change in the laws is too pessimistic;
and that most humane and thoughtful people in this country would
welcome early implementation of the report's findings on this
subject."[7]

Wolfenden himself told Tony that a public campaign would probably
be counter-productive. But Tony disagreed and years later would argue
that without his campaign the 1967 Sexual Offences Act would have
been severely delayed.[8]

Two months after his letter, Tony single-handedly set about
changing British society forever. In his support for Dr Reid's letter in
The Spectator he had written that he would "gladly belong to any
society which existed to help the victims and their families of our
homosexuality laws. But even more to the point would be the
formation of a society concerned to work for a change in the laws
themselves."[9]

In the absence of others, Tony set up a society. With some of the
signatories to *The Times* letter he brought together a group of
like-minded people to form a law reform society. As he said, "My hope
had been that a change in law, if accomplished, would return the
subject to the realm of private life. I was concerned with liberty to live,
work – without fear, without persecution – restoring normality to men
who differed only in sexual orientation from their fellows."[10]

Tony sent out even more letters, again in his own time and at his own
expense, asking people to join the society. Peter Wildeblood declined
but offered his support. He wrote, "I am entirely in favour of such a
step provided that the 'Board' is really representative – a
preponderance of clergymen, psychiatrists or professional do-gooders
(or indeed homosexuals) would not be a good thing". Lord Longford
refused to join saying it would hamper his efforts if seen to be
representing a group, but his wife joined. Eventually ninety-one people
joined the society.

Its first meeting was held on 12 May 1958 at the Harley Street
surgery of Dr Kenneth Walker. Walker was a surgeon and sexologist
who co-wrote a book with Jungian psychiatrist E.B. Strauss, *Sexual
Disorders in the Male* – but like many of his time he believed
homosexuality was arrested development. Tony could not escape his

teaching commitments at Bangor, and only three people attended. But it was here that the Homosexual Law Reform Society (HLRS) was officially launched. Walker was elected as the first chairman with Tony as vice-chair.

The society quickly swung into action and put a small ad in a number of national newspapers: "The Homosexual Law Reform Society is working for the implementation of the major Wolfenden proposal. Details from the Hon. Secretary, 219, Liverpool Road, London, N.1." In the first week there were 250 replies. There were no members, only supporters, which meant the Executive Committee retained control. Most of the supporters were heterosexual but it also included people like the humanitarian Victor Gollancz, the writer Stephen Spender, the radical Anglican priest Canon John Collins, psychiatrist Dr E.B. Strauss and MP Kenneth Younger. The writer J.B. Priestly and his bisexual wife Jacquetta Hawkes were to play a prominent role in helping set up the Albany Trust, named after their address, which aimed to promote psychological health and pioneered counselling for LGBT people. It is still in existence today.

Over the years other organisations formed and evolved, fighting for equality, but all grew from the HLRS. Eventually its work led to the passing of the Sexual Offences Act of 1967, which saw Wolfenden enacted after ten years.

Whilst spending time in London at the Albany Trust Tony met his long-time partner Cliff Tucker. Born on 18 December 1912 in Monmouth, Cliff was the son of Rev Frederick Charles Tucker and Mary. He attended Monmouth School and St David's College, Lampeter. In 1936 he worked for ICI before leaving for BP in 1946 where he remained until his death.

When he came to London Cliff "brought with him his Welshness and the memory of his Nonconformist background. These influences were to remain with him all his life."[11] His father had been a Baptist minister and Cliff had grown up in an area of high unemployment and widespread poverty which left him with a lifetime regard for the 'horny-handed sons of toil'. He travelled extensively with BP working on labour relations and staff matters in the Middle and Far East. Returning to head office, he was manager of industrial relations until he retired. He used to say that membership of the Labour party 'didn't exactly help me' with some senior managers but he was trusted by them and by the unions. In later life he looked back with pride on strikes he had averted or settled.

Cliff also said that his childhood gave him an understanding of Oscar Wilde's saying that 'martyrs are those who have to live with saints'. As a youth he joined the Labour party, inspired by Ernest Bevin, and worked as a local councillor for Stepney, St Pancras and Camden, and was secretary of the Holborn and St Pancras Labour Party.[12] He was also a magistrate and was described as reliable, hard-working and caring. Towards the end of his life however he believed that Labour had lost its way and he became disenchanted with the party. Once asked about his hobbies he replied, "trying to fight poverty and prejudice".

That fight was to take many forms. In December 1976 Mary Whitehouse attempted to prosecute *Gay News* for its allegedly blasphemous poem 'The Love That Dares To Speak Its Name' by James Kirkup. The editor was given a nine months suspended sentence and fined £500, and *Gay News* was fined £1,000. Cliff fought against censorship and resigned his membership of the Church of England following the result. Tony too was upset at the publication but thought "the poem really was blasphemous, and disgusting, and feeble".

Together they fought tirelessly for equality. Tony left Wales in 1962 and spent some time teaching in America. He and Cliff wrote to each other almost every day. They were to live together for thirty-five years before Cliff died in 1993. Tony followed Cliff's wishes and bequeathed the proceeds of their London home to Cliff's alma mater, the University of Wales, Lampeter. Where there is now the Cliff Tucker lecture theatre and the Dyson Fellowship in Poetry.

Tony died from leukaemia in 2002.

21. A Social Revolution begins

Ten years passed and despite much talking, much campaigning and many letters and articles Wolfenden had not been enacted. The Homosexual Law Reform Society had attempted to establish local committees around Britain to share the work on activism, but only one was successful, the North Western Homosexual Law Reform Committee, set up in 1964. Led by the indefatigable Allan Horsfall it was this group, after the collapse of the HLRS, that went on to dominate the fight for equality. Little had been achieved since A.E. Dyson had written an open letter to *The Times* in 1958. In 1960 Labour MP Kenneth Robinson introduced the first full-scale Commons debate asking for the Wolfenden's recommendations to be enacted, as the previous chapter has described. But the then Home Secretary, Rab Butler, refused, saying that society was not ready for the suggested reforms. What was needed was someone to spearhead a new campaign. And that someone was Leo Abse.

Leo was born on 22 April 1917, in Cardiff. He came from a prominent local family: his father Rudolf was a solicitor and cinema owner, his brother Dannie was a doctor and a well-known poet, and his elder brother Wilfred was a psychoanalyst. Leo was educated at Howard Gardens High School before working in a local factory and then going to study at the London School of Economics. Like many people of the time he had fleeting communist sympathies, and even clandestinely visited Spain in 1939 during the Civil War. During World War II he served in the RAF, then returned to Cardiff to study law. He set up his own law firm, Leo Abse & Cohen, which grew to be the largest in Cardiff and which still exists today.

Leo was involved in politics from an early age and from 1953 to 1958 he was a member of Cardiff City Council. He was defeated as Labour candidate in Cardiff North in the general election of 1955 but was elected in 1958, and arrived in the House of Commons a year after the Wolfenden Report was published. Throughout his life he was very involved in Welsh politics, being the chairman of the Welsh Parliamentary Party from 1976 to 1987 and leader of the Labour anti-devolution campaign in Wales before the 1979 Referendum.

Leo was an MP for nearly thirty years. He was a spirited character who dressed in flamboyant suits on Budget Day. He remained a backbencher in a safe seat, which gave him the freedom to tackle controversial subjects other MPs preferred to ignore. Over the years Leo addressed many social issues particularly around marriage, families and disabilities. But probably the issue he is most remembered for is the campaigning he did to partially decriminalise homosexuality.

Leo had been influenced by his brother Wilfred on the theories of Sigmund Freud. Freud, the father of psychoanalysis, believed that people were fundamentally born bisexual, but that they matured into heterosexuality. Leo told the *Observer* in 2007, "I am a Freudian. And I had been taught by Freud that men and women are bisexual. People should come to terms with their bisexuality, not repudiate it and become homophobic."[1] However Leo, like many people of his time, believed that homosexuality was 'faulty' or infantilised, and that young people had to be protected and educated into not following that route.

In Cardiff Leo experienced the effects of the law at first hand. A number of criminal cases he had been handling were all paid for by one man. With a little research he discovered that a local vicar was being blackmailed. Calling one of the criminals into his office he told him if he received one more cheque from the vicar he would get the man sent down for ten years; he also told the vicar to contact him if he was approached by the criminals again. Another person who may have helped form his view of blackmail was George Thomas, later ennobled as Viscount Tonypandy, who would become Speaker of the Commons. Writing in his book *Tony Blair: The Man Behind the Smile*, Leo claimed that Thomas, a secret homosexual, had been blackmailed and that he had on a number of occasions helped Thomas financially – at one point lending him £800 to pay them off. Leo also came across homosexual men regularly through his artist wife.

Driven by these experiences and his broader beliefs, in 1962 Leo introduced into parliament a small bill. In it he proposed that the police should not prosecute those homosexuals being blackmailed, and that all cases of adult male homosexuality should automatically be referred to the director of public prosecutions before proceedings were advanced. He was concerned that homosexuals were the second largest class of criminals apart from motorists.[2] The bill failed.

Two years later a new Labour government under Harold Wilson came into power. In May 1965 Lord Arran[3] introduced a bill similar to Leo's into the House of Lords. Despite fierce opposition from some it was passed. However it could not go through the Commons as parliament had ended. Two days later Leo tried to re-introduce his bill in the Commons, but was again defeated. Ten months later Lord Arran re-introduced *his* bill and the Conservative MP Humphry Berkeley put an identical bill before the Commons. However both were shelved due to the second general election in just two years.[4] Wilson, despite supporting the bill privately, had said in 1961 that endorsing Wolfenden would cost the party six million votes and he did not want the boat to be rocked.

Labour was returned to power with a landslide victory, and there was one person now who was about to effect huge changes: Welshman Roy Jenkins was appointed Home Secretary. In 1954 following the highly publicised trial of Lord Montagu of Beaulieu, Jenkins had argued for the decriminalisation of homosexuality. He believed private relations between adults were not the affairs of the state[5] and had supported Berkeley's bill without success. Berkeley lost his seat in the 1966 general election due in part, he said, to supporting homosexual reform. Leo, perhaps disingenuously, was convinced he would never have succeeded: "The House didn't like Humphry Berkeley," he claimed. "He was gay and everyone knew. He was an enfant terrible who never grew up. I don't think he could have got it through."[6]

When Leo re-introduced his bill Roy Jenkins was in a much better position to help. In cabinet he was able to get Wilson to agree that Leo must be heard. Wolfenden also supported the bill. Lord Arran told the House of Lords that Wolfenden had sent him a letter saying that he approved of both Arran and Abse's bills – that they had 'the basic principles' of the report.

Leo's bill was not the enactment of Wolfenden. Rather, it was a watered down version, a collection of minor changes to the law, limiting the way in which prosecutions were brought, curbing blackmailers and requiring no court sentence be passed on a homosexual without a doctor's report. The latter point may have resulted from Leo's position on the Council of the Institute for the Scientific Treatment of Delinquency. The Institute had been responsible for creating the Portman Clinic, members of which had submitted testimony to the Wolfenden Report. They were strongly oriented to psychoanalytical approaches to crime and criminality. Leo like them felt that "imprisoning homosexuals for long periods in male jails is like incarcerating a sex maniac in a harem."

He was backed by five other MPs, one of whom was the Liberal party leader Jeremy Thorpe. In the early 1970s Thorpe became embroiled in a homosexual scandal with Norman Scott. When Scott moved to Talybont in north Wales he told a friend of how he had been mistreated by Thorpe; she reported this to the Welsh Liberal MP Emlyn Hooson who precipitated a party inquiry. The story dragged on until Thorpe was forced to resign in 1976.

Leo's bill also received the support of the Rev. Llywelyn Williams MP, from Abertillery. Williams, who had supported Wolfenden back in 1958, said "While society could never give moral approval to [homosexual] behaviour, nevertheless, since it takes place in the privacy of a household, it should not rank as a criminal offence, any more than heterosexual behaviour between consenting adults in private, such as adultery and fornication, to which again society could never give moral approval, should rank as a criminal offence."[7]

Despite much opposition and manoeuvring Leo juggled innumerable amendments until finally, after an all-night filibustering, the bill was passed 101 to 14 – one hundred supporters were required. Later Leo said, "I get so damned annoyed when people say Wolfenden was a watershed. We got that bill through on one vote."[8] Support came from surprising quarters, including both the Church and the medical profession – though it was partly based on the wish to offer spiritual and medical help. If people could not freely or legally access their services, they could not openly offer help or 'cures'.

Jenkins, for his part in getting the bill passed, was criticised for lending the government's authority and time to get the legislation through.[9] He assured people that "it would be a mistake to think that we are giving a vote of confidence or congratulation to homosexuality. Those who suffer from this disability carry a great weight of loneliness, guilt and shame. The crucial question ... is should we add to those disadvantages the full rigour of the criminal law?" However he did celebrate the bill as 'an important and civilising measure'. And while Leo Abse is the MP most commonly associated with the Sexual Offences Act we should remember that other Welshman, Roy Jenkins. His biographer John Campbell wrote, "these reforms would not have happened when they did – well ahead of most European countries –

without Jenkins' drive and determination." Interestingly another MP who voted for the bill was Margaret Thatcher, who in 1988 introduced Section 28 into the Local Government Act which outlawed the ill-defined 'promotion' of homosexuality.

So the bill was passed. It was not what many had hoped for, but it was better than nothing. However, the arrests did not stop. Between 1967 and 2003 over 30,000 gay and bisexual men were convicted for behaviour that would not have been a crime had their partner been a woman.[10]

Sexual Offences Act 1967   Ch. **60**   I

ELIZABETH II

1967 CHAPTER 60

An Act to amend the law of England and Wales relating
to homosexual acts.   [27th July 1967]

B E IT ENACTED by the Queen's most Excellent Majesty, by and
with the advice and consent of the Lords Spiritual and
Temporal, and Commons, in this present Parliament
assembled, and by the authority of the same, as follows:—

1.—(1) Notwithstanding any statutory or common law provi- Amendment
sion, but subject to the provisions of the next following section, of law
a homosexual act in private shall not be an offence provided homosexual
that the parties consent thereto and have attained the age of acts in private.
twenty-one years.

(2) An act which would otherwise be treated for the purposes
of this Act as being done in private shall not be so treated if done—

    (*a*) when more than two persons take part or are present; or

    (*b*) in a lavatory to which the public have or are permitted
        to have access, whether on payment or otherwise.

(3) A man who is suffering from severe subnormality within
the meaning of the Mental Health Act 1959 cannot in law give 1959 c. 72.
any consent which, by virtue of subsection (1) of this section,
would prevent a homosexual act from being an offence, but a
person shall not be convicted, on account of the incapacity of
such a man to consent, of an offence consisting of such an act
if he proves that he did not know and had no reason to suspect
that man to be suffering from severe subnormality.

(4) Section 128 of the Mental Health Act 1959 (prohibition
on men on the staff of a hospital, or otherwise having responsibility
for mental patients, having sexual intercourse with women

Reaction to the bill was mixed, but mostly positive. William Wolff of the *Daily Mirror*, in a piece entitled 'A Social Revolution Begins', said it turned out to be "not so much a battle as a walkover".[11] The *Church Times* called it "a great triumph for those, including some leaders of the Church of England, who have been campaigning."[12] Tony Dyson wrote that the passing of the bill was a great triumph particularly as Wolfenden had estimated it would take seventeen years to bring about. Some say Leo should have fought for more changes, others feel that it was the best he could do at the time. Despite its flaws it was now possible for men to live together as a couple and not face arrest or blackmail. It also encouraged supporters to campaign further. Yet in practice it had peculiar quirks. It was still illegal for two men to meet or even telephone each other to arrange to have sex. Therefore arranging something legal was in itself illegal.

Around the world the changes were watched with interest. Commonwealth countries followed Wolfenden and the Sexual Offences Act to reform their laws. Other countries such as the USA can trace their sexual orientation criminal laws to Britain. [13]

Despite achieving a huge social change Leo was not always happy with 'the gays' and complained that they lacked gratitude: "I never had one word of thanks from any gay activist or lobby. When I've shown any reservations about the gays, they haven't forgotten."[14] Despite his fascination with psychoanalysis he never saw things from 'the gays' perspective. Leo, and many like him at the time, was more concerned with discouraging homosexuality. "How can we diminish," he asked the House of Commons "the number of those who grow up to have men's bodies but feminine souls?"[15] He believed that adult sexuality had to be learnt, and like others blamed the parents: absent, jealous or loveless fathers could make their child homosexual just as overprotective mothers could. Both created auras which the child was never able to fully break away from and assert their independence. He referred to homosexual men as 'faulty males'.

Protecting children or allowing freedom to religious bodies and the medical profession to offer 'cures' was more important. The freedom to be oneself was still controlled. Homosexuality was not allowed outside the house and even private didn't really mean private. In 1996 five men were prosecuted for having group sex in a house. They took their case to the European Court of Human Rights in 2000 which upheld their complaint that the police had violated the fundamental principle of a person's right to privacy. It was not until 2003 that amendments to the Sexual Offences Act meant that sexual activity between more than two men was no longer a crime.[16]

In addition, throughout all his campaigning for the Sexual Offences Act, Leo never invited the Homosexual Law Reform Society (HLRS) set up by Tony Dyson and others to any discussions. Neither did Lord Arran. Antony Grey, the secretary of the Sexual Law Reform Society[17], was unhappy at the concessions Leo was arranging but was constrained by the fact that Leo was an executive member of the HLRS and Grey had to limit his criticisms.

Leo also did not believe that the Age of Consent should be lowered from twenty-one. In the years that followed the passing of his bill he was horrified at the calls made for more equality. He thought that the subject was closed.

In April 1971 there was a Commons debate on annulling marriages after one party had undergone a sex change, brought about by the case of April Ashley who had gone to court when her husband wanted to annul their marriage due to her transgender status. Alexander Lyon, Labour MP for York, put forward a bill to make a marriage void if the parties were not male and female. Leo, adding his own amendment, drew attention to the fact that this was the first time that problems of the 'trans-sexual or pseudo-hermaphrodite' had been discussed in the House. The amendment he wanted to add was that "no marriage would even by implication ever come into existence if, for example, two homosexuals knowingly deceived the registrar by one of them deliberately masquerading as a woman"[18]

With regard to the Corbett v Corbett (April Ashley) case Leo argued citing the Flora case: "The judge insisted that sex and gender must not be confused and he made his judgment ... finding April Ashley a male by applying only the biological tests and ignoring psychological factors," Leo said. "In the present developing knowledge of depth psychology" he doubted the wisdom of such a ruling. We are in danger, he said, of the law pulling away from and not towards medical science. He added, "because biological tests proved her to be a male, what one is saying to the doctors, psychiatrists and surgeons is that although they are treating the patient and giving the best opportunity for her to live out her life as a human being, we at law will condemn her to be a non-person. I find that unacceptable." Leo did not want the words 'male and female' used in the bill as they ignored gender: "If a person believes that she is a woman, even if the biologically male characteristics are present, such a person should be acknowledged as a person and should not be placed in this limbo".

With regard to marriage it was argued in the Commons debate on 'Grounds in which a marriage is void' that if two people lived together one person could be kicked out of the home without any means. Leo proposed that financial relief should be available only when there was evidence of a sex change operation. However the Commons upheld the verdict in Corbett v Corbett, although they recognised the state of uncertainty they faced. It was left open for the courts to decide in future cases exactly how 'male and female' was to be defined. For the meantime marriage was to rely on biological sex not gender.

Unable to accept Leo's watered down version of Wolfenden, and determined to fight for equality, the Campaign for Homosexual Equality was set up in 1969 followed by the Gay Liberation Front in 1970. Stonewall UK was formed in 1989 to lobby against Section 28. These groups pushing through legal changes meant that the UK was the leader in Europe for LGBT rights for four years running on the scale established by the International Lesbian, Gay, Bisexual, Trans and Intersex Association. Its ranking slipped to third in 2016 due to better gender identity rights elsewhere.

The Sexual Offences Act was a milestone in the journey towards the Single Equality Act 2010. Some question why homosexual men should have their convictions quashed – and the answer is because it was an unequal law. Heterosexual people could have sex, gay women could have sex, but gay men could not. For a law to be effective it has to be universal. Which is why the Single Equality Act said people could not be discriminated against for who or what they were. Those calling for a re-criminalisation of homosexuality are trying to open the doors again for society to discriminate against certain groups of people. And that is a slippery slope. Criticised during his own time, modern historians have been kinder to Leo Abse. There was only a limited amount he could achieve in the face of the prejudices of the time, but he was able to open a door which can never be shut again.

22. Not on our seafront

After the Wolfenden Report recommended the *partial* decriminalisation of homosexual men, it lay dormant on the Government's shelves for years. As the previous chapter noted, frustrated by the unwillingness of the Government to act groups began to form, campaigning to raise awareness and to force the Government to enact Wolfenden.

One was the North Western Homosexual Law Reform Society (NWHLRS)[1], set up in 1958. Over the next few years however the aims of the HLRS were criticised for not, according to some members, being ambitious enough in their demands for changes to the law. Many didn't want just the Wolfenden recommendations put into place: they wanted more wide-ranging laws covering life outside of an empty house. The NWHLRS re-formed as the Committee for Homosexual Equality (CHE) in 1969[2] and later the Gay Liberation Front was formed in 1970.

An early member of CHE was Griffith Vaughan Williams. Born in Bangor in 1940, he was educated at a local grammar school before studying journalism in Cardiff. Griff worked as a freelance journalist on a number of provincial newspapers around the country, and from 1979 to his retirement was the press and information officer for the Institution of Mechanical Engineers. "He didn't look like anyone's idea of a gay man," Ross Burgess told *Pink News* after Griff's death, "which probably helped him get his message over in the early days."[3] His North Walian "twang was instantly recognisable across crowded rooms."[4]

As activism in the 1960s grew, Griff was on the front line. He was a volunteer working for Antony Grey, the secretary at the Homosexual Law Reform Society from 1962 to 1970, before becoming a member of CHE. He later joined the London Information Centre which had been established in 1972. Griff also broadened the CHE from just homosexual men to include lesbians and other gay groups. Many 'gay' groups of the 70s and 80s actively discouraged bisexual people.

When Peter Mitchell stood as an MP in 1977 for the City of London and Westminster as the 'Campaign for Homosexual Civil Rights' candidate, Griff acted as his election agent. It was intended, as Peter Scott-Presland said in his book *Amiable Warriors*, as a dummy run to see how many "homosexuals, of whom there were many thousands migrating to the capital and fleeing narrow-minded provincialism, would vote for 'their man/woman'." He went on to say, "That the suggestion should come from Vaughan Williams is no surprise. He was nothing if not a drama queen, and an election had all the confrontational theatricality he could wish for, as well as thrusting him into the limelight as election agent. Moreover he was right that fielding a candidate would generate more publicity than CHE had ever achieved so far". Peter Mitchell came fifth, out of ten candidates.

One of Griff's jobs at CHE was to organise the annual conference, and in 1976 he applied to Scarborough council to hold it in the town. They turned him down. The council claimed their staff would refuse to serve gay people and Mrs Sheila Bradbury, the council's conference organiser said, "Our council decided that as there were a lot of young people in the town it would be better the conference was not held here."[5] However, Griff and CHE refused to walk away. They set about campaigning, urging unions and other groups to boycott the resort. This proved highly successful, costing the town millions in lost revenue.

The year after Scarborough, Griff turned to Llandudno for the conference. It is not known why he chose Llandudno, though it could have been due to the publicity surrounding a 24-hour gay helpline that had been set up after a number of suicides in the area. A newspaper article entitled 'Hell in Llandudno' stated that in the previous two years at least five gay men had killed themselves, "most of them young, ashamed and inexperienced. They have often been so unhappy that it is only after their deaths that their gayness came to light." One such young man, said the article, was an "an attractive youth in his teens". His partner and his friend, named Brian, had tried to convince him not to be ashamed, that things would get better and that he could find happiness and fulfilment. But the young man distanced himself from them. They lost touch and shortly afterwards came news that the young man had killed himself. Horrified at yet another suicide in the town, particularly of one so young, Brian and the friend decided to fight for change. Brian installed two telephones in his home, at his own expense, and operated the helpline 24 hours with volunteers.[6]

Brian's comments echoed ones made in Cardiff in 1972. At a Socialist Society meeting the Cardiff branch of the Gay Liberation Front outlined their aims and discussed practical activities. Stuart Neale, "a soft-spoken unassuming member of the group", said "While the GLF campaigns for legal changes, it is aware that this will do little to alter the image of homosexuals as freaks or somehow evil people." He continued that the law was "merely an expression of deep-rooted attitudes embedded in our society that are based mainly on ignorance and fear." Howard Llewellyn, another member, argued one of the best ways to change attitudes was to bring people into direct contact with gays.

Whatever his reasons for choosing Llandudno, Griff put out feelers to Aberconwy Borough Council outlining plans for CHE to bring an estimated 1,700 delegates to the town.[7] The dates he wanted to discuss were Easter of 1977 or the August Bank Holiday. The council responded by sending him promotional material and said they would be pleased to make any of five venues available free of charge for conferences in the town. On the list was the Astra Theatre. Griff contacted them and received confirmation that the theatre would be available for the August Bank Holiday 1977.

Ten days later Griff visited G. Roy Bentley, the supervisor of the Astra cinema, who made a very attractive offer. Shortly after however, that offer was withdrawn. Griff went back to the council to seek another venue but Peter Hall, a council tourist officer, refused the application. Hall said he had discussed the matter with the chairman of the Hotels and Restaurants Association and claimed that they did not have any building available for a conference of that size. Griff made a second application in October 1976 asking to be accommodated for August Bank Holiday in 1979. But Peter Hall once again replied saying that the Arcadia and the Pier Pavilion were booked and once again there was not enough room for the delegates.

Griff began to suspect that the refusal had more to do with discrimination than reality, and began to say so. He took to the press to accuse the borough committee of discrimination. "If we had been Rotary International we would have got red carpet treatment," he claimed. By turning away the conference for 1977 and 1979, he said, Aberconwy Borough Council was losing Llandudno between £50,000 and £100,000 each time. And he warned the town might lose other conferences just as Scarborough had.

The media turned to Scarborough to confirm Griff's statement and Sheila Bradbury agreed it was true. The Liberal Party had refused to hold their conference in Scarborough in future, as did the National

Union of Students and the National Association of Probation Officers.[8] "A factor in their decision," she said, "was doubtless the turning away of the CHE conference."[9] Peter Hall meanwhile hit back describing Griff's comments as 'totally biased' and accused him of putting "a sinister interpretation" on his department's handling of the application.

As the press interest grew Griff, writing from his home in Fulham, began to be more open in his accusations of 'prejudice'. He claimed the Llandudno decision was unfair to hoteliers.[10] The choice, he argued, should have been put to the whole council and not left to one individual. "Local traders," he said, "ought to be made aware that there is an element in the conference industry which is being selective in who it encourages to hold a conference at the Queen of Welsh resorts." He went on to say that he had inspected both the Grand Theatre and the Astra cinema, and was satisfied they could be used. "I also surveyed," he said, "the numbers of bedrooms available in hotels and guest houses and came to the conclusion that there would be sufficient room for CHE members as well as resort holidaymakers."

Councillor Jim T. Williams, chairman of Llandudno's Hotels and Restaurants Association, supported Peter Hall's decision. His argument was that it was impossible to accommodate CHE, partly because not all the hotels were open and those that were had regular visitors who couldn't be turned away. He said it was up to individual hoteliers who to accept.[11] G. Roy Bentley, Astra's supervisor, also distanced himself from the offer made to CHE until Griff sent a copy of the original letter to the *North Wales Weekly News*. In it Bentley had written, "I would suggest that our Astra theatre is best suited to your purpose with its 1,645 capacity, licensed bars and full stage equipment". He went on to describe all the amenities at the theatre before concluding, "I am quite certain that we can make all arrangements for your conference. Perhaps you will contact me again at your earliest convenience." Bentley countered saying that it was impossible to make specific arrangements so far in advance and that this was a standard letter sent to everyone who made an enquiry.[12] He chose not to mention the meeting that had taken place between himself and Griff.

By January 1977 the media were reporting that CHE intended to be at Llandudno come what may. Griff told the *Western Mail*, "I have no doubt that their attitude is, 'They are homosexuals and we don't want them walking along our seafront'.[13] We have met the same response from other towns. So far," he added, "Aberconwy have only spoken through Peter Hall's typewriter. The council has been silent in its attitude to CHE". Griff invited the people of Llandudno to write to him at his address at 849 Fulham Road, to let him know their views.[14]

The decision to revisit the matter prompted Griff to write the council a letter in which he warned how the town could suffer financially, adding, "We are quite prepared to arrange for a public forum to be held in the town, to which everyone would be welcome." He commented that some people in the town seemed to be scared of the council. "It really is surprising," he said, "that the Queen of the Welsh resorts can't cope," before adding that gay power, a weapon as yet little used may be mobilised. "The Liberal Party has said it won't hold its conference in Scarborough until the CHE is allowed into the town."[15]

On Saturday 23 April Griff visited members of the Gwynedd CHE branch to assure them they would be coming to Llandudno, "even if we have to pitch tents under the Great Orme"[16]. Then Griff met with Peter Hall. The decision would be revisited, and would go to a full council, said Hall.[17]

At the council meeting Hall repeated, "It is the policy of this council to encourage conferences early or late season, or during the winter months," adding that the councillors were "anxious to point out that, of course, they have nothing at all against CHE." Various councillors came out in support of Hall including W. Glynne Jones, director of leisure and amenities, who echoed that it was not normal practice to encourage conference use during summer months.

Jim T. Williams complained that the Hotels and Restaurants Association of Llandudno were being made a scapegoat in the whole affair. He blamed Peter Hall for attributing to him that there was no room in the town, and stated that it was completely untrue that he had made such a statement – conveniently ignoring his previous statement to the press. "Thousands of people," he said, "will have heard Mr Griffith Vaughan Williams, CHE conference organiser, say on the radio this morning that I would welcome the CHE conference. For the record I want to say that this is completely untrue. At no time have I stated that I would welcome or not welcome this particular conference. I would repeat what I have said in the past in press statements; that the booking of accommodation in hotels is the concern of the hotelier, and not the Llandudno Hotels and Restaurants Association ... If there is a continuance of this harassment of misquoting, or taking out of context, anything which I have said, or may say in this connection, I will be forced to seek legal advice, as to what future action I should take. Furthermore I would suggest that the BBC should give the same prominence to my statements as they gave to Mr. Vaughan Williams on the radio this morning."

However, a correspondent in the *Guardian* joined the row by pointing out that "Just about every organisation of any standing, from the Conservative Party to the pawnbrokers' national body has at some time held its annual conference at Llandudno. Jo Grimond sent his Liberal Party into battle from there in the high post-Orpington summer of 1962 and only a couple of days ago the National Association of Chief Education Welfare Officers debated truancy at the Hydro Hotel" – this at the height of summer, in June.

Despite meetings with a representative from the Hotels and Restaurants Association and a representative of the Hutchinson Leisure Group, owners of the Astra Theatre and Winter Gardens Ballroom,[18] CHE never did hold its conference in Llandudno – they went to Nottingham.

Griff worked for CHE for thirty-five years and was a forceful advocate for LGBT rights. The historian Keith Howes described him as "passionately, noisily committed to gay rights but never pompous or elitist; always politely eloquent, even at his most bombastic. His was a powerful gay voice, devoted to truth and equality."[19] In 1974 he consulted on and participated in a pioneering documentary for ITV, *Speak for Yourself,* about homosexual equality which portrayed CHE's work.[20]

Concerned about the violence against LGBT people Griff worked closely with the police, improving relations with them. In 1980 Griff worked with Julian Meldrum on the CHE publication *Attacks on Gay People* which described the violence they suffered. He approached the Metropolitan Police in the early 1990s with the idea of working together – something not welcomed by all CHE members. They remained wary of the hostility generally shown to them by the police. However the success of this meeting saw the setting up of the London Lesbian and Gay Police Initiative which met regularly throughout the 1990s.

After the horrific bombing of the Admiral Duncan pub in 1999 Griff was asked by the police to advise the Met on working with the LGBT community in such a trying time. As a result the Met extended its links with groups throughout London resulting in the formation of the LGBT Advisory Group – 'Policing Watchdog for LGBT People in London' (still in existence today). Griff remained closely involved with this group up to his death, and was an important adviser on the murder of LGBT people. In 2002 Griff decided at the group to investigate the ways that murders were being handed by the police. Five years later *The Murder Review* (2007) by the LGBT Advisory Group was published; it claimed that many investigations of murders were hampered by the institutional discrimination within the police force. Griff undertook most of the research, and Bob Hodgson, co-chair of the group, said, "He scoured local papers and visited coroner's courts to discover pieces of information on LGBT cases which had been overlooked or badly investigated."[21] The report scrutinised six investigations (five gay men and one transgender woman) in London from 1990 to 2002, and stated in the Introduction: "The investigations in the early 1990s were hampered by a lack of understanding and sensitivity towards LGBT people and also by deep mistrust of the police within the LGBT community due to historical policing practice. Later investigations, on the other hand, were more effective in engaging with the community through the use of LGBT Liaison Officers and independent advisors."

In summary the report said,

> Police at the time failed to deal adequately with LGBT life and culture. The initial investigations of the first murders seemed to us to be more focussed on determining promiscuity and risk taking, and seemed predisposed to interpreting circumstances as sex acts 'gone wrong'.[22]

The report made twenty-two recommendations for improvements in the Met – all of which were implemented. And the Met awarded Commendations to Griff and his colleagues for their work. In the years that followed other police forces followed the Met's lead and implemented changes which all ultimately originated from the CHE report and Griff's research.

Bob Hodgson described Griff as "a character, and a gay activist who had an encyclopaedic knowledge of LGBT issues and details of past and current cases. He was well known at many LGBT forums across London. To Chairs like myself he could be challenging in the extreme. If he thought an issue had been brushed aside he would persist with specific questions until satisfied with the answer.

He was also a stickler for meeting protocols and doggedly refused to embrace electronic communication technology. At the ends of meetings his lists of items under 'any other business' were legendary but he delivered them with good humour and a characteristic twinkle in his eye."[23]

It was due to the work done by organisations like CHE and people like Griff Vaughan Williams that lives for LGBT people across Britain were made better. Griff died in 2011 survived by his partner of thirty years Paul Cannon.

23. We All Fall Down

In 1981 an unknown epidemic swept through America. By the end of the year over a hundred people had died. The disease had existed since the 1970s but its symptoms had been missed and attributable deaths had not been recorded. By 1980 it had already spread to five continents and throughout the following years the death figures rose. Four years later the virus was isolated medically and in 1986 it was given the name Human Immunodeficiency Virus (HIV), with late symptoms referred to as AIDS (Acquired Immune Deficiency Syndrome). In the same year the World Health Organisation reported that it had been notified of 43,880 cases in 91 countries.[1]

The British press headlines, like others around the world, screamed fear and pointed fingers at homosexuals and intravenous drugs users as plague carriers. Discrimination, horror and ignorance prevailed. The famous 'tombstone' advert crashed down on British television screens in the world's first major government-sponsored national AIDS awareness drive, and leaflets were sent to every house. Awareness increased and so did fear. Nurses were afraid to touch HIV and AIDS patients, firefighters refused to administer the kiss of life, and an ignorant public thought haemophiliac was another word for homosexual. The Sports Council for Wales banned all AIDS victims from using public swimming baths, in the days when infection was believed to be from any source. Only later was it recognised that the transmission of bodily fluids could cause infection.

In the early days most portrayals of HIV and AIDS in plays and films were American. In 1985 *The Normal Heart*[2], *As Is* and *A Quiet End* appeared on American stages, and the TV film, *An Early Frost*, was screened, followed by *As Is* a year later. In Britain the first play to be staged was *The Normal Heart* (March 1986) which had its European premiere at the Royal Court Theatre with Martin Sheen in the lead role. Both the play and Sheen were nominated for Laurence Olivier Awards.[3]

Little, however, had been produced in Britain until August 1986 when the first British play[4] about HIV and AIDS was written in Swansea. For three months second year students from Swansea University, under the guidance of their drama lecturer Paul Heritage, researched and wrote *We All Fall Down*. Forming a production company, Principal Parts, they managed and produced the play. They had intended to stage it at the university but realised they could reach more people performing at a public venue in the centre of town. They approached the Dylan Thomas Theatre and the play was booked in for October 19 and 20 as part of the Swansea Fringe Festival. The students also decided that after each performance there should be a debate, and invited health officials and representatives from political parties to take part.

The aim of the play, said the students, was to combat the stereotypical image of AIDS as a 'gay plague'. Other plays, such as *The Normal Heart* (still on in London at the time), dealt with the political and emotional side of gay people with the condition whereas *We All Fall Down* was designed to show that AIDS could affect anyone. Paul Heritage hoped it would be shown in schools as the information it contained had been based on advice from leading AIDS experts, including the West Glamorgan Health Authority's Chief AIDS adviser Dr Colin Griffiths, who had been instrumental in creating one of Britain's most comprehensive AIDS education programmes.[5] Principal Parts were also supported by Eddie Ramsden, Swansea council's environmental health officer[6] and the proceeds from the play were to go to the Terrence Higgins Trust, a HIV/AIDS charity named after Welshman Terrence Higgins.

Almost as soon as plans for the performance started, so did the controversy. Swansea was not new to criticism of gay plays. A year earlier in February 1985 Gay Sweatshop[7] had staged the play *Poppies*, inspired by the peace movement of the early 1980s and exploring the nature of masculinity. Theatre workers and cleaners at Swansea's Taliesin Theatre went on strike, refusing to work on the play in case they caught AIDS.

When details about *We All Fall Down* appeared in the press and its theme became apparent, panic set in. The professor of English at the University withdrew the £3-400 which his drama department had promised[8] and the management at the Dylan Thomas Theatre met to discuss a possible ban. They had not been told, they claimed, that AIDS was the topic. They too were not unfamiliar with controversy around gay plays. Three years previously a campaign led by Conservative Councillor Richard Lewis against the notorious *Romans in Britain* by Howard Brenton had seen the play banned because it contained a scene of a male rape.

Paul Heritage, speaking against the ban in the *South Wales Evening Post* said, "If plays like mine are banned AIDS will spread quicker than ever. The Little Theatre are setting themselves up as censors. They are without doubt anti-gay and much more dangerous than AIDS itself. We want to dispel ignorance and prejudice and this is the reaction we get."[9]

The secretary of the Dylan Thomas Theatre, Finvola Clifford Davies, responded that the theatre was forbidden by the terms of its lease to stage any production which was deemed political. "It depends," she said, "on how crude it is. Obviously if this is just a homosexual exercise I don't think we would be too happy about it."[10] They would take advice from the West Glamorgan Health Authority's chief administrative medical officer Beverley Littlepage before deciding if the play could go ahead.

Swansea Council then joined the fray by stating that in their view the performances of *We All Fall Down* should go ahead, and even threatened to close the theatre if it was banned. Swansea Fringe Festival administrator Dave Downes also came out in support.

By the end of August the Dylan Thomas Theatre officials had met and discussed the matter. They had been 'dismayed', they told the press, "and disturbed at the misrepresentation of the issue by the news media,"[11] and Principal Parts were told they could go ahead. It was also confirmed that the play would continue to receive financial backing from the university's drama department.[12]

That'll Be the Day, a second play also by Principal Parts and written and directed by Paul Heritage, was due to open at the St Phillips Community Centre in Swansea as part of the same Fringe Festival.[13] A musical, described as boy-meets-boy, girl-meets-girl play, it dealt with all the issues affecting young gay people, including problems in school and with parents. It was to "be a celebration of homosexuality, designed to counter sexual bigotry and prejudice against homosexuals."

Councillor Richard Lewis was strongly critical of that play too, and said, "Shows like this only further the cult of homosexuality."[14] However fellow Swansea City Councillor Tim Exton came out robustly in its defence, saying the play should be welcomed as a positive step in the campaign to educate the public. Criticising Lewis he said, "He's undermining the ability of the public in Swansea to make up their own minds on the subject." Addressing both plays, Exton said, "This is something that should be welcomed. It's a positive step forward and I would like to see it tour all our community centres rather than it being confined to just one."[15] Both Tim Exton and Richard Lewis had attended a seminar on AIDS a couple of weeks earlier and Exton was surprised at Lewis' views. "I'm very disappointed," he said "that having attended this seminar, he is determined to be so alarmist. AIDS is not confined to homosexuals and trying to censor what is a very important public debate in this way is wrong."[16]

By early October Lewis had announced that he intended to take legal advice and was confident of getting a court injunction to stop the play, adding that he feared there could be a serious public disorder if the musical were allowed to continue.[17] He also wanted to stop all gay plays being performed at the Swansea Fringe. Paul Heritage responded that if necessary he would take the show to the streets, "It seems this man will stop at nothing to prevent a show which he had not even seen."

Despite Lewis' efforts the musical went ahead. There were forty-two people in the audience, including the councillor, and despite being the only protestor he claimed he represented the 'moral majority.'[18] "They were trying to persuade people that gay is the in thing," he said. "It left me cold and feeling sick, but the music wasn't too bad." Despite his liking the music Lewis continued his attacks. He threatened the St Phillips Community Centre with an examination of its licence, with a view to restricting use of the premises as a community centre for local people only. Today the St Phillips Community Centre is still open and welcoming everyone.

On the whole *That'll Be the Day* was well received, with the *South Wales Evening Post* describing it as "Daring, different, and yes, gay, the performance was a wonderful tongue-in-cheek send-up of heterosexual prejudices and it portrays homosexuals as human beings."[19] The story concerned a shy lesbian, played by Gill Prewitt, who runs away from home and meets a crowd of gay people in a café which proves to be a sanctum from the cruel world. The group is made up of colourful characters, Danny the Deviant, (played by Simon Machin) a male cross-dressing singer; Doris, a mother who's baby was removed by the state because she was a lesbian; Jo the café owner who had left her husband when she realised she was gay; Arnold, a straight man; Les, a macho gay who hated effeminate 'queers'; Spike, a butch dyke; and Johnny, a male prostitute. The *South Wales Evening Post* advised their readers, "Ignoring the controversy ... on its merits, its entertainment value is high. Propaganda or educational? Judge for yourself."[20]

Opinion still raged about both plays. That venerable journal, *The Stage*, entered the controversy[21] with an article headed, 'Tory tries to bring an absolute end to gay plays', which prompted the Watford Palace Theatre, one of the first companies to develop 'Theatre in Education', the interaction of education with stage, to write to Swansea City Council leader Tyssul Lewis. In their letter they said, "It is ironic that some persons in positions of authority pay lip service to the principals of free speech, but in practice seek to undermine it. Freedom of artistic expression is an essential aspect of free speech."[22] The letter called on Tyssul Lewis and the city council to do everything in their power to resist attacks on freedom of speech and to oppose those responsible for them.

Nearer to home Tom Edwards, secretary of the Swansea Free Churches Council, expressed his members' deep concerns. He presented a petition with a meagre fifteen signatures saying, "We urge the city council to convey to officials of the Fringe that such propaganda is unacceptable and that any future monetary grant will be withheld unless such productions ceases."[23]

At the next full council meeting in December Councillor Lewis proposed half the £4,500 financial support for the Swansea Fringe Festival to be withdrawn. But he faced opposition. Councillor Lawrence Bailey claimed he had no objections to Lewis making an idiot of himself,[24] and Councillor Colin Hammacott said Lewis was trying to destroy a grant which promoted a wide variety of performances because he found one play offensive.

Lewis, however, was determined to continue his attack. In December 1986 he produced a leaflet which was distributed to 5,000 people in his council ward, condemning gay people. *Uplands Newsline*, edited by Lewis and distributed by him, openly attacked Principal Parts: "AIDS ... the EVIL on our doorstep!! ... Homosexuality has rightfully been scorned by most self-respecting people .... but what about Swansea City Council and the Labour members who run it, what have they done ... we called for a ban, but we were ignored." The plays "soured the entire event and to us it became the festival of shame.

We can do without weirdos who are a few pence short in the pound when it comes to their sexual tastes."[25]

A member of the Gay Society at Swansea University spoke out against the leaflets: "We are not perverts. Child abuse, rape and other perverted activities are predominantly heterosexual." In the newsletter Lewis called for the closure of the university drama department and reported that he had written to the Conservative Education Secretary Kenneth Baker asking for their funding to be withdrawn.[26]

In response to Councillor Lewis' offensive actions his Kattoys business in Oxford Street was picketed by twenty members of the university, who were arrested for obstruction. "They came down on us like a ton of hot bricks," Andy Buurman told the *Gay Times*. "That's because we were protesting about AIDS hysteria. When we had a picket on a porn shop recently the police were very helpful and took us in to talk to the managers of the shop."[27] The behaviour of the police, Buurman claimed, 'was appalling' and he went on to say that a complaint against their treatment whilst in police custody would be lodged.

Paul Heritage 29, Tracey Hind 21, Andrew Buurman 21, Adrian Benbow, and Katy Barrett were all charged with obstruction. The police said ten people had gathered outside Kattoys on 13 December and as the street there was narrow pedestrians were being forced onto the road.[28] The protestors were, said the police, physically stopping people and thrusting leaflets into their hands. Giving evidence, PC David Hill said the students had been blocking the pavement and PC David Tomas said he saw Paul Heritage point at a passer-by and shout "There is nothing wrong with the gays". However the five defendants stated that they had been walking up and down the street and had not congregated outside the shop. Barrett said they forced no leaflets on people as it would not have been in their interest. "We did not want to confront people," she said, "we wanted them to understand it and why we were there. We want sympathy not confrontation." Paul Heritage said he had not shouted anything and as he had been talking to a journalist some distance from the shop he was surprised at his arrest.

Meanwhile Lewis had been invited by the university's Conservative Society to speak on the subject of 'Why homosexuals should not be allowed to teach'. Paul Heritage and a group of fifty students gathered to prevent the Councillor from entering the students' union building where the talk was due to take place. Lewis was taken by several college porters to a lecture theatre where he proceeded to give his talk to an audience which included TV and media journalists. Lewis declared that all gay teachers and lecturers should be sacked. "The biggest mistake this country ever made," he said, "was to decriminalise homosexuality. To anyone with moral values the practice is evil and the rise of AIDS is I believe directly connected with our attitude towards homosexuality." According to several reports by journalists Lewis was subjected to spitting, shouting, jeering and jostling by students after the lecture. Paul Heritage faced disciplinary action for his part in the demonstrations, and possibly dismissal. At a meeting of the College Council both the university's principal, Brian Clarkson, and the president of the college, ex-prime minister James Callaghan, defended Lewis' right to freedom of speech.

Paul Heritage defended his actions and those of the students, and their right to freedom of speech by saying, "Councillor Lewis is a racist and an extreme homophobe. The college authorities are ignoring the direct provocation to gay students. The college should not allow the councillor to advocate violence in the way that he does." Lewis had described gay people as 'evil, perverted and wicked' and he had called for vigilante groups to be set up to attack gay people. "In South Wales and Swansea in particular, people like Councillor Lewis are allowed to make this sort of statement in the press any time they like. No one is allowed to stand up to that. The newspapers are not prepared to let the other side have a voice."

Tim Exton wrote to the *Western Mail* correcting 'inaccuracies' and 'omissions' in the reporting of Lewis' lecture. "The heckling he suffered," said Exton, "was not at the hands of the college Gay Society, but was an expression by groups and individuals within the campus of their anger at his viciously anti-homosexual behaviour. Is it not strange," he asked, "that Mr Lewis steadfastly upholds the right of miners to choose which union they belong to, yet he denies people the right to freely determine their own sexuality – surely a case of double standards?"[29]

Paul Heritage was not sacked and is now Professor of Drama and Performance at Manchester, but the Students Union was fined. The police never responded to the students' complaints of unfair treatment and the court case against the five arrested took place on 27 March

1987. They were all found guilty and fined £25 each. Judge David Williams said he had come to the conclusion that what happened during the protest probably lay somewhere between the completely differing accounts heard by the court. All five appealed and in June 1987 the convictions were quashed.

In March 2013 Lewis, as a Roman Catholic, spoke against equal marriage. He said: "I can't support this because of my faith, I'm sorry. I sympathise and I don't have a problem with civil partnership, that's fine."[30]

HIV and AIDS are still prevalent today and at the time of writing the current global deaths are twenty-two million, with sixty million infected. If precautions are not taken anyone can be infected.

24. A Purpose in Life

In 1915 Mrs Margaret Mackworth was on her way home on board a luxury liner. She had travelled with her father, D. A. Thomas, to America on business, and as they were having lunch she was in 'a fog of gloom and depression'.[1] The First World War had meant giving up her militant activism on female suffrage and it was becoming necessary to end her marriage. It had been a societal necessity and she had not loved her husband. Not until 1922 would she fall in love – and then it was with a woman.

As Margaret and her father finished lunch, she heard a loud noise. She thought something terrible must have happened, but D.A. dismissed her concerns. However as they made their way to the lift a second torpedo struck. D.A. rushed to see what was happening as she ran to their cabins to collect lifejackets. In her room the lights had gone out and the ship was listing heavily but she managed to get back to the deck searching for her father to no avail. Margaret could not swim and had a fear of heights but before she had time to worry the water had risen to her waist and swept her off the ship. Dragged under she struggled back to the surface and grabbed a floating board but lost consciousness in the freezing water.

Despite Germany advertising in American newspapers that it considered the *Lusitania* a legitimate target as she was carrying arms, the ship had sailed. When she was struck she sank in just eighteen minutes. 1,198 people were killed including, millionaire Alfred Gwynne Vanderbilt, and the outrage caused by the sinking propelled America into the First World War. Margaret, her father and his secretary were among the 761 people who survived.[2] Margaret's mother and husband rushed to Dublin to be with her, but suffering from bronchial pneumonia she took time to recover. Later she would say that she believed being saved meant she had a purpose in life.

Margaret Haig Thomas was born in 1883 to Welsh coal magnate David Alfred Thomas and his wife Sybil. She was born on 12 June at Princes Square, Bayswater but four years later the family returned to Wales, to Llanwern House on the outskirts of Newport. She was later educated in Scotland before going on to Oxford University's Somerville College.

D.A., as he was known to all, gave his only child an education and involvement in his business affairs unusual at the time. Women, especially of her station, were predominantly expected to marry, have children and concern themselves with domestic life. Instead, D.A. cultivated Margaret's intelligence, and they would have long political and social discussions: he wanted nothing more than for Margaret to be a businesswoman in her own right. Her father was not her only inspiration. Sybil was an intelligent, politically active woman and D.A. treated her, and Margaret, as his equals. In her autobiography *This Was My World* Margaret says that her mother "had prayed passionately that her baby daughter might become a feminist." Other members of the family, aunts and cousins, were also feminists in the suffrage movement.

Despite her wealthy upbringing Margaret was proud of her father's working class roots. D.A. was born at Ysguborwen, Aberdare in 1856 the fifteenth of seventeen children. His father Samuel had been a grocer in Merthyr Tydfil before becoming a mining entrepreneur and a pioneer in the Welsh coal industry, but when D.A. was born his father was close to bankruptcy. At twenty-six years old D.A. married Sybil Margaret Haig the daughter of a landowning family. By then he had taken over his father's mining concerns, made a fortune, and served as an MP in Merthyr between 1888 and 1910.

Despite Margaret's liberal upbringing and independence it was still expected that she marry and in 1908 she wed a neighbour, Sir Humphrey Mackworth, twelve years older than her. Their wedding took place at the old parish church of Holy Trinity, Christchurch, Caerleon, and D.A. gave Llanwern village the day off. But the marriage was doomed from the start. Their personalities were radically different and while Mackworth loved active sporting pastimes like fox hunting, and was a military man, Margaret had interests in reading and politics. In her autobiography, *My World*, she admitted the marriage had been for societal reasons and that they had little in common: "Humphrey held that no one should ever read in a room where anyone else wanted to talk. I, brought up in a home in which a father's study was sacred, held, on the contrary, that no one should every talk in a room where anyone else wanted to read."[3] He also disapproved of Margaret's politics.

Just four months after her marriage, Margaret, aged twenty-five, joined the Women's Social and Political Union (WSPU), the militant wing of the suffragette movement. Activists had become dissatisfied with the lack of progress made by the Union of Women's Suffrage Societies and felt something more than discussions was needed. They adopted the slogan 'Deeds not words', and members were known for breaking windows, cutting telegraph wires and targeting men's leisure places such as cricket pavilions, golf courses and boat houses by setting them on fire at night when nobody was in them.

In September 1909 Margaret spoke at a meeting of the Aberdare Liberal Club at Llanwern, her family home. She received a polite reception and said she hoped the current Liberal government would be true to the traditions of Liberalism and would grant ratepaying women the vote. However, her first major speech was made at the inaugural meeting of the WSPU in November 1909 at the Temperance Hall, Aberdare. It quickly became apparent that a number of men were aiming to disrupt the meeting and the speakers were shouted down. As the women stood on the stage the crowd threw rotten vegetables, dead mice and even set live ones onto the stage. Windows were broken and general mayhem threatened, forcing the women speakers to leave.

In December fellow Welshman David Lloyd George, Chancellor of the Exchequer, stayed with the Thomases at Llanwern. The *Evening Express* published a picture adding to the caption "… a party of passive suffragettes on the lawn …"[5] Margaret is the 'passive suffragette' on the

far left. That passivity was short-lived: Margaret is most famous for setting a bomb.

Even with the militant action, progress on women's rights was slow. In *My World*, Margaret writes that her branch in Newport had performed a few small acts of militancy, but nothing dramatic. In 1912 Olive Fontaine, a member of the Newport WSPU, was imprisoned in London for window-breaking.

Margaret's decision to place a bomb had been escalated by the death of Emily Davison in June 1913, who was killed by the king's horse during the Epsom Derby. Later that month Margaret collected ammunition from a suffrage-friendly pharmacist in London, travelling back in a crowded third-class carriage with incendiary tubes carried in a flimsy basket. Her nervousness during the journey was compounded when a woman leant her elbow on the basket! On the 25 June Margaret approached a letter-box set in a low wall in the leafy suburbs on Risca Road, Newport, "my heart beating like a steam engine, my throat was dry."[6] She threw the tubes into the box and smoke billowed forth. A crowd gathered, the police arrived and witnesses who had seen Margaret were quick to identify her. She was charged with "unlawfully placing in a certain post-office letter-box ... a certain explosive substance"[7] and pleaded guilty. She was faced with a £10 fine and £10 costs, or a month's imprisonment. She refused to pay and was sent to Usk Prison where she immediately began a hunger strike.

The militant suffragettes had been using hunger strikes since 1909 when officials released Marion Dunlop, the first woman to strike, to prevent her from becoming a martyr. The tactic was quickly adapted, and hunger strikes became so common the government introduced forced feeding. A cat and mouse strategy was devised in which strikers would be released and then re-arrested once they had recovered their health. After six days Margaret, reported to be "in a very weak condition as the result of her hunger-striking"[8] was released. To her annoyance she found that the fine imposed on her had been paid, probably by her husband.

With the outbreak of World War I the WSPU abandoned militant action in order to work for the war effort, and Margaret too turned her attention elsewhere. When D.A.'s general manager left to join the war she took over his duties, and when her father was away she was placed in charge of his businesses. Their relationship was close and in *My*

World she said that he was her greatest influence. Of her, he said that had he had lost her on the *Lusitania* "my life would have been blighted for ever, and everything would have become a blank for the future. She is more than a daughter to me; she is a real pal."[9]

When D.A. was given new appointments by David Lloyd George, now Prime Minister, he travelled extensively and was made Viscount Rhondda in 1918. He accepted the honour on the condition that it would pass on to his daughter. Margaret also devoted herself to women's war work becoming Director of the Women's Department of the Ministry of National Service.

D.A. died in 1918 and was cremated in London, his ashes being brought back to Llanwern. Flags all over south Wales flew at half-mast and even President Hoover sent a message of condolence. Margaret now became Viscountess, or Lady, Rhondda but the loss of her father was a huge blow to her. As a result of his death she became financially responsible for his mistress Evelyn Salusbury, from Tredunnoc near Caerleon, who had been one of his private secretaries, and her two half-siblings.

As a peer Margaret sought to take her seat in the House of Lords. Originally the Sex Disqualification (Removal) Act, which allowed women to take up many professions previously denied them, meant that women peers were able to take seats in the House and so she applied. But in response that part of the act was repealed. She fought tenaciously for many years but women were not permitted to sit until 1958.

By the early 1920s Margaret's marriage was one in name only. It ended in divorce in 1923 on the agreed grounds of Humfrey's desertion and misconduct – though these grounds were fictitious. Later she admitted "we simply never fitted – though we tried to pretend we did for thirteen years."[10]

Margaret turned her attention in a new direction and founded her own magazine in May 1920 in Fleet Street, London. *Time and Tide* was a weekly liberal journal with essays, reviews and letters. Margaret, who funded it from her inheritance, had initially intended it to be a political review which would influence people.

Two years after founding the paper Margaret had her first serious same-sex relationship. Helen Archdale, like Margaret, came from a family experienced in activism for women's rights, and in 1901 she had

married Captain Theodore Montgomery Archdale. They had two sons and a daughter whilst stationed in India but seven years later she returned to Britain having become estranged from her husband. Like Humphrey Mackworth, he did not approve of his wife's activism.

Almost immediately Helen joined the WSPU and was an active member, having been imprisoned in 1909 with Adela Pankhurst for a breach of peace. They had amassed a number of people outside the Edinburgh hall at which MP Winston Churchill was due to speak. The four women convicted of this offence went on hunger strike but were released after four days. Helen moved to London in 1911 and continued her militant action. Her daughter Betty recalls collecting stones for her mother for breaking windows, for which Helen received a two month prison sentence. In 1918 her husband was killed when his ship was torpedoed. In the same year she worked at the Ministry of National Service, where she was Margaret's assistant.

By 1922 they were living together in a London flat and a house in Kent where they received streams of literary and artistic visitors on the weekend. But within four years their relationship was strained. The first editor of *Time and Tide* had not worked out and was quickly replaced by Helen who became the only women editor of a weekly paper at that time. However when it ran into difficulties Margaret proposed changes which Helen resisted. Eventually Margaret replaced an embittered Helen as editor, and Helen believed she had been blamed and sacked for the paper's poor sales.

As their relationship struggled Margaret wrote a letter to Helen which was found in her papers after death although it is not known if she ever sent it. It summed up Margaret's feelings, "I wonder if you too are realising how near the end we are getting? I don't know whether you ever ask yourself why we live together; if you ever go back to the time when we first came together. We began it for the only reason that can make living together possible, because we were very fond of one other." She added "I have paid heavily for believing that your love…was real, when in fact it can only have been a passing surface schwärm [passion], much as I've seen you several times. I gave you all I had to give and for years now I have been struggling not to see, what you were making only abundantly clear, that the only value I had in your eyes was some one who could give the children treats … when I tried to tell you I cared you sneered."[11] Helen spent time abroad, and of the cottage they shared at weekends, she wrote to a friend, "but we do not necessarily go together in fact it is rarely that we coincide."[12]

Angela John, in the most comprehensive biography written on Margaret, *Turning the Tide*, and the only one that details her same-sex relationships, shows that their connection was not a solid one. They had widely different beliefs, and Margaret was under considerable strain, managing her father's businesses, as the owner of the journal and with her activism on women's rights. Yet despite their differences they stayed together until 1933, by which time they were barely speaking.

In the meantime Margaret had formed a new friendship with a woman fifteen years younger than herself, Winifred Holtby. Winifred is most remembered these days for her novel *South Riding*. When she and Margaret met she had been in a 'friendship' with the writer Vera Brittain – although Vera would vehemently deny it was a sexual one. Her memoir of their relationship, *Testament of Friendship*, provides a forced and defensive view of heterosexuality aware as she was of the rumours that surrounded first her and, later, Margaret.

A hundred years after the deaths of the Ladies of Llangollen same-sex relationships were still being portrayed as 'perfect,' 'noble' although the term 'romantic' had been dropped. "Her friendship with Vera Brittain," says Marion Shaw in her biography of Winifred, *The Clear Stream*, "and throughout Vera's subsequent writings, was a model of female friendship, a 'noble relationship' equalling, as Vera maintained, the great male friendships of history ... The friendship became an iconic feminist example of 'sisterhood' at its most admirable."[13]

Vera went to great pains to distance herself and Winifred from "scandalmongers who invented for her a lurid series of homosexual relationships, usually associated with Lady Rhondda or myself."[14] They had reason to be worried. By the late nineteenth and early twentieth century, society was becoming more aware of what lesbianism was. There was a lot of publicity about the openly lesbian culture in Paris and in *My World* Margaret admits to reading Havelock Ellis's *Studies in the Psychology of Sex* when she was younger – a book that was notoriously difficult to obtain. She recalls how it was necessary to have a statement from a doctor or lawyer as to the good character of the person before they could buy it. She had obtained her copy from the women-only Cavendish Bentinck library and recalls her father's 'amused indignation' that he could not get hold of a book his daughter had read.

Lesbianism continued to be socially unacceptable, and in the 1920s the subject was often in the headlines. The 1921 Criminal Law Amendment Bill had aimed to criminalise lesbianism but it was defeated on the grounds that it would "draw attention to lesbians and do harm by introducing into the minds of perfectly innocent people the most revolting thoughts."[15] Seven years later the trial of Radcliffe Hall for her novel *The Well of Loneliness*[16] put the subject firmly in the public eye and lesbians had to take great care not to be found out.

However, as with all histories of sexual orientation it is often difficult to retrosexualise individuals. The terms we are familiar with today would either not have been used or had different connotations. People from the early twentieth century would not have defined themselves as lesbians in the way we do today. Radclyffe Hall's book caused consternation as women in same-sex relationships would not have seen themselves as 'inverts', in the way that the character Stephen Gordon was portrayed. Winifred wrote, "Radclyffe Hall taught me a lot. She's all fearfully wrong, I feel. To love other women deeply is not pathological. To be unable to control one's passions is."[17] Or more importantly, to control how other people saw one's passions!

Marion Shaw clarifies Winifred's position on sexuality and gender, "I think we have to return to her own comments about the construction of sexuality, made variously in her later years, the 'feminine' and 'masculine' are very artificial categories and that the human personality, is, in varying degrees, an admixture of both. "We do not ... know," as she had written at the end of *Women*[18], "hough we theorise and penalise with ferocious confidence – whether the 'normal' sexual relationship is homo- or bi- or heterosexual. Perhaps like many women, given an appropriate context and a willing partner whom she loved of either sex, she could have been lesbian, heterosexual or both."

Winifred and Margaret had met when she had submitted an essay on education to *Time and Tide* which impressed Margaret. Two years later they met again at Margaret's flat and "talked for nearly three hours about everything in the world."[19] Another two years and she was appointed to the board of directors. Their friendship deepened when Vera Britten married and Margaret was becoming estranged from Helen. They would go down to Margaret's Kent country house at weekends and spent frequent holidays together. However Winifred maintained her close relationship with Vera even though her association with Margaret caused jealousy. Vera, who also wrote for *Time and Tide*, described Margaret as "desperately shy when tête-à-tête ... a nice woman, but rather a lonely one."[20]

Unfortunately Winifred died of Bright's Disease in 1935, aged only thirty-seven, a year before *South Riding* was published. She never saw how successful her novel became. Both Brittain and Margaret agreed on the need to be circumspect in an effort to memorialize and protect the reputation of their deceased friend.

Shortly before Winifred died Margaret had met another writer, Theodora Bosanquet, and it was she who was to prove Margaret's most significant relationship. Born on the Isle of Wight in 1881, she spent many years as the assistant to writer Henry James, himself a subject of speculation as to his sexual orientation. Theodora wrote four books, was the Executive Secretary of the International Federation of University Women, and had been an active suffragette. From 1935 to

1958 she was editor of *Time and Tide* and later a director.

In 1933 Margaret, on a holiday cruise with Theodora, wrote to Winifred telling her that they had decided to live together. "Emotionally," she wrote, "I feel happy and at rest as I haven't for years."[21] But she was still aware of the need to keep the relationship secret. "When her god-daughter suggested to her that a member of the *Time and Tide* staff might be a lesbian," wrote John in *Turning the Tide*, "Margaret's response was: 'That is a *slimey* thing to say. You might say the same of Theodora and me'. With the term connoting erotic relationships there was concern about labelling and portraying a personal lifestyle as deviant and unacceptable." John's use of the word 'lifestyle' is uncomfortable reading because nobody has a 'lifestyle', they have a life.

In her letter to Winifred, Margaret explained her cover story. Her accommodation was just too big so she would ask Theodora to take a couple of rooms as they were intending to write a book together and would share the house until it was done. The book never appeared. In 1937 they took a house in Surrey where they would spend the weekends, and in 1949 took a flat near the Ritz Hotel in Piccadilly, where they received many famous guests. They were together for twenty-five years, from 1933 until Margaret's death in 1958, and John describes their relationship as Margaret's "deepest and most enduring partnership".

In 1957 Margaret's health began to deteriorate. She handed over the running of *Time and Tide* to her friend Charles Peaker, but Theodora was worried that without the paper "Margaret wouldn't really have much to live for."[22] She was diagnosed with cancer of the stomach and taken into hospital, where she died on July 20, 1958.

Margaret was cremated and her ashes interned with those of her beloved father and mother at the church of St Mary's, Llanwern. Theodora did not attend. Margaret's finances did not cover her will and so her properties were sold, making Theodora homeless. She rented a flat in London and died on June 1, 1971.

In her usual self-deprecating way Margaret once wrote, "I had a profession. I was rich. Owing to being my father's daughter I had, almost by accident and much to my own surprise, made a name. A name is a platform. Life was before me to do what I chose with." And she chose to fight for those issues which needed change. She died the same year that women were finally allowed to take their seat in the House of Lords although, given how much she fought for that right, her portrait was not hung there until 2011.

It seemed that her belief in being saved from the *Lusitania* for a purpose was correct. She achieved an enormous amount for women's rights.

25. Pride in Wales

The Stonewall Inn is a bar in New York. It was there that arguably the most important event in the history of sexual orientation and gender identity took place. In the 1960s it was an established venue for LGBT people, the largest in America, although it was subject to frequent raids by the police. Originally owned by the Mafia they regularly paid off the police but one night on June 28, 1969 a raid went wrong, provoking a riot that lasted for two days. Six months later two of the main organisations, the Gay Liberation Front (the first to use the word 'gay' in its name) and the Gay Activists Alliance, dedicated to LGBT activism were formed, and the rest is history.

The Gay Activists Alliance organised the first gay parade on June 28, 1970 in New York. Thereafter annual parades were intended to raise visibility and to fight against discrimination. London was the first city to follow suit. There had been an unofficial walk by 150 men through Highbury Fields in November 1970 but the first official UK Gay Pride Rally took place on July 1, 1972 – the nearest weekend to the anniversary to the Stonewall riots. Around two thousand people turned up.

France held its first Pride rally five years later, followed by Australia in 1978 and a year later Canada, Germany, Mexico and Spain. Ireland was next in 1983, and in 1985 Wales became the tenth country in the world to hold a Pride march. It was organised by the students of Cardiff University. They had complied with the regulations in notifying the county council and had received authority in May for the event to go ahead in June. Student Tim Foskett wrote to the police saying, "In the spirit of all this year's Gay Pride events, it is less a protest, more a celebration of the existence of homosexuals and our consequent pride in being lesbians and gay men. Before the march we shall instil into the marchers the importance of a peaceful, happy march both for the image of lesbians and gay men and to ensure the structure of Cardiff remains sound." It was intended, they said, to counter "lesbian and gay oppression", and about 250 people were expected to march. The organisers estimated that about five percent of the Cardiff population were homosexuals and they wanted to show pride in who they were.[1]

Superintendent Dave Hatch of the South Wales Police was supportive and agreed that officers would keep a low profile. "It is the first march of its kind in the city," he said. "They are exercising their freedom of speech and we do not anticipate any breaches of the peace that we would not be able to handle." He continued, "We will treat it like a march of Girl Guides, Boys' Brigade or any other youth gathering".

The march was to go from Park Place on the university campus to the shopping centre in Queen Street at 2pm on June 20. They would be handing out 'non-offensive' leaflets requesting that the public treat gay and lesbian people 'normally'. Frances Brown, a twenty-three year-old sociology student, said "Unless people have a friend or relative who is gay then they never know how often they come across us. But there are many of us around and we want to be treated the same as everybody else. This will be less of a demonstration than a statement of our pride."[2]

However a row was brewing over support for the students. A motion was due to be discussed at a Students Union general meeting in the university. The general secretary Stephen Baird protested, "I object on Christian principals. I have objected to their actions on several occasions and I don't believe the student's union should get involved in sexual politics."[3] However, the opinions of Baird, and others, did not stop the march going ahead.

What little objection there was came, as usual, from religious groups. The *South Wales Echo* published a letter from a Mark Carroll headed 'March of the sinful gays,' which began "I read that there is to be a march in Cardiff in June by homosexuals. I write this letter prayerfully believing that this shows how sinful and away from God we have strayed in this world."[4] He added the traditional Biblical 'clobber quotes' and encouraged people to read the Bible for themselves. If they did they would find that although Leviticus 18:22 states that "thou shalt not lie with mankind, as with womankind. It is an abomination", according to Exodus 35:2 whoever works on a Sunday should be put to death. Throughout LGBT history the Bible has been cherry-picked to prop up discrimination, with Christians carefully avoiding calling for those Biblical sins which carry a death penalty to be enacted.

I. and C. Jones from Cardiff responded to Mark Carroll's letter asking if he was as pure as God or Jesus to sit in judgement on others. They also pointed to the plight of the Jews in Nazi Germany persecuted because they were different, and asked if he wished to see the same fate befall homosexuals in Britain. "To persecute anyone is a great injustice," they wrote "and can destroy one's own soul in the process. It is better to show love and compassion towards your fellow man than hate."[5]

In the end the march was hailed as an overwhelming success. More than 100 'homosexuals' turned up give out leaflets and to carry banners – some reading '2-4-6-8 Gay is good as straight' and 'Lesbians unite and fight'. A small group carried a banner with 'Straights against violence against Gays'. The media managed to find one objection. A pensioner selling charity tickets from a kiosk thought the march was a load of rubbish and that the police presence was a waste of time and money.[6] Tim Foskett said he was happy with the public's response and that it was intended to make the march an annual event.

The Pride march was a snapshot of the issues faced trying to put on a LGBT event in 1985. Although small political and social gains had been made by the beginning of the 1980s, the AIDS crisis produced a backlash of public feeling. The fear of being identified as 'gay' was also still strong. These attitudes affected other events in the same year.

In February 1985 the Lesbian and Gay Group from Bangor University complained in the student magazine *Y Seren* (The Star) that attendance at their stall at the Serendipity Clubs and Society Fair event was very low. They estimated that with 2,000 students at Bangor there should be at least 150-200 potential members for their group but they had only half that. They believed the reason for the low membership was fear, in part. Fear of being seen talking to gay men and women. "… please remember," they said in their monthly article, "that a few words of visible support can make a hell of a lot of difference to a hell of a lot of people."[7]

Fear had played a part in court case that January for the assault of an Iraqi student Hussain Mohammed Omed. The two students accused of assault said the trouble had been started by a hoax letter sent to the Bangor University Lesbian and Gay Group. The letter concerned another student Said Tofeek who said he had lost his temper and struck Hussain when he suspected Hussain was the author of the letter. Said's wife had threatened to leave him after two members of the Gay Society had called at their home. Talal Shoker had been trying to separate Hussain and Said, and he was found not guilty of assault.

Hussain denied writing the letter to the group.[8] No convictions followed and the matter dropped from the public record.

The Bangor University Lesbian and Gay Group, which met weekly, determined to organise more social events, which they acknowledged would be a struggle. North Wales was regarded as a club wasteland by heterosexual people, and for LGBT people it was even worse. The only places were The Cavern in Llandudno, with a fairly large clientele, and Olivers over the border in Chester which was nearly always packed. It was a situation reflected throughout Wales.[9] As Daryl Leeworthy has noted in his research, LGBT people from South Wales often went across the border to Bristol and Bath.[10] The Bangor group also spent more time across the border than in Wales.

In March the Bangor students were still struggling to organise events for LGBT people. They invited members from various religious denominations to participate in a discussion about 'Homosexuality and the Bible' – but only two members of the Catholic society attended.[11] The 'Christian' voice was more loudly heard in Cardiff when a row flared up at the Welsh College of Music and Drama over the organisation of a 'Lesbians in Wales' get-together in March. About forty women had been granted permission by the governors to hold weekend workshops on 'the problems of lesbianism in Wales'.

The student Christian Union accused college governors of being 'irresponsible' for allowing the Gay Rights conference at a time when children were being taught at the college. Jane Barry, of the CU, said, "It is a grave matter because children from the age of 10 attend the college on a Saturday morning when the lesbian meeting will be going on. We don't believe it is right they should be open to this sort of influence."[12]

Protest letters were sent to the principal and governors, and displayed around the building. However the chairman of the Governors, Councillor Emyr Currie Jones, defended the decision: "I believe a little more Christian charity is called for in a matter like this." And president of the Gay Society, Carlon Spencer said, "It is disgusting how these so-called Christians are acting ... It is the first time we've have this sort of freedom conference at the college and we in the Gay Society hope to increase our activities in future." Miss Barry, a trainee teacher, argued that the matter had not come up for discussion at the college and it should have been in order for the

Christians to have a voice. However students' union president Chris Ricketts pointed out that this was not the first time an external conference had been held at the college and that other conferences such as Liberal party meetings had been conducted without objection.

Outside of the university Howard Ashton of Ashvale, Tredegar wrote to the *Western Mail* letter's page objecting to the 'Lesbians in Wales' get-together. He was heartened to see that it was strongly opposed by the Christian Union, who were following God's command to "have nothing to do with the worthless things that people do; things that belong to the darkness. Instead, bring them out to the light" (Ephesians, Ch 5, v11). Ashton continued, "I understand that the Christian Union has been accused of lacking Christian charity. If anyone is to accuse Christians of their lack of charity in this matter, then that person had better accuse God himself of it, since he declared himself solidly against homosexuality."[13] Ashton, like many, insists on forcing into the Bible, and into God's mouth, a word that did not even exist before the late nineteen century. Nowhere in the Bible is homosexuality mentioned. Another non-university person, Terence Jones, replied to Ashton's letter attacking his "interpreting the Bible to suit his own religious convictions."[14] That is a sentiment familiar to thousands of people.

About the same time Francis Brown, Secretary of the Cardiff University Lesbian and Gay Society and a co-organiser of the Pride march was writing of his disgust and amazement at the comments of Cardiff Councillor Derek Allinson. A front page article in the *South Wales Echo* discussing the possibilities of increasing policing of Bute Park included comments by Allinson who equated homosexuals with alcoholics, glue sniffers and other 'undesirables'. Bute Park was a popular meeting place for LGBT people who often had nowhere to go or lived in places hostile to those who were gay. Francis pointed out that LGBT people were not given funding to run safe spaces and so tended to congregate in coffee shops and public parks. They did not break the law and were entitled as tax payers to use public areas. LGBT people were denied access to public areas, so where were they supposed to go? "The people of this city need to realise that lesbians and gay men are not 'undesirables'," he said, "but law-abiding ratepaying responsible adults and so long as unresponsible [sic] adults, such as Mr Allinson, propagate such lamentable sentiments about homosexuals being 'undesirables' our work will be in vain."[15]

The argument about safe spaces for LGBT people was to continue later in the year. In December, Wales' very first 'Gay Centre' was proposed, providing social and recreational facilities for the gay community. A co-operative had been formed, its members were fundraising and writing letters to every local authority in the area and to all trade unions with branches in South Wales. A centre was needed because "Apart from public houses and night clubs in Newport, Cardiff and Swansea, South Wales does not have any facilities where gay people can meet in a relaxed and convivial surrounding. Many gay people simply do not like such places, the unemployed cannot afford them and those under 18 cannot use them ... the South Wales Gay Group recognise that there is a need for social recreational and welfare facilties that is not being catered for by the Commercial Sector. It is hoped that the proposed Gay Centre would be able to provide a café area, meeting room, lounge, offices and confidential areas from which the already well established counselling services could operate ... The basic objective is to provide a Community Centre for the gay people of South Wales so that interest and needs currently ignored by the commercial sector can be more fully developed."

The public was asked to contact their councillors to back the project, which would be the first of its kind in Britain. They were also seeking views on gay rights from candidates for local elections. John Stevenson, who headed the group, said the centre was not about building a ghetto but a means of removing barriers. "It is essential to heal the rift between gays and the community at large" and would be a "beacon of hope in what was often a sea of despair" for many men and women who felt isolated.[16]

Ogwr councillors branded the organisers as 'perverts' and 'drug takers' with a corrupting influence on young people. Labour councillor Muriel Williams suggested that the request merely be noted but Conservative Don Rutter wanted the committee to establish a clear policy on homosexuality. He argued if gays were encouraged then it would open the door to drug taking. Councillor Jennie Gibbs said that despite knowing many gay people of both sexes she did not think public funds should be used to encourage their 'rather peculiar habits'. "I do not think this council's ratepayers should be asked to support what is after all a private hobby and I am concerned about young children." Councillor Joan Spurgeon went even further: "We are speaking about perverts. We are being asked by perverts to donate money that could be spent elsewhere to more deserving causes." Like many she deliberately ignored the fact that LGBT people are ratepayers too.[17]

Councillor Bill Evans was also strongly against, saying that homosexuality was an illness and should be treated as such. He had already caused offence at the Labour conference in October when he was booed off the stage for branding homosexuality a sickness when the conference debated equal rights for lesbians and gay men. As he was slow-handclapped he had said, "The people we are talking about should be educated, and the country should be educated, that this is an illness and sickness in our society because it is an unnatural act." He was the only person to speak against the motion.[18] Jo Richardson, MP and Labour's front bench spokesperson on women's rights, said Evans' speech showed that society still had a long way to go before it was educated on the subject. The vote was in favour of equal rights by 3,395,000 to 2,805,000 and was acclaimed by gay-rights activists as a historic victory.

A letter writer to the *Western Mail*, E. Parry from Cardiff, wrote that he was sad to see Evans' attack on gays. He highlighted the problem of LGBT people living in small valley communities "streaming into Cardiff's gay clubs at the weekends." Confessing that he too once held views similar to Evans he had changed his attitude having met a number of gay people and discussed the problems they faced.[19] However Bill Evans was unrepentant and on returning home the Maesteg Workingman's Club congratulated him on his stand against gays. He boasted to the *Western Mail* "I have had dozens of telephone calls congratulating me on the stand I took ... I think these people (homosexuals) are sick ... I was down in the club having a pint and people were coming up to me and saying 'Good for you Bill – well done'. It seemed they were all in agreement with what I had to say ... personally, I don't know how anyone can get involved in this sort of thing – it sends shivers down my spine."

When plans were made to open the centre in the Taff Ely area instead local councillors discussed the matter. Bill Evans from Ogwr repeated his comments about homosexuals being 'sick'. They only thing which should be supplied for them, he said, is a medical centre. Councillor George Fairley stressed the link between homosexuals and AIDS and that to support the group would be 'retrograde step'. Councillor Ted Merriman said they were seeking approval of what had become 'fashionable and acceptable'. "If we give them one glimmer of support they will grow and grow in strength and put more and more pressure on us. We have to nip this in the bud." The committee voted unanimously to give no support to homosexuals.[20]

The letters pages of the South Wales press were full of opinions provoked by the debates of local councillors. 'P.A.' from Swansea wrote a letter to the *South Wales Evening Post* headed 'Dangers of Ignorance' in which he said he was sad that communities were led by such ignorant people. "It is incredible in this day and age Mr Merriman can have such dangerous views. After years of persecution it seems that at last gay people were being accepted. Now we find ourselves the scapegoats of AIDS and dangerous lies." He suggested instead of special medical centres, special centres of education be set up as a matter of urgency. "They are certainly not in touch with the real world and should retire as soon as possible before they cause real harm!"

In November Peter Washer from Swansea also wrote to the letters page saying a number of issues that had been raised needed answering. He criticised Ted Merriman for saying the group were seeking the council's seal of approval for unacceptable activities, and pointed out that they were seeking funding, not moral approval. He added Bill Evans' suggestion for a medical centre was twenty years out of date and that the long term failure rate of homosexuals as patients was 100%. "This surely goes to show that people are born gay, not made gay, or struck down with a bad case of 'gayness'."[21] Jane Spurgeon was also criticised for her 'farcical' remark that homosexuality was being made acceptable to youngsters: "As long as publicity-seeking local politicians manage to make the front page with this arrant nonsense, gay youngsters will be left in no doubt as to how acceptable their sexuality is." Jenny Gibbs "completes the package of totally unfounded prejudice". Washer concluded by saying "Public proclamations of homophobia are not only extremely irritating, but make very uncomfortable reading. They reveal much more about the speakers than they do about the minority which they are attacking. I'm sure I'm not the only one who could do without such nonsense."

However, Mrs M. Robinson from Waun Goch, Nantymoel writing in the *South Wales Echo* congratulated the councillors of Ogwr for taking a stand in refusing the 'appallingly brazen' request for a centre to enjoy their 'odious activities'. She thought it unfortunate that the councillors did not give the 'true' scriptural reason for their refusal, and blamed the spread of AIDS to 'prove' the harm homosexuals were doing to others. Like many others who use a bullwhip Bible, Mrs Robinson did not take responsibility for her views but blamed God: "Let me say this very clearly I am not the judge in this matter – God is, and His word says though we are to love the sinner, we are to hate the sin and not condone it in any way."[22]

The Leisure and Recreation Committee at Pontypridd also received a letter asking for support and financial help in setting up a Gay Centre, but that committee also overwhelmingly rejected the request. Councillor Judith Burford was in favour of helping the group and was sympathetic to their cause. But the decision was quickly shut down. After the meeting she said she was disappointed that there had not been a discussion which she regarded as 'quite interesting'. In the end, no gay centre was set up at this time.

Three years later in 1988 the Conservative government brought in Section 28 which banned the 'promotion' of homosexuality. And so the fight for safe spaces and the fight against discrimination became even harder. The next Pride march in Wales did not take place until 1999, although Section 28 was not repealed until 2003. At the time of writing this in 2017 only children under the age of fourteen have lived in Britain free of legal persecution.

Notes

One: Here lived Peggy Evans

1. Pennant, Thomas *A Tour in Wales*, Vol 2 The Journey to Snowdon Henry Hughes, London 1781
2. Hutton, William *Remarks Upon North Wales* Knott and Lloyd, Birmingham 1803
3. Prichard, Thomas Jeffrey Llewelyn *The Heroines of Welsh History: Comprising Memoirs and Biographical Notices of the Celebrated Women of Wales* W. and F.G. Cash, London 1854
4. Foulkes, Isaac Cymru Fu; Yn Cynwys Hanesion, Traddodiadau yn Nghyda Chwedlau a Dammegion Cymreig Hughes and Son, Wrexham 1862
5. James, Dr E. Wyn *Ballard Implosions and Welsh Folk Stanzas* 2006 http://orca.cf.ac.uk/42469/1/implosions.html#fortysix Retrieved 9 January 2015
6.. Lloyd-Morgan, Ceridwen 'Marged ferch Ifan' *Oxford Dictionary of National Biography*, Oxford University Press 2004 [http://www.oxforddnb.com/view/article/62908, accessed 2 June 2016

Two: The Welsh Sappho

1. Aubrey, John *Brief Lives* Vol 2, Clarenden Press, Oxford 1898
2. There have been suggestions he was in his twenties but the consensus is that he was much older than Katherine. It was common at this time for older men to marry young women.
3. Friendship
4. These are the opening lines of 'Injuria Amici'.
5. The Greek poet from the island of Lesbos (from where the word lesbian originates) who was known to have same-sex relationships.

Three: The man with the upside down arms

1. Doherty, Paul *Isabella and the strange death of Edward II* Robinson, London page 30 caption for de Spenser image 2003
2. Nicholas, Thomas *The History and Antiquity of Glamorganshire and its Families* Longmans, Green & Co, London 1874
3. Warner, Kathryn *Edward II: The Unconventional King* Amberley Publishing, Stroud 2015
4. However there are arguments that this was not the actual place of capture and that Morien perpetrated the myth for his own gains. The plaque was knocked off its post by a car and now languishes in a rather messy state in a shed as can be seen by the picture.
5. In 2008 research into a partial skeleton from Hulton Abbey strongly suggests that these are the remains of Hugh. Hulton Abbey was in Hugh's family and he was probably quietly buried here to avoid attention.
6. http://www.ianmortimer.com/EdwardII/death.htm

Four: Extraordinary Female Affection**
1. Webb, Alfred John *A Compendium of Irish Biography* M.H. Gill & Son, Dublin 1878
2. Mavor, Elizabeth *The Ladies of Llangollen: A Study in Romantic Friendship* Moonrise Press Ltd, Ludlow 2011
3. Pritchard, Rev. A *Short Memoir of the Ladies of Llangollen* Hugh Jones, Llangollen 1918
4. The black and white effect was added by General Yorke who bought the house in 1876.
5. Mavor, Elizabeth *A Year with the Ladies of Llangollen* Penguin Books Ltd, London 1986
6. Stanley, Liz 'Romantic Friendship? Some issues in Researching Lesbian History and Biography' *Women's History Review*, 1:2, 1992 193-216
7. Ellis, Megan *Mary Parker (Lady Leighton) and 'The Ladies of Llangollen'* Cylchgrawn Llyfrgell Genedlaethol Cymru/ National Library of Wales journal Cyf. 5, rh. 3 (Haf 1948), p. 207-208.
9. Published by the Hogarth Press owned by Leonard and his bisexual wife Virginia Woolf. Virginia herself had an interest in the Ladies – the original concept of *Orlando* her most famous novel was based on the Ladies but this later changed.

Five: Frances and Mary
1.*Cambrian News* 'Death of Miss Frances Power Cobbe' April 8 1904
2.Mitchell, Sally *Frances Power Cobbe: Victorian Feminist, Journalist, Reformer* University of Virginia Press Charlottesville 2004
3.Mary Somerville, a Scottish scientist.
4.Mitchell 2004
5.Hosmer, Harriet Goodhue & ed Carr, Cornelia *Harriet Hosmer letters and memories* The Bodley Head, London 1913
6.Cobbe, Francis Power *The Duties of Women. A Course of Lectures* Women's Temperance Publication Association, Chicago 1887
7. Mitchell 2004

Six: Cranogwen
1. Aaron, Jane '"Gender difference is nothing": Cranogwen and Victorian Wales' *Queer Wales,* University Wales Press, Cardiff 2016
2. *South Wales Daily News* 'Women and Shipping Casualties' September 24, 1878
3. Cosmos 'Wives on board ship' *South Wales Daily News* June 25, 1892
4. Aaron 2016
5. Davies, Russell *Hope and Heartbreak* University Wales Press, Cardiff 2005
6. Aaron 2016
7. *The Cambrian News* 'Noted Welshwoman: Death of Cranogwen' June 30 1916

8. *Seren Cymru* 'Eisteddfod Cymrodorion Rhymni' January 6 1865
9. *Y Quiet a'r Dydd* 'Canol Ceredigion' August 15 1873
10. John, Angela V. *Our Mother's Land: Chapters in Welsh Women's History, 1830-1939* University Wales Press, Cardiff 2011
11. Gramich, Kate & Brennan, Catherine *Welsh Women's Poetry 1460-2001* Honno Classics, Dinas Powys 2003
12. John 2011
13. Aaron 2016

Seven: Too absurd to be seriously entertained
1. Edith's story was covered extensively in the *Carmarthen Weekly Reporter; Pembrokeshire Herald & General Advertiser; Tamworth Herald; Weekly Main; Cardiff Times*
2. The Carmarthen Arms pub and the Bluebell Inn were so close together that they impeded traffic and was referred to as the throttle valve.
3. *Weekly Mail* 'Dying Merthyr Girl' 13 February 1904

Eight: The Girl Who Would a Sailor Be
1. King James version
2. *The Welshman* 'Gaieties and Gravities' March 31 1843
3. A type of boat.
4. *The Welshman* 'A Female Sailor' September 23 1842
5. *Cambrian* (no title – page 3) November 19 1842
6. *Wrexham & Denbighshire Advertiser* 'The Rhos Heroine Again' August 29 1857
7. *Pembrokeshire Herald* 'A Female Sailor' August 24 1855
8. *Cardiff & Merthyr Guardian* 'Local and Provincial: A Female Sailor' June 2 1860
9. *Evening Express* 'Girl Ships as a Sailor' October 29 1898

Nine: The Butterfly Dancer
1. The words Marquess and Marquis are the same.
2. Gault got five years in prison, was released, went back to France, committed a murder during a burglary and was guillotined.
3. Lockley, Mike 'Inside the Amazing World of the Midland Toff they called Lord Gaga' *Birmingham Mail* March 27 2016
4. It is unknown which year he wrote about Henry.
5. Aldritch, Robert & Wotherspoon, *Garry Who's Who in Gay and Lesbian History* Routledge, London 2002
6. Hyde, Montgomery H. *The Other Love: An Historical and Contemporary Survey of Homosexuality in Britain* William Heinemann, London 1970
7. Hyde, Montgomery H. *Lord Alfred Douglas: A Biography* Dodd Mead, New York 1985
8. Costello, Peter *Conan Doyle, Detective* Carroll & Graf, New York 2006

9. Gardner, Viv 'In the Eye of the Beholder' in *Theatre History and Historiography: Ethics, Evidence and Truth* edited by Claire Cochrane, Jo Robinson, Palgrave Macmillan, London 2015

10. Slide, Anthony *The Encyclopaedia of Vaudeville* Greenwood, Westport, Connecticut 2012

11. Breward, Christopher The Hidden Consumer: Masculinities, Fashion and City Life 1860-1914 Manchester University Press, Manchester 1999

Ten: A Valley Song Cut Short

1. Gordon, Cliff 'Testament' *Wales* Sept No 42/44 1959 pp69-71

2. Maggs, Grafton An Ephemeral Encounter with a man called Cliff Gordon Oystermouth Parish Online newsletter

3. Cross, Will *The Abergavenny Witch Hunt: An Account of the Persecution of Over Twenty Homosexuals in a Small Welsh Town in 1942* Will P. Cross publishing, 2014

4. B.B.'s Gag Book *Daily Mirror* May 30 1945

5. *Yorkshire Post* 'Noel Coward's Revue' August 24 1945

6. Betts, Ernest 'Coward without a kick' *Daily Express* August 23 1945

7. Isherwood, Christopher *The Lost Years: a Memoir: 1945-1951* ed Katherine Bucknell, HarperCollins 2000

8. *Daily Express* 'Entertainment' 12 July 1948

9. Williams, John L. *Miss Shirley Bassey* Quercus, London 2010

10. The recording can be heard on http://i1os.com/Choir_Practice_by_Cliff_Gordon_(BBC_1946)/UsM8_TW0pto.video

11. Trueman, Matt 'Ivor Novello's final musical, Valley of Song, to come to the stage in January' *The Guardian*, December 18 2013

12. Gordon 1959

13. *News of the World* 'B.B.C. Artist Charged' January 31 1954

14. Ferris, Paul *Caitlin: The Life of Caitlin Thomas* Hutchinson, London 1993

Eleven: Like a shadow I am

1. Tamboukou, Maria *Nomadic Narratives, Visual Forces: Gwen John's Letters and Paintings* Peter Lang Publishing Inc, New York 2010

2. Italian for 'light-dark'

3. John, Augustus *Chiaroscuro: Fragments of an autobiography* Pellegrini & Cudahy, New York 1952

4. Chitty, Susan *Gwen John, 1876-1939* Hodder & Stoughton Ltd, London 1981

5. Roe, Sue *Gwen John* Chatto & Windus, London 2001

6. Holroyd, Michael *Augustus John: The New Biography* Vintage, London 1997

7. Ottilie's long-time partner was Elisabeth Winterhalter, one of the first female doctors in Germany.

8. Chitty 1981

9. Roe 2001

10.Ida it is believed to have had a long relationship with the painter Jelka Rosen who married the composer Delius.
11.Lloyd-Morgan, Ceridwen *Gwen John: Letters and Notebooks* Tate Publishing, London 2004
12.Chitty 1981
13. Tickner, Lisa & Jenkins, David Fraser *Augustus and Gwen John* Harry N. Abrams, New York 2004

Twelve: There are no rules
1. Reynolds, Gwyneth *Benton End Remembered* Unicorn Press Publishing Group, London 2002
2. Hale, Kathleen *A Slender Reputation: An Autobiography* Frederick Warne & Co, London 1998
3. Blythe, Ronald *Outsiders: A Book of Garden Friends* Black Dog Books, Norwich 2008
4. Brace, Marianne 'Nine Lives of a Cat Woman' *Independent* May 5 1998
5. Grieg, Geordie *Breakfast with Lucian* 2013
6. Blythe 2008
7. Reynolds 2002
8. Brown, Bernard 'Cedric Morris at Benton End' *Art New Zealand* Summer, No 25 1982-83
9. Hale 1998
10. Reynolds 2002
11. Wakelin, Peter 1999
12. Despite Giardelli being heterosexual the bisexual American artist Fairfield Porter was in love with Arthur Giardelli. Giardelli was also a student at Benton End.
13. *Daily Telegraph* 'Glyn Morgan, artist – obituary' August 7 2015
14. Brown 1982-83
15. Reynolds 2002

Thirteen: A tangle in my life
1. *Daily Express* 'The Nightmare of being trapped in the wrong body' March 4 1997
2. Toomey, Philippa 'Chronicle of a journey from male to female' *The Times*, April 3 1974
3. Holden, David 'Books: James & Jan' *The New York Times*, March 17 1974
4. McSmith, Andy 'Love Story: Jan Morris – Divorce, the death of a child and a sex change … but still together' *Independent* June 3 2008
5. Lerman, Leo 'Jan Morris, The Art of the Essay No 2' *The Paris Review*, Summer No 143 1997
6. Morris, Jan *Pleasures of a Tangled Life* Barrie & Jenkins Ltd, London 1989

Fourteen: The Veronal Mystery

1. Eric's death was covered extensive in the *Daily Express; Cambrian Daily Leader; Daily Sketch; The Times*

Fifteen: A Wonder of Nature

1. Boswell, John *The Marriage of Likeness: Same-sex Unions in Pre-modern Europe* Harper Collins, London 1995
2. Wales, Gerald of & O'Meara, John (translator) *The History and Topography of Ireland* Penguin Classics, London 1982

Sixteen: And the pray was granted

1. *Cambrian* 'Hermaphrodite Child: Curious Phenomenon at Cardiff' May 25 1906
2. *Pembrokeshire Herald and General Advertiser* 'Extraordinary Circumstance' November 14 1851
3. White House on the Taf
4. Richards, Melville The Laws of Hywel Dda (The Book of Blegywryd) Liverpool University Press, Liverpool 1954
5. Owen, Aneurin *Ancient Laws and Institutes of Wales* Public Record Office 1841
6. Preves, Sharon E. *Intersex and Identity: The Contested Self* Rutgers University Press, New Jersey 2003
7. United Nations Human Rights: Office of the High Commission https://unfe.org/system/unfe-65-Intersex_Factsheet_ENGLISH.pdf retrieved 24.08.2016
8. His father, also William Jones, is the noted mathematician famous for devising the use of the symbol π for pi
9. *Monmouthshire Merlin* 'Hermaphrodite Salmon' July 31 1858
10. Morris, J.A. Letters to the editor: 'Cefn-y-Wrach (The Witches's Ridge)' *Western Mail*, April 3 1878
11. *The Observer* 'In Ancient Greece, she'd have been a god. In Wales, they spit on her' May 24 1998

Seventeen: I have a certain amount of regrettable nororiety

1. Non-transgender person
2. At 3 June 2016
3. Randell, John *Sexual Variations* Priory Press Ltd, London 1973
4. Randell, John *Transvestism and Transsexualism. A study of 50 cases*, British Medical Journal, December 26, 1959, 1448-1452
5. Tully, Bryan *Accounting for Transsexualism and Transhomosexuality* Whiting & Birch Ltd, London 1992
6. Digital recordings of the symposium can be listed to and downloaded from http://digitallibrary.usc.edu/cdm/ref/collection/p15799coll4/id/1571/rec/7
7. All England Law Reports, *All ER 1970* Volume 2, Corbett v Corbett

(otherwise Ashley) (No 2)

8. Lithman, Adella 'Oh Please God, change me into a boy while I'm asleep' *Daily Express* July 27 1976

9. Rees, Mark *Dear Sir or Madam: The autobiography of a female-to-male transsexual* Cassell, New York 1996

10. Russo, Francine 'Is there something unique about the transgender brain?' *Scientific America* 2016

11. Hamzelou, Jessica 'Transsexual differences caught on brain scan' *New Scientist* January 26 2011

12. Savage, Helen Changing Sex?: transsexuality and Christian theology Durham theses, Durham University. Available at Durham E-Theses Online: http://etheses.dur.ac.uk/3364 2006

13. Last, Richard 'Stepping out of line' *Daily Telegraph*, October 17 1980

14. King, D., 2002, *Pioneers of Transgendering: John Randell, 1918-1982*, GENDYS 2002, The Seventh International Gender Dysphoria Conference, Manchester

Eighteen: Dear Ernest... we disagree with you

1. A member of the British Association of Psychotherapists, Chair of the Psychoanalytic Section and Vice Chair of the Council. He is in private practice in North London.

2. Twomey, Daniel DSM 'British Psychoanalytic Attitudes Towards Homosexuality', *Journal of Gay & Lesbian Psychotherapy* 7:1-2, 7-22, 2003, DOI: 10.1300/ J236v07n01_02

3. Jones, Ernest *Free Associations: Memories of a Psycho-analyst* Hogarth Press, London 1959

4. Thyer, Bruce A. 'The X Club and the Secret Ring: Lessons on How Behaviour Analysis Can Take Over Psychology' *The Behaviour Analyst* No 1 (Spring), 18, 23-31 1995

5. Makari, George *Revolution in Mind: The Creation of Psychoanalysis* Harper Perennial, New York 2008

6. Garber, Marjorie *Bisexuality and the Eroticism of Everyday Life* Routledge, London 2000

7. Ruitenbeek, Hendrik M. (ed) *Psychoanalysis and female sexuality* Rowman & Littlefield Publishers, Lanham 1966

8. Maddox, Brenda *Freud's Wizard: The Enigma of Ernest Jones* John Murray, London 2006

9. Malcolm, Janet *Psychoanalysis: The Impossible Profession* Vintage Books, London 1988

10. Cooper, Emmanuel *The Sexual Perspective: Homosexuality and Art in the Last 100 Years in the West* Routledge, London

11. The full letter can be read on Wikisource under 'A Letter from Freud (to a mother of a homosexual)'.

12. Drescher, Jack & Lingiardi, Vittorio *The Mental Health Professions and*

Homosexuality: International Perspectives CRC Press, London 2003
13. Rosario, Vernon A. *Homosexuality and Science: A Guide to the Debates* ABC-CLIO, Santa Barbara 2002
14. Mattioli, Guillermo 'Psychoanalysts facing homosexuality' 2009 http://guillermomattioli.com/en/psychoanalysts-facing-homosexuality/ Retrieved 16.06.16
15. Abelove, Henry, Barale, Michele Aina & Halperin, David M. (eds) *Lesbian and Gay Studies Reader* Routledge, London 1993
16. Roudinesco, Elisabeth 'Other Sexualities – I' *Psychomedia*, J E P No 15, Winter 2002
17. Segal, Hanna *Yesterday, Today and Tomorrow* (The New Library of Psychoanalysis) Routledge, London 2007
18. Dresher 2003
19. Chabin, Broderick S. *Adolescent Males and Homosexuality: The Search for Self* Brave Dog Press 2014
20. Lewis, Brian *Wolfenden's Witness: Homosexuality in Postwar Britain* Palgrave Macmillan, London 2016
21. Williams College, Massachusetts, USA
22. Shapira, Michal *The War Inside* (Studies in the Social and Cultural History of Modern Warfare) Cambridge University Press, Cambridge 2015
23. Abse, Leo *The Bisexuality of Daniel Defoe* Karnac Books, London 2006
24. Davies, T.G. *Ernest Jones 1879-1958* University Wales Press, Cardiff 1979
25. *The Times* 'Obituary: Dr Ernest Jones' February 12 1958
26. Maddox 2006
27. Davies, T.G. 1979
28. No 2 in WalesOnline's 'Pinc List: The 40 most influential LGBT people in Wales', 2015
29. Personal comment to author.

Nineteen: A most intimate friend

1. Carradice, Phil 'Desmond Donnelly, mercurial but doomed' BBC Wales, 2013 http://www.bbc.co.uk/blogs/wales/entries/197740a7-6f91-3a83-aa8d-d2d b0082d19a Retrieved 8.6.16
2.Boothby, Sir Robert 'Sexual Offences' *Hansard* vol 521 cc1295-9 1953
3. Lewis, Brian *Wolfenden's Witnesses: Homosexuality in Postwar Britain* Palgrave McMillian, London 2016
4. French, Philip 'We Saw the Light, but too late for some' *The Observer* June 24 2007
5. Lewis 2016
6. Boothby, Robert *Boothby: Recollections of a Rebel* Hutchinson & Co, London 1978
7. Rees, Goronwy *A Chapter of Accidents* Chatto & Windus, London 1972
8. Boothby 1978
9. Rees Jenny *Looking for Mr Nobody: The Secret Life of Goronwy Rees*

Weidenfeld, London 1994
10. Rees, Goronwy 1972
11. Rees, Jenny 1994
12. Rees, Goronwy 1972
13. Rees, Jenny 1994
14. Wolfenden, Sir John *Turning Points* Bodley Head Ltd, London 1976
15. Faulks, Sebastian 'Jeremy Wolfenden' in *The Fatal Englishman: Three short lives* Hutchinson, London 1996
16. Mort, Frank *Capital Affairs: London and the Making of the Permissive Society* Yale University Press, New Haven and London 2010
17. Whose mother was Welsh.
18. Self, Helen J. *Prostitution,Women and Misuse of the Law:The Fallen Daughters of Eve* Routledge, London 2003
19. Mort, Frank 2010
20. Houlbrook, Matt *Queer London: Perils and Pleasure in the Sexual* Metropolis, 1918-1957 University of Chicago Press, Chicago 2005
21. Rees, Jenny 1994
22. Mort 2010
23. Rees, Jenny 1994
24. Mort 2010

Twenty: I was concerned with liberty
1. With the exception of indecent assaults.
2. Grey, Antony *Quest for Justice:Towards Homosexual Emancipation* Chatto and Windus, London 2011
3. Hansard Homosexual Offences and Prostitution HL Deb 04 December 1957, Vol 206 cc733-50
4. However Lord Longford then went on to support Section 28 and oppose equal age of consent.
5. *The Times* 'Lack of Action on Wolfenden Report' September 3 1958
6. *The Times* 'A.E. Dyson' August 13 2002
7. *The Times* Letters to the Editor April 19 1958
8. *The Independent* 'A.E. Dyson' August 1 2002
9. Dyson, A.E. Letters to the Editor: 'Vice Prosecutions' *The Spectator* January 10 1958
10. Scott-Presland, Peter *Amiable Warriors: A History of the Campaign for Homosexual Equality and its Times* Paradise Press, London 2015
11. *The Times* Obituaries: Clifford Tucker June 9 1993
12. Bradley, Ian 'Faithful band salutes the 'Saint of Socialism'' *The Times*, December 1 1980

Twenty-one: A Social Revolution Begins
1. Bedell, Geraldine 'Coming out of the dark ages' *The Observer*, June 24 2007
2. Loghead, George 'Vice Bill voted in by MPs' *Daily Express*, July 4 1966

3. He had inherited the title because his older brother, who was gay, had committed suicide.

4. Labour, only 17 months in government, only had a majority of 4 MPs due to local elections so had to go back to the country.

5. He also voted to legalise the Age of Consent and against Section 28.

6. Bedell 2007

7. Johnson, Paul & Vanderbeck, Robert *Law, Religion and Homosexuality* Routledge, London 2014

8. Bedell 2007

9. Campbell, John *Roy Jenkins* Jonathan Cape, London 2014

10. Bedell 2007

11. Wolff, William 'Spotlight on Yesterday (and some of the day before) in Parliament' *Daily Mirror*, July 5 1967

12. *Church Times* 'Comment on the News: Sexual Offences' July 14 1967

13. Kirby, Michael 'Lessons from the Wolfenden Report' *Commonwealth Law Bulletin* Vol 34, No 3, September 2008

14. Bedell 2007

15. Sinfield, Alan *Literature, Politics and Culture in Postwar Britain* Continuum, London 1989

16. Gleeson, Kate 'Freudian Slips and Coteries of Vice: The Sexual Offences Act of 1967' *Parliamentary History*, Vol 27, pt 3 2008 ,pp 393-409

17. The Sexual Law Reform Society was the successor to the HLRS in 1970 and went on to fight for further legal changes.

18. Hansard 'Grounds on which a marriage is void' HC Deb 02 April 1971, vol 814 cc 1827-54

Twenty-two: Not on our seafront

1. Later the Sexual Law Reform Society.

2. It adopted the name Campaign for Homosexual Equality in 1971.

3. *Pink News* Obituary November 17 2010

4. Scott-Presland, *Peter Griff Vaughan Williams* obituary December 21 2010

5. Edwards, Margaret '"Campaign No" sets off Protest' *North Wales Weekly News* December 30 1976

6. *GW* (unknown publication) 'Hell in Llandudno' 1976

7. *North Wales Weekly News* '"Gay Lib" campaigners set on Llandudno date' April 28 1977

8. *North Wales Weekly News* 'CHE accuses committee of "smokescreen"' June 16 1977

9. When the union of National Association of Teachers in Further and Higher Education held their conference in Scarborough in 1980 many of the delegates objected by wearing 'Glad to be Gay' stickers and generally protesting in memory of the CHE ban. No national LGBT conference was subsequently held in Scarborough until the Gay Community Network held an event in 2005 – the first in 29 years.

10. *Liverpool Daily Post* 'Llandudno has snubbed us – homosexuals' January 3 1977

11. Edwards, Margaret 'Campaign No' sets off Protest' *North Wales Weekly News* December 30 1976

12. *North Wales Weekly News* 'CHE accuses committee of "smokescreen"' June 16 1977

13. *Western Mail* 'Homosexuals 'barred' from seaside town' January 3 1977

14. *North Wales Weekly News* '"Gay Lib" campaigners set on Llandudno date' April 28 1977

15. *Guardian* 'Last resort for Gays' June 6 1977

16. *Manchester Evening News* '"Gay Libs' for resort' January 30 1977

17. Owen, Colin 'No again to CHE conference' *North Wales Weekly News* June 2 1977

18. *Llandudno Advertiser* 'Determined delegates' April 30 1977

19. Bourne, Stephen 'Griffith Vaughan Williams: Champion of gay rights who fought institutional homophobia' *The Independent* January 25 2011

20. The documentary can be seen on YouTube 'Speak For Yourself' (London Weekend Television 21/7/74)

21. Bourne 2011

22. LGBT Advisory Group to the Metropolitan Police *Thematic Review of Lesbian, Gay, Bisexual, Transgender Related Murders* LGBT Advisory Group, London 2007

23. Bourne 2011

Twenty-three: We All Fall Down

1. National Archives 'AIDS Monolith' 2005 http://www.nationalarchives.gov.uk/films/1979to2006/filmpage_aids.htm Retrieved 4 June 2016

2. It was turned into a TV film in 2014 and has a positive critics score of 94% on Rotten Tomatoes in 2016.

3. Best play went to *Les Liaisons Dangereuses* and best actor to Albert Finney in *Orphans*.

4. *South Wales Evening Post* 'UK's first AIDS play for festival fringe' 28 August 1986

5. Greaney, Shaun 'AIDS play Anger' *South Wales Evening Post* 4 September 1986

6. *South Wales Evening Post* Letters: 'Cruel and ignorant gay bashing' 18 September 1986

7. One of the first gay theatre companies designed to combat stereotypical portrays of gay people.

8. Gay Times 'Swansea Students face AIDS drama blow' October 1986

9. Greaney 1986

10. Neville, Sarah 'AIDS play may be banned' *Western Mail* 29 August 1986

11. Greaney 1986

12. *South Wales Evening Post* 'AIDS play will get cash help' 17 September 1986

13. *Western Mai* 'Ban demanded on play about gays' 30 September 1986

14. *Western Mail* 'Alarmist gay play call' 1 October 1986

15. *ibid.*

16. *South Wales Evening Post* 'Alarmist gay play call' 1 October 1986

17. *South Wales Evening Post* 'Injunction bid to stop gay musical' 3 October 1986

18. *South Wales Evening Post* 'Councillor fails to halt gay musical' 9 October 1986

19. *South Wales Evening Post* 'A gaily gay send-up of prejudice' 9 October 1986

20. Greaney, Shaun 'A gaily gay send-up of prejudice' *South Wales Evening Post* 9 October 1986

21. Swift, Elizabeth 'Tory tries to bring an absolute end to gay plays' *The Stage* 9 October 1986

22. *South Wales Evening Post* 'Freedom of speech attack' 9 October 1986

23. *South Wales Evening Post* 'Protests on gay play' 3 November 1986

24. *South Wales Evening Post* 'Call to stop Fringe finance' 8 December 1986

25. Lewis, Richard 'AIDS ...the EVIL on our doorstep!!' December 1987. Also *Gay Times* 'Students arrested in Swansea protest' January 1987

26. *The Observer* 'AIDS demo arrests' 14 December 1986

27. *Gay Times* 'Swansea lecturer defends protest demo' March 1987

28. *Western Mail* 'Lecturer and students win demo appeal' 24 June 1987

29. *Western Mail* 'Not only gays who heckled councillor' 22 December 1986

30. Keates, Helen 'Swansea Council motion supports equal marriage and commends MPs who voted in its favour' *This is South Wales* 16 March 2013

Twenty-four: A Purpose in Life

1. Rhondda, Viscountess *This Was My World* Macmillan & Co, London 1933

2. Another American who died was Charles Frohman a famous theatrical producer. His long term partner was theatre critic and producer Charles Dillingham. Frohman was travelling to London to help J.M. Barrie put on his play *Peter Pan: or The Boy Who Wouldn't Grow Up* and as the ship went down he paraphrased 'Why fear death? It's the greatest adventure of all." He wanted to be remembered as the man who gave Barrie's Peter Pan to the world.

3. Rhondda, Viscountess 1933

4. *Merthyr Express* 'Aberdare Liberals at Llanwern' September 4 1909

5. *Evening Express* 'Mr Lloyd George at Llanwern' December 22 1909

6. Rhondda, Viscountess 1933

7. *Aberdare Leader* 'Suffragette Outrage' July 19 1913

8. *Aberdare Leader* 'Release of Mrs Mackworth' July 19 1913

9. Rhondda, Viscountess *D.A. Thomas, Viscount Rhondda* Longmans Green and Co, London 1912

10. John, Angela V. *Turning the Tide: The Life of Lady Rhondda* Parthian, Cardigan 2013

11. *ibid.*

12. *ibid.*

13. Shaw, Marion *The Clear Stream* Virago Press, London 1999

14. Brittain, Vera *Testament of Friendship: The Story of Winifred Holtby* Macmillan & Co, London 1940

15. Thorp, Angela 'The Sexual Offences (Amendment) Bill: "Age of consent" and abuse of a position of trust' House of Commons Research Paper 99/4 January 21 1999

16. From a Welsh LGBT history perspective it's worth noting that the love interest in *The Well of Loneliness*, Mary Llewellyn, is Welsh.

17. Shaw, Marion 1999

18. *Women and a Changing Civilisation* by Winifred Holtby, 1933

19. John, Angela V. 2013

20. Shaw, Marion 1999

21. John, Angela V. 2013

22. *ibid.*

Twenty-five: Pride in Wales

1. *South Wales Echo* 'Gay march for city gets the go-ahead' May 15 1985

2. *South Wales Echo* 'Hundreds expected at gays march' June 19 1985

3. *South Wales Echo* 'Gay march for city gets the go-ahead' May 15 1985

4. *South Wales Echo* Letters: March of the sinful gays May 20 1985

5. *South Wales Echo* Letters: Homosexuals May 28 1985

6. *South Wales Echo* Gays plan march as an annual event June 21 1985

7. Lesbian & Gay Group U.C.N.W. 'With A Little Help From Our Friends!' *Y Seren* February 14 1985

8. *Western Mail* 'Hoax letter led to assault, court told' January 23 1985

9. Lesbian & Gay Group U.C.N.W. 1985

10. https://historyonthedole.wordpress.com/book-reviews/queer-wales/

11. Lesbian & Gay Group U.C.N.W. A Religious Note March 14 1985

12. *South Wales Echo* 'College row as lesbians set to meet' March 22 1985

13. Ashton, Howard Letters *South Wales Echo* April 4 1985

14. Jones, Terence Letters *South Wales Echo* April 6 1985

15. *South Wales Echo* 'Gay protest: We are not law breakers' March 21 1985

16. *Pontypridd Observer* 'No cash for the gay centre' December 12 1985

17. *South Wales Echo* 'Attack on gays in plea for funds' November 14 1985

18. Hibbs, John 'Labour Party Conference: Victory and fury in debate on gay rights' *Western Mail* , October 5 1985

19. Parry, E. Letters 'Ordinary men and women' *Western Mail* October 11 1985

20. *South Wales Echo* 'Attack on gays in plea for funds' November 14 1985

21. Washer, Peter Letters: 'Arrant nonsense on gays' *South Wales Evening Post*, November 16 1985

22. Robinson, M. 'Letters: Breaking God's law' *South Wales Echo*, November 25 1985

Index

About the author

Norena Shopland has extensively researched the heritage of LGBT people and issues in Wales for over sixteen years. She devised *Welsh Pride*, the first project in Wales to look at placing sexual orientation and gender identity into Welsh history, and managed *Gender Fluidity*, the first funded transgender project in Wales. Her work has appeared in the Welsh and British press, radio and TV and she regularly provides advice and support in the history of LGBT people in Wales. She lectures extensively, including staff networks such as the Welsh Government, and to numerous museums, archives, charities and other events such as BiFest, Sparkle and Pride. She is the former chair of the Cardiff & Vale LGBT Forum and is Vice Chair of Plaid Pride.

Norena Shopland has a Master's degree in heritage studies and has worked for the British Museum, National Museums Scotland and the Museum of London. Now living in her native Wales she has worked with leading heritage organisations including National Museums Wales, Glamorgan Archives and Cardiff Story. In 2017 she was invited to speak at the Parliamentary Archives at the House of Commons to commemorate the Sexual Offences Act (1967).

SEREN

Well chosen words

Seren is an independent publisher with a wide-ranging list which includes poetry, fiction, biography, art, translation, criticism and history. Many of our books and authors have been on longlists and shortlists for – or won – major literary prizes, among them the Costa Award, the Jerwood Fiction Uncovered Prize, the Man Booker, the Desmond Elliott Prize, The Writers' Guild Award, Forward Prize and TS Eliot Prize.

At the heart of our list is a beautiful poem, a good story told well or an idea or history presented interestingly or provocatively. We're international in authorship and readership though our roots are here in Wales (Seren means Star in Welsh), where we prove that writers from a small country with an intricate culture have a worldwide relevance.

Our aim is to publish work of the highest literary and artistic merit that also succeeds commercially in a competitive, fast changing environment. You can help us achieve this goal by reading more of our books – available from all good bookshops and increasingly as e-books. You can also buy them at 20% discount from our website, and get monthly updates about forthcoming titles, readings, launches and other news about Seren and the authors we publish.

www.serenbooks.com